FATHERHOOD

FATHER HOOD

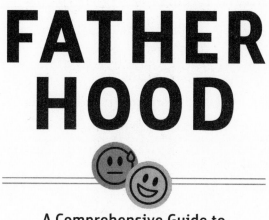

A Comprehensive Guide to
Birth, Budgeting, Finding Balance,
and Becoming a Happy Parent

THE EDITORS OF FATHERLY

HARPER HORIZON

Contents

SECTION III
Growing Your Own

SECTION IV
Reference

Introduction
The Known Unknown

Your father knew nothing. Well, next to nothing—at least, next to nothing when it came to the likely effect he would have on you or your life. At most, when you were born, he had an inkling of what his presence and participation could offer. You inherited that same inkling. You're considering it now, an undistinguished mass like an uncut diamond. Your sense is that you can make something priceless of it, but even the first cut requires a decision you might not be ready for. After all, you don't know the first thing about diamond cutting.

Maybe your father loved you, maybe he didn't. Whether he was present or absent, understanding or harsh, "good" or "bad" in your estimation, he was most likely unaware of what he held—because there was nobody to teach him to shape it. Like others before him, he progressed through the experience of fatherhood, trying to refine the raw white stone and trying to make it shine. Someone just needed to help him find the correct angles.

Since 1950, the US government has spent roughly $600 billion on NASA programs and nearly $10 billion collecting data on mothers; the $15 million in change it found between the couch cushions went to research related to fatherhood. But the bulk of that research has been conducted in just the last decade. Which is all to say that humanity knows more about Alpha Centauri than we know about whether your old man fucked you up.

But we know more than we used to. And here's what the data says: fatherhood is a silly word used to market a ridiculous idea. Fatherhood implies that having a kid automatically offers men access to an altered state of being. It really doesn't.

Want to know what will happen to you in the moment your child is born? Not much. As birth releases an oxytocin flood to your wife's brain, overwhelming her with feelings of love so profound she ugly cries into low-thread-count hospital sheets, you may very well be tempted to check the Browns' score (spoiler: they're losing). You may feel this runs counter to the favored sentimental and celebrity narrative—"the first time I saw that face, my whole world changed!"—but birth experiences are as unique and varied as the men who have them. Instant love may be the story, but it's not necessarily the norm.

So, when does Mom pass Dad the oxytocin? When she passes the baby. Men receive the biological benefits of dad-status only when they start taking care of their kids. Odd as it may sound, those initial dirty diapers become a gateway drug to care. You'll want more. But only if you keep doing it. And it goes on like that forever: kid and Dad passing the good feelings back and forth like a joint until, if all goes well, the former delivers the latter a heartfelt eulogy. But Dad has to start, because the kid's hands are too small to roll one and because that's the one thing that we absolutely know for sure, peer-review and all: whatever seriously good vibes are going to be have to start with you.

While your father might have known nothing, he was particularly in the dark about the things he did know—which was actually a lot. He was pretty much parenting all the time. And surprise, surprise, most of the time, he was probably doing fine. Roughhousing was parenting; watching television with you was parenting; talking to your mother at the dinner table was parenting. Fatherhood is only a state of being in that it's the act of being who you are. Because the fact is that the person you are before you have a kid will not be appreciably different than the person you are after you have a kid. And that person is the template your kid will use to learn how to live in the world. So becoming a good father is about knowing yourself and leveraging all that's good in you toward raising someone who knows better than you. That's love.

But love isn't always easy, and loving as a parent can be even harder. It's easy for the bad times (and there will be bad times) to eclipse the wonder that is raising another human. It's not for nothing that some dads go out for a pack of cigarettes and decide not to come back. Some men let the hard times lie to them. Some men fall into the trap of thinking parenthood will always be tough and they will never be tougher.

You get maybe eighteen good years to lean into being a truly active and effective father. If you're lucky, your relationship with your kid will continue to bloom into their adulthood and your own old age. If you're really lucky, you get to see how they turned out.

Those eighteen years, though. They go by fast. And if you get lost in the tough times you miss the profound beauty of your kid becoming a person. You'll look up one day and there will be a man or a woman standing in front of you and you'll think, "What the hell just happened?"

That inkling that you have? That inkling that your father had? There's no great secret in turning it into fatherly knowledge. All you have to do is be present. All you have to do is stop sometimes and observe a supposedly mundane moment. Because none of them are truly mundane—each one contains a look exchanged, a moment of communication, or a physical touch that is laying the foundation for your child's personhood.

This book is about helping you create, recognize, and acknowledge those moments. And that you're holding it in your hands is a damn good sign that you're on the right track. Don't sweat what you don't know, because if you know yourself, you know fatherhood.

FATHERHOOD

SECTION I

PREGAMING

In the best-case scenario, expecting parents have a full nine months to get ready for a kid. But instead of building a nursery, the best parents-to-be build an emotional foundation to be great parents and solid partners.

CHAPTER 1

Life–Life Balance

It's morning on a workday. Your baby is awake, which means you're probably awake as well—far too early. And because babies aren't born with a snooze button, you'll be staying awake. You stare at the ceiling for a moment, relishing the last bit of cozy comfort, maybe playing a game of who'll-get-the-baby chicken with your partner. But you can't stay in bed. Might as well get some coffee in your system and get on with it.

You've shaken away the dim edges of sleep, stretched, and held your kid for some morning cuddles. Literally nothing could be better than your child. And yet, the world pulls you away.

As you prepare for your day, you find yourself caught in the liminal space between being at home and being at work. Your body is making breakfast, but your mind flits between home responsibilities and work concerns, be it deadlines, projects, or quotas. The milk sloshes in the cereal bowl; your partner coos to the baby; you worry about all those TPS reports and how much vacation time you have left.

A working dad's morning (whatever time of day it occurs) is one of the daily pivot points between work and life. It's a time where the balance, or lack of balance, can be most keenly felt. It's evident in the pang of guilt and worry while getting a kid ready for day care or preschool. It's evident in a partner's exhausted expression. It's evident in the gratitude that there is work to go to at all.

These pivot points bring a parental truth into focus. As undeniably incredible and transformative having a child is, a new kid can make relationships more difficult. For all of the wonder and love and goodness kids bring to your life, the fact of their birth can create relationship conflict: with your work, your partner, and counterintuitively, with the kids themselves.

MAKING IT. WORK.

Financially speaking, kids are like cement water wings, making it much harder to stay afloat. The fun folks at the US Department of Agriculture (yep, the cabbage-yield people) calculate that the average American family spends $12,980 per year per child.[1] Practically speaking, that means new fathers are more dependent on their employers at precisely the moment when they have fewer extra hours to offer. As such, the post-baby struggle to balance professional and personal obligations can feel like a government appropriations process: it's confusing, rules are involved, and any compromise breeds contempt on both sides of the aisle.

Determining the rules of your new existence as a father—what it means to be a father at work and at home—isn't particularly easy. But as with all things, management, tactics, and goal-setting are key. Sure, the exercise of sitting in a room and ranking one's priorities can feel ridiculous, but it's worthwhile. Fatherhood changes a person, and you have to come to grips with that. In management-speak, you're the only one to "onboard" the new guy.

Becoming a father doesn't fundamentally change the underlying mechanics of balancing home life and work life, but it does shift the fulcrum, destabilizing the whole system. You may be able to exert the proper pressure to get things back on the level, but you will likely never achieve long-term equilibrium. Raising a kid is a dynamic process. Birth is just the first of many seismic shifts that will mess up whatever balance you think you've achieved. Still, it's a place to start.

Understand that balancing your family life and your work life isn't a one-and-done proposition. It's a long and evolving process. Starting that process in the proper headspace and being proactive and thoughtful about the discussions you have, the stands you take, and the concessions you make in the run-up to the birth of your child can set a good precedent for both you and your employer. But instability will inevitably become the status quo, so the best bet is to get strong sea legs early on. In this case, that means figuring out your personal goals and getting into a tactical mindset.

Here's something you're going to notice during these preliminary conversations with your manager: you're in a crap bargaining position. Parenthood requires that employees ask their employers for more—more understanding, more access to benefits (which shouldn't be a problem but often is), and more flexibility—at exactly the moment when they need a job the most. Expecting dads and new dads who sense this dynamic but don't address it directly wind up playing well-intentioned defense. For instance, many new fathers refuse to ask for flextime arrangements. According to a 2013 study, nearly 70 percent of fathers engage in informal flextime, but only 10 percent formalize those arrangements. That leaves many practicing the art of "passing"—a term McMaster University researcher Erin Reid coined to describe the act of cheating on your employer with your family (think: pretending a call with your wife was business related).[2] This is both understandable and avoidable.

Here's how to avoid it. Try not writing scripts in which your child plays the villain, you play the hero, and your work plays the damsel in distress. Own the fact—verbally, to your employer—that you plan to put your kid first. When in doubt, treat conflicts like car accidents. Don't apologize.

THE TRUTH ABOUT PATERNITY LEAVE

Barring a national paternal leave policy, fathers are largely reliant on a patchwork of state laws that may or may not allow them paid time at home in the first weeks of their child's life. Currently, that patchwork of laws isn't the greatest. Five states currently mandate paid parental leave. New York State, California, New Jersey, Rhode Island, Washington State, and Washington, DC, now have laws in place requiring employers to provide paid leave to employees. Leave amounts run from four to twelve weeks and cover anywhere from 60 to 90 percent of wages, depending on the hours a parent works.

Any other leave a parent might receive comes at the discretion of an employer. The best businesses recognize the benefit of allowing a family time to establish long-term care patterns and bonding. They'll offer three months of leave to both parents. The worst companies allow paltry leave or offer it only to mothers, often considered the "primary caregiver." And it will remain this way until laws change.

But laws and policies are only half the battle. Office culture can be toxic even when managers are not. According to Ferne Traeger, a psychotherapist who specializes in helping individuals and corporations navigate major transitions, this should give new parents pause.

"Frequently, managers are not even aware of their biases. They think they actually get it, but they don't," Traeger says. "The undercurrents of workplace culture can have a tremendous effect on how fathers feel about taking time off."[3] So recognize this and differentiate between your employer (the company) and your employer (the human in charge of you). Your workplace has an agenda, and that agenda is for you to work more.

Need more freedom? Ask for it. And keep discussions with your manager focused on your work deliverables and due dates.

Ultimately, good managers care about results more than keeping asses in seats. If you have a bad manager, think about moving on. Intervene on your own behalf. It behooves even happily employed expecting and new fathers to shore up their professional networks and discuss new opportunities. Taking an aggressive negotiating stance may be unwise; emailing that guy Phil you met at the conference in Tampa is not. Sure, Phil may have halitosis, but he knows people who know people. Unlikely as it may sound, Phil is a hero. Phil is the smelly guy who helps you calm down.

THE PATERNITY BONUS

Now we're calm, which means that it's time to prepare for the long haul. Happily for you, fatherhood does not represent a long-term professional liability. To the contrary!

According to a study conducted by Boston College researchers in 2016, some 97 percent of fathers see job security as important or extremely important.[4] Employers tend to understand this (implicitly if not explicitly) and assign value to the perceived loyalty and consistency of their working dads. A seminal 2014 study by sociologist Michelle Budig found that American employers consistently described fathers as committed employees with more skin in the game than their coworkers. And that's not the best part. The best part is that Budig found men's earnings increase on average more than 6 percent when they have a child.[5] This "Fatherhood Bonus" explains the statistical discrepancy between the average earnings of dads and non-dads, which are unequal even when adjusted to account for employee age. Whether employers are smart to count on dads or just culturally biased in their favor is an interesting academic discussion—for other people.

For fathers, the key takeaway is to ask for more money within the first year. Even if a raise isn't forthcoming, it will make your manager reconsider your compensation, and the evidence suggests that will likely end well.

The best defense is, to twist the saying, a good offense. Fathers often forget this because they feel like they are underperforming in the office or at home. That's fine, but it's important to practice a bit of compensation pattern recognition and take advantage of the privileges life throws at you.

Work inevitably feels different for a new dad than for a non-dad. Time away from the home—whether for business trips or happy hour drinks—is now subject to negotiation with both your boss and your spouse. This is the new normal, and it dictates that you will miss out on some things workwise. There will be happy hour drinks undrank, LinkedIns unlinked, and meetings unmet.

Commitments have a cost, and no one gets to have it all (except Dwayne "The Rock" Johnson, for some reason). You might become the guy who declines all meetings at 5:00 p.m. You might have to send a colleague on a trip you'd like to go on. You might have to delegate or let things slide a bit more than you'd like. The key is to decide what concessions you plan to make, then stick with the plan. Otherwise, you'll have to get used to living not just with kids but with disappointment too.

PARTNER-LIFE BALANCE

Since the mid-twentieth century, the number of two-income families has skyrocketed. Currently, just over half of American fathers have working partners.[6] That said, the pursuit of work balance isn't just about financial stability and scheduling—it's about allowing partners to pursue their own growth.

On a fundamental level, everyone is comparing the home life they're building to a model family. And model families—like actual models—are often unrealistically proportioned. Many, if not most, men believe not only that they will be primary breadwinners but that they should be. They believe this despite being avowed feminists, and their wives may believe it too (the dynamic is slightly different in gay couples, who make more than straight couples). In the wake of a child being born, more mothers than fathers reduce their hours, take significant time off, or quit their jobs entirely, which is fine as long as they're not being pressured into it. But assumptions can and do often make the proverbial ass out of everyone involved.

For example: think it's the fault of hardworking people when they go broke? Think again. Home economics matter, but macroeconomics are just as (if not more) important.

Imagine this: day care calls and your kid is running a slight fever. Both you and your wife have super important afternoon meetings. Who buckles first and sends the text "Childcare emergency. Can we re-sked?" It's remarkably easy to default to making these sorts of things into mommy problems. And you'd better believe that day care providers and teachers will make it even easier by calling mom first. But unless that's the deal that's proactively been struck, it's likely to foment resentment because such gender role play is utterly unequal. That's why it's better to get ahead of it. Have an on-call schedule or at least an explicit understanding. This matters not only because relationships are key but because two successful parents are better than one, and mothers are fighting an uphill battle against workplace bias. A little bit of overcompensation—say, picking up the kid three times a week—is more than just an act of love. It's a smart investment.

And if that's not enough incentive, consider that Stew Friedman of the Wharton Work/Life Integration Project has conclusively demonstrated that children benefit when their mothers feel empowered at work—more so than when their fathers do.[7] So, to the extent that you can support your spouse's professional advancement (and the entailing control), know that the benefits aren't all arriving via direct deposit. Remember that work isn't just your work.

KID-LIFE BALANCE

Though it's tempting for new parents to focus on the impact of family life on work—after all, an addition to the family is what changed everything—the impact of work on family life is generally more keenly and negatively felt. So the question of how work affects your home life, and the ways in which you're likely to let it, is much more profound than its inverse.

The long-term danger faced by working fathers is falling into what Brad Harrington, executive director of the Boston College Center for Work & Family, calls the "conflicted father" role. Harrington divides modern fathers—baby boomers, Gen Xers, and millennials—into three types: egalitarian, conflicted, and traditional. (Surprisingly, the distribution is relatively constant intergenerationally.) The "too long/didn't read" version goes like this:

- Traditional fathers feel their wives should take the lead on childcare, and they do. (It's worth noting these are mostly straight guys, so *wives* is the right word.) Most traditional fathers—roughly 60 percent—are sole breadwinners.

- Egalitarian fathers think they should share caregiving equally with their partners and do. Most egalitarian fathers—over 60 percent—are not sole breadwinners.

- Conflicted fathers believe they should share caregiving equally with their partners and don't. Most conflicted fathers—a lot more than 60 percent—are miserable.

"Conflicted fathers wanted to climb the corporate ladder but at the same time wanted to spend more time with their children," Harrington explains. "Conflicted fathers asserted that their children's interests were their top priority but were highly susceptible to the work demands of their corporate cultures."[8]

The takeaway? There's no ideal equation for a balanced life—being woke doesn't change that—but there is a perfect formula for unhappiness: hypocrisy. Men who want to put their kids first but don't wind up suffering for their sins. The consequences are very real and keenly felt.

And sometimes those consequences aren't just felt by Dad.

Children were more likely to show behavioral problems if their fathers were overly involved psychologically in their careers. This tends to occur when overinvolvement manifests itself as what Stewart Friedman calls "cognitive interference." The most common form of cognitive interference? "Techno-interference."[9] This is what is known in common parlance as failing to put down the fucking phone.

It's easy to conflate being at home with being *present* at home, but these two things are growing ever more distinct. As the cubicular nine-to-five gives way to a nebulous 24/7—Unlimited vacation days! Work from home! Flex-time! Why didn't you answer the phone?!—the desire to be present at home has in many cases transformed into an unwitting obligation to be available for work all the time. We live in an era of the bedtime Slack ping. And that's bad news for children, who can tell the difference between present and accounted for (infants, it's worth noting, cannot, so you've got about ten months of cushion). In other words, you can take the work out of the office, but you can't take the office out of the worker—that is, unless you realize that when you walk through your door, you are no longer a man with a title. To them, you are just "Dad."

Interestingly—and actually this may change your life and ease your suffering—Friedman and his coauthor Jeffrey Greenhaus have proven that cognitive interference is more harmful to children than a dad spending extended hours at work.

Children of fathers who work long hours and then clock out tend to fare better than children of fathers who go home but keep checking their email. So, finish what you're doing, then move on.

The truth is, work can be alluring—a siren song calling you from the adult world to drop the blocks and see what your peers are up to. The truth is, you might always have best intentions and love in your heart for your child, but you will also have your phone in your pocket. And from that phone there will issue beeps and boops just as from your child will issue pees and poops, squeals and peals and cries. Your baby doesn't have a touch screen. It's not that interactive. There are no games on it. At times, this baby will be very boring. And then, the temptation to dance alone to the rhythm of work—the comforting patter of emails, the ping of texts, and the timpani of subscription-based time-management software—is real. Bear down and deal with being present for your kid.

YOU-LIFE BALANCE

We started off the chapter talking about the seesaw of work-life balance. And it would be naive not to acknowledge the competing demands of both home and work. But here's the buried lede: balance isn't . . . real. The human resources phrase "work-life balance" contains a logical fallacy. (Never trust anyone who has to have "human" in their job title to seem relatable.) The dash implies an opposition that simply isn't possible. In truth, it's all part of the same experience. There is no zero-sum game. Spending time with your kids may make you a better employee. Working will likely make you a better father. Understanding is not a finite resource. It's a habit.

It's also something you owe yourself.

You made a decision by having a child and choosing to be in that child's life. That decision affected your work life. And the subsequent decisions you make at work will affect that child's life. Every day you will make the decision to return home from work instead of going out to buy a pack of cigarettes, heading to the bar with the guys, and . . . that's a decision, as well. And these are mostly if not all decisions based on love, which is far more stable than anything your boss can offer and far more worth it than any annual bonus.

CHAPTER 2

Nine Months, Six Conversations

In the lead-up to the birth of a child—specifically a first child—many parents focus on their health, the hospital, and readying their home. This translates to countless doctor appointments, carefully wrought birth plans, and, most obviously, a whole lot of stuff—all those cribs and strollers and binkies. No matter how valuable, stuff matters less than values. What babies need, more than even a place to poop and sleep, is an emotionally stable environment. And if that sounds easy to provide, rest assured it isn't. Babies are, after all, a profoundly destabilizing force.

Many happily married couples assume that the love that brought them together will organically and naturally create a healthy environment for their children. This is demonstrably untrue. As Ian Curtis so presciently moaned, "Love, love will tear us apart." The difference between mutual love and shared love is, as anyone who ever watched their crush dance with someone else well knows, that shared love can exist in opposition.

Couples are usually unprepared for the stress and struggle that descends with a newborn. So there's good reason why University of Wisconsin sociologist E. E. LeMasters called birth a "crisis" for marriage.[1]

From 2005 to 2011, researchers at the University of California, Berkeley documented the experience of one hundred couples experiencing new parenthood, including during the transition from late pregnancy to birth with regular follow-ups into the grade school years. They found that nearly a third of these couples experienced "clinical ranges" of distress in their marriages within a year of the birth of their first child.[2] This means that simply by becoming a parent, men and women could experience diagnosable depression, anxiety, and stress.

A similar 2009 study followed 216 couples over the first eight years of marriage and measured how the birth of a child changed the functional quality of their relationships. Researchers found that the birth of a child was linked to a distinct and sudden drop in relationship satisfaction compared to couples who remained childless.

Drops in relationship satisfaction were strongly correlated with uneven or mismatched expectations—not values, but actual expectations—about what life after a baby would be like: who will be changing diapers, when are we returning to work, who is doing night feedings?

A 2002 study by UNC Greensboro researcher Marion O'Brien drilled down on this dynamic, finding that husbands who held more traditional attitudes regarding child-rearing and those whose beliefs about child-rearing differed from their partners saw the steepest declines in intimacy—meaning, in this case, less companionship and sex. This isn't just a dad problem; two-thirds of mothers experience a decline in marital satisfaction as well.[3]

But the significant and growing body of research on relationship outcomes does not suggest that postbaby rancor is inevitable. To the contrary, it suggests that men and women can avoid conflicts by making an effort to actively avoid conflicts. They just need to understand when those conflicts are mostly likely to arise so that they can operate from a shared premise. They need to have what every functional business has and what many dysfunctional families do not: a value proposition and some clear goals. The only way to get there is to talk.

NEED TO KNOW

The Six Traits that Make Marriages Divorce-Proof

Before John DeFrain's research led him to the six culturally universal traits that make a strong family, he was practicing as a family therapist. It was the early 1970s and DeFrain notes that the American view of marriage and family wasn't exactly rosy. Much of that was because the divorce rate had climbed to around 50 percent. The doom and gloom was so pervasive, as DeFrain recalls, that many studying American marriage didn't believe that there was such a thing as a strong family, nevermind figuring out how to track them down.

It struck DeFrain that the best way to find a strong family was to leave the definition to those who felt they had one. So he sent out press releases calling for members of strong families to contact him and his research partner.

A full six weeks passed without response. There seemed to be a distinct possibility that strong families really didn't exist. Then a hundred or so letters arrived from Connecticut, and as the press release was finally picked up around the country more responses rolled in until they had a sample of thousands.

DeFrain and his colleagues responded with questionnaires—the gist of which he boiled down to "What works?"

Surveys relating to qualities of strong families from places as diverse as Soweto, South Africa, and Indonesia were all remarkably consistent. While they might use different language, metaphors, and allusions to describe what made their families strong, they all shared six distinct and culturally constant traits: Appreciation and affection, commitment, positive communication, enjoyable time together, spiritual well-being, and successful management of stress and crisis.

"People are people are people and families are families are families. What makes us work as families is remarkably similar," DeFrain says. "As an academic you think, we're all so different, we can't possibly understand each other. It's baked into the human mind. But in families, it seems that the strengths remain the same."

Trait #1:
Appreciation and Affection

Sometimes parents and kids might think affection means cuddling or that appreciation shouldn't be a two-way street. That's not the case. Appreciation can be understood as giving someone the time they need to complete tasks, keeping promises, and saying thank you (yes, to the children too).

Likewise, affection can be more than hugs. It can also be a desire to forgive or a belief that the love you share between you is a source of strength. It can even mean playing physical games like wrestling or holding hands. Which is not to say that hugs doesn't count. Hugging always counts.

Trait #2:
Enjoyable Time Together

Strong families like to hang out with one another. In fact, they feel that spending time together is valuable and necessary. There are no real specific enjoyable activities that strong families prefer, but they do tend to show an appreciation for group adventures–even ones as simple and inexpensive as a spontaneous Sunday hike.

In general, enjoyable time together means appreciating family rituals, sharing laughter, and having gratitude for a home everyone can return to.

Trait #3:
Communicating Effectively with One Another

Strong families give family members room to share their feelings and emotions. They listen before talking and seek explanations before assigning blame.

While humor and jokes are valued in strong families, they tend to avoid put-downs and name-calling. Sarcasm is rare and everyone's point of view is appreciated and respected.

Trait #4:
Demonstrating Commitment

For strong families, commitment isn't lip service. It's not just a promise or a pledge. Instead, commitment is displayed in acts. Families that are committed to one another will share responsibility and operate democratically to the extent that it's feasible.

But more than that, commitment means showing appreciation for who each individual in the family is and celebrating that person's perspective. Strong families have a high regard for one another while keeping expectations reasonable and working to boost everyone's self-esteem.

Trait #5:
Spiritual Well-Being

The idea of spiritual well-being should not be confused with a specific religious doctrine. Strong families without a church can still share spiritual well-being by understanding that there is a greater power outside of themselves. They will appreciate family history and their connection to ancestors, while acknowledging responsibility to care for their community of the natural world. They will share a sense of peace, hopefulness, security, and safety even if those feelings aren't connected to a deity that holds the keys to their common salvation.

Trait #6:
Managing Stress and Crisis Effectively

Just because a family is strong doesn't mean that sometimes it won't be buffeted by adverse situations. After all, you can't control every health issue, natural disaster, or political shift. If anything, most families discovered exactly this in 2020, with lockdowns and a fractious political season.

So what's more important is how families address adversity. The strongest families do so with an understanding that, together, they can get through anything. They believe they have a support network that will see them through, both among themselves and with friends, and that every crisis offers a chance to learn and become stronger. They are resilient because they bend rather than break and find some good even in the darkest times.

Putting Traits into Action

Importantly, there's no specific magic to these qualities of strong families. While each can be explored in detail, as an aggregate they boil down to a simple notion. People in strong families genuinely feel good about one another and share a mutual concern for one another's health and well-being.

Strong families are strong because they understand what their strengths are and they lean into those strengths despite living in a society that DeFrain says "just murders families."

"We're just trying to produce and be seen and succeed. It's a beehive. And we don't have any time to connect with each other on an emotional and spiritual level," he says. "If you just know what your problems are you have nothing. You need to know what your strengths are and focus on those and spend time together and enjoy each other."

SO, WHAT EXACTLY IS THERE TO TALK ABOUT?

John DeFrain of the University of Nebraska–Lincoln has spent the last three decades trying to answer that question by observing and interviewing some twenty-four thousand American families.[4] All that *Brady Bunch*–style sleuthing helped him develop the International Family Strength Model, which suggests that precisely six characteristics make for strong family units.

1. Appreciation and affection.

2. Commitment to the family.

3. Positive communication.

4. Enjoyable time together.

5. Spiritual well-being.

6. Successful management of stress and crisis.

These don't map perfectly to specific conversations—asking a spouse if they're committed to a family is generally a nonstarter—but they do suggest that setting specific goals for the future is necessary to achieving anything resembling happiness and that the emotional process of preparing for a child's birth is unlikely to be entirely organic. Conversations need to happen. If Google Calendar invites are what it takes, so be it.

CONVERSATION ONE:
Should Past Be Precedent?

When it comes to parenting, adults rarely order "off the menu," the menu consisting largely of the behaviors they observed when they were young. Children of remote fathers become remote fathers. Children of overbearing mothers become overbearing mothers. Children of abuse disproportionately become abusers, and children raised by supportive parents disproportionately become supportive parents.

The heritability of parenting behaviors can be good or bad but is almost inevitably confusing for married couples who often feel that they *come from the same place* in some profound way but don't in any literal sense.

Couples bring unique views on child-rearing into a relationship and, more often than not, inconsistent expectations for themselves and each other. This is particularly true when couples come from different religious or cultural backgrounds—a truth relevant to over half of modern couples.

History, therefore, is *not* common ground. Real common ground is a landfill constructed with intention.

What to Ask:

What were the qualities of your upbringing that you remember with fondness?

* Do you feel you had enough love and respect from your parents?

* Did you feel you were safe?

* Were there family rituals that you miss that made you happy and gave you solace?

* Do you feel you had room to play and friends to share your life with?

What are the qualities of your upbringing that you wish had been different or better?

* Do you feel your family dealt with conflict appropriately?

* Do you feel that your discipline was fair or unfair?

* Did you have enough to make you comfortable?

* Were you given too little freedom? Not enough? Or just enough?

CONVERSATION TWO:
Division of Labor

When parents have expectations of the division of labor that aren't met after a child arrives, the result is resentment, increased stress, and a strain on the relationship. But the division of labor discussion isn't just about who's changing diapers and washing bottles; it's also about professional expectations. Division of labor outside the home must be considered with the division of labor inside the home too.

These conversations can be fraught, particularly if couples are striving to reach some kind of even split (not gonna happen). Yet what's more important than parity is consensus.

What to Ask:

How will we approach parental leave, and who will go back to work first?

- Are there financial considerations that make one person's work more crucial to family outcomes?

- If we consider the cost of childcare, does it make sense for someone to stay home?

- How will we foster family time if we are both working?

How will we divide home tasks during paternity leave, and maybe after?

- How will we divide feedings and nighttime duties?

- Is there a way we can agree to split diaper duty?

- Are there certain chores we'd prefer to take on? Are there chores we hate? How can we divide these equitably?

- How will we divide administrative tasks like scheduling doctors, researching day care, paying bills, or managing bank accounts?

CONVERSATION THREE:
Faith

Spiritual well-being is fundamental to a strong family. That doesn't necessarily mean a connection to a religious organization or congregation is required. It simply means that families have a shared belief in a power larger than themselves that helps organize and guide their world. That power might be God writ large. The power might come from nature, the mysteries that lie in the mathematical theorems of physics, or maybe a well-developed belief in the principles of the wizardly world of Harry Potter. The point is that families need to have something greater to believe in to help focus their values and behaviors.

What to Ask:

What does faith mean to us personally?

- Are we spiritual or are we religious?

- Are we practicing our faith or are our observances strictly cultural?

What cultural or religious traditions are most important to us?

- Are there rituals and rites that are obligatory to be a part of our religious community?

- Are there traditions that we can agree to leave up to our children when they are old enough to decide on their own?

CONVERSATION FOUR:
Health

A family's values around health can affect myriad factors of their daily lives, from their diets to how active they are to how and when they seek medical care. When a couple's ideas about what improves family well-being are out of sync, parents might find themselves struggling and, in the most extreme circumstances, placing a child at risk for disease and poor health outcomes. Before a child arrives, couples need to agree on fundamentals, including an agreement that vaccines are necessary and important; which parent (if not both) will be responsible for communicating with medical professionals on behalf of their child; and ways in which a family's nutrition and physical activity can be supported.

Importantly, mental health should be a part of this conversation. A consideration of health care should not stop at keeping a family physically healthy. Emotional and psychological well-being is crucial to health as well.

What to Ask:

How seriously do we take scientific guidance in relation to our health?

- Do we both believe that vaccines are necessary and that the science is well established?

- Do we trust medical professionals?

- How reactive do we want to be if and when our child displays symptoms of illness?

How will we continue to support each other's health?

- Can we align our diets and exercise?

- Are we giving each other enough time and space to practice mindfulness?

CONVERSATION FIVE:
Discipline

A consistent disciplinary approach is crucial for the success of any discipline style. Children are more apt to push boundaries when styles are inconsistent, and uneven discipline between parents can create resentment by making one parent the bad guy. The key to consistent discipline is to have built rules that are connected to values. So when a kid inevitably asks "Why?" the answer isn't "Because I said so"; it's "Because that's what this family stands for."

This conversation is crucial before a baby arrives because it will build a foundation for discipline when a child is older. Discipline shouldn't even be a consideration for babies. (Anyone who suggests a baby should be disciplined is plain wrong.) In fact, discipline is not effective until children have learned that other people have thoughts and ideas that are different from their own, which doesn't occur until four years old.

What to Ask:

Can we agree on a boundary now that we will put in place from day one?

- Can we abide by that boundary if it's applied evenly to everyone in the family, including adults?

- Are there boundaries we fundamentally disagree on?

When boundaries are broken, what should the consequences be?

- Is corporal punishment consistent with the moral boundaries that we agree on?

- How did the consequences we experienced as children affect us as adults?

- How do we feel about time-outs? Grounding? Talking it out with a child?

- What are the discipline strategies we've seen or read about that we'd like to try?

CONVERSATION SIX:
In-Laws

Grandmothers and grandfathers are part of the emotional environment of a family too. Whether closely involved or distant, they have an effect on the way a family operates. Their presence can add much-needed support, but their demands may also foster undue stress. That stress is amplified when couples have conflicting expectations about how involved in-laws will be in child-rearing. Understanding how to navigate holidays, rules and spending time with in-laws will help reduce friction in marriage and set good expectations for in-laws from the start.

What to Ask:

What do we want from our in-laws?

- Do we want them to provide an opportunity for children to interact with their family history and develop empathy for older people?

- Do we want them to provide support in terms of childcare?

What do we expect from our in-laws?

- Is there family history to be concerned about?

- Are there health concerns that should be considered?

- How often will we visit and/or accept visits?

With careful consideration of these issues in relation to shared values, parents will provide more than a well-feathered nest for their child. After all, a child needs more than a safe and cozy environment. They need a loving, respectful, and supportive one too.

THE CASE FOR A MISSION STATEMENT

If you've read *A Game of Thrones* you know that every clan has a motto—the "words" they live by. Famously, House Stark's words are "Winter is coming," which focuses the characters to values of preparation, grit, and stoicism that guide them on their epic journey.

Those mottoes essentially act as mission statements. In the business world, a mission statement is text that guides an organization. It's the promise that a company seeks to fulfill for its customers and shareholders, acting as a gut check. Therefore, every decision a company makes should be aligned with its mission statement.

When applied to a family, a mission statement, motto, or "words" can have the same function. They are the foundation on which the family makes decisions. The late author and businessman Stephen Covey makes a strong argument for making a family mission statement.

"Your mission statement becomes your constitution, the solid expression of your vision and values. It becomes the criterion by which you measure everything else in your life," he writes in his book *The 7 Habits of Highly Effective Families*. "If you have a family mission statement that clarifies what your purpose is, then you use that as the criterion by which you make the decisions."

Family mottoes were largely left in the Old World when America was first colonized, replaced mainly by the foundational guidance of the Bible. After all, who needed a family motto when you had hard-core commandments? But as time has gone on and the nation has become more secular, many families no longer guide their house by a religious text, leaving a vacuum of meaning that can make parenting harder.

It's easy for a child to question a parent's decisions when the decisions aren't based on a foundation of values. "Because the Bible tells me so" was eventually replaced by "Because I said so" or, in some cases, aphorisms like the Golden Rule.

What's transformational about a family mission statement is that it removes a tremendous amount of ambiguity from parenting. As much as it provides structure for decision-making—"we're going outside because we value being healthy"—it also offers quite a bit of freedom. Because so many requests kids make are unlikely to be in opposition to a mission statement— "can we play superheroes?"—there is less reason to say no out of hand, meaning this value gives you the freedom to say yes and enjoy your partner and children.

If you've ever tried to start a company, you know that writing and revising a mission statement can be quite a process. But all mission statements have some very basic commonalities. First, they describe the nature of the organization—what it looks like and how it feels. Second, it talks about what the organization does and the fundamental goals that drive it. Finally, it describes how the organization interacts with the outside world.

To the extent that mission statements have these similarities, it means that you can build your household mission statement on an existing scaffolding, almost like a Family Values Mad Lib. Does it make it any easier to narrow down the values? Not necessarily. That requires the conversations detailed above, and those conversations take time. But once you've talked, you're ready to fill in the blanks.

OUR MISSION

The _____s are a/an _____ family who believe that their
     [family name]   [adjective]

time together is best spent _____ing, _____ing, and
                   [verb]   [verb]

_____ing. Our job is to grow together and support one another through
[verb]

hardship and good times with _____,
                               [core value, such as honesty, faith]

_____, and _____. Beyond our home, we treat others with
[core value]   [core value]

_____ and _____ so that our family
[social value, such as respect, kindness]   [social value]

members are a valuable and active part of our neighborhood and

community.

CHAPTER 3

The Trouble with Birth Plans

As cavalier as the Marine Corps saying "Do or Die" sounds, the doing still requires a set of steps, instructions, and expectations—a plan. In the Marine Corps Doctrinal Publication titled *Planning*, the process of creating a plan is described with distinct martial clarity:

"Planning encompasses two basic functions—envisioning a desired future and arranging a configuration of potential actions in time and space that will allow us to realize that future."[1]

For ex-Marine Eric Raszewski of San Diego and his wife, the desired future was to deliver a healthy baby into the world. And the configuration of potential actions in time and space that would allow them to realize that future was a birth plan.

A birth plan is usually a single page, given to the hospital staff and referenced by parents, that lays out their hopes for labor and delivery. It's more of a guide than anything else—a kind of best-case-scenario wish list in the case of a typical birth. Birth plans cover important issues, like how a woman will deal with pain, whom she wants for support in the room, mobility during labor, episiotomies (to have them or not), denying continuous fetal monitoring, requests on birthing position, as well as care right after birth, like immediate breastfeeding and prolonged time on the umbilical cord.

While there's little data suggesting that one mode of birth is better than others, it's still important for couples to be able to communicate their wishes clearly. In the 1970s, as parents looked for ways to make their birth less medicalized, the concept of the birth plan was created to help them communicate their wishes to midwives, doctors, and nurses. After all, medicine thrives on documentation, so building a document that itemizes preferences—from the presence or absence of the father in the delivery room to the desired level of medical intervention—became a standard practice.

Standard, of course, doesn't necessarily mean easy or uncomplicated. The Raszewskis built their plan during birth classes connected to the hospital where they were planning on delivering their child. But despite the fact that Eric had a leadership role in the corps, and guidance from hospital staff, building a plan was still difficult.

"There was still a lot of confusion about what our options actually were," Raszewski recalls. "We didn't know what to expect. You can read a hundred articles on a hundred blogs and they all tell you something different."

That's no small wonder. Like death, birth is a largely hidden process. Many women go into labor without having ever seen labor. Many men go in so entirely unprepared they leave the delivery room traumatized. The man gawking at the horror of vaginal delivery has become a movie trope (*Knocked Up, 9 Months,* and *The Back-Up Plan,* just to name a few).

The intensity of that moment—"I can't do this!" screams Cameron Diaz in the movie *What to Expect When You're Expecting*—is juxtaposed against the beauty of the moment after, when the baby is handed to its joyful parents. Conflict. Resolution. And the studio makes 53 percent of the gross.

That clean scene is cinema verité compared to the TV shows that document modern birth. According to a study from Trinity College, 68 percent of pregnant women turned to reality shows like *A Baby Story* on The Learning Channel to help prepare for birth. The problem is, in an analysis of programs like these, complications are far more common than they are in real life.[2] The reason for this isn't because more mothers are having traumatic births; it's that normal, uncomplicated births lack the rich drama that reality television thrives on.

"As an example," writes study author Rosemary Theroux, "the situation of a breech delivery was overrepresented as 14 percent of births, even though it is typical in only 3 percent to 4 percent of births."

A broad read of the birth-related numbers in the United States cools the drama significantly. In 2018 there were 3,791,712 registered births in the United States. Of these births, 3,729,199—or just over 98 percent—occurred in a hospital. The mean age of birth mothers was about twenty-seven years old, and most of them, a full 61 percent, were married at the time they gave birth. During delivery, 75 percent of laboring mothers were given an epidural or spinal anesthesia to manage pain, and only a third of those labors were induced.

Of all the babies born in 2018, 65 percent arrived vaginally and 94 percent entered the world headfirst. Most of them arrived during business hours between Tuesday and Friday. A vast majority of the babies emerged fully baked, with 90 percent born at full term. Only 9 percent of newborns in 2018 required admission to a neonatal intensive care unit. In fact, infant mortality rates have been on a long, steady decline for nearly a century. And although it's true that far too many women die in childbirth in the US compared to the rest of the industrialized, wealthy nations, only fourteen maternal deaths occur per every hundred thousand live births.

Despite these reassuring statistics, the raft of options presented to expectant parents, combined with what they've seen of birth in the media, can throw people off.

WHAT KIND OF BIRTH EXPERIENCE DO YOU WANT? AND CAN YOU REALLY PLAN FOR THAT?

Of the over three million births in the United States, couples like the Raszewskis have to wonder what their specific birth will look like. There are a lot of questions to be answered, and they can feel overwhelming. In reality, birth plans are largely created to answer three questions: How will you manage pain? Where will you deliver? Who will be there? But these are reasonable and necessary questions that boil down to an essential query: What kind of birth experience do you want?

"The first birth plan opened us up to options that she didn't really know about," says Eric Raszewski. And considering the options, he felt the plan wasn't the place where he should flex his corps-built leadership skills. "I took a step back and let her lead. It's her body. I was just focused on making it as comfortable as possible."

Many fathers-to-be take on a subordinate role in answering these questions, and a couple of reasons account for this. One is simply that the questions are addressed to women by default. But anthropologist Richard K. Reed of Trinity University points out there's more to it than polite deference to the person growing the baby.

"They're both engaged in this process of getting ready for childbirth and getting to grips with it," explains Reed, the soft-spoken Wisconsinite who studied the anthropological role of fathers for his 2005 scholarly work, *Birthing Fathers: The Transformation of Men in American Rites of Birth*.

In fact, men tend to lag behind women in concern for pregnancy, according to Reed. But that's not from laziness or lack of will. It's because men simply do not have the biological cues that allow women to focus on reproduction.

"Women have distinct physical experience that gives them a clue that something is happening. Men experience it more cognitively and emotionally, not physically. So they are a little bit slower to come to an awareness," Reed says.[3]

That places men at a bit of a disadvantage when it comes to jumping in and helping make decisions. They aren't necessarily primed to do so. And that's okay.

"The father's help is unnecessary. If it happens, that's great. But to say that something he should do sets parameters around the process ... that can lead to trouble," Reed explains. "The expectation is that men are there to help women in the process of childbirth. But men should be there for themselves. They should be team members with unique experiences and emotions."

Also, men operate largely free from the pressures placed on women, whether it be the moral judgments of medicating pain or the implications that bonding is improved outside of medical settings. Because they have a perspective outside of the birth-industrial complex aimed at moms, they are in a prime position to provide support and act as a sounding board. A dad-to-be, if he is thoughtful and willing to take on the role, can offer a calm, reasonable voice to help sort through seemingly unreasonable choices.

Fathers-to-be can't give birth, but they will experience the birth process, cognitively and emotionally, nonetheless. And while an expectant father's particular needs and concerns may be unique in many ways, by working in parallel with their partners to build a birth plan, they can help drill down on the issues at hand, such as:

+ Is there value in experiencing the pain of birth or watching the person you love endure the pain of birth?

+ Is it more important to stay relaxed through birth or to closely monitor the labor and delivery despite the stress that might entail?

+ Is there something inherently wrong with opting for obstetric intervention like cesarean section, or is a natural birth better?

The final Raszewski plan was to have a vaginal birth with as few medical interventions as possible. But sometimes things don't work out as planned.

A VERY BRIEF AND TOTALLY MISOGYNISTIC
HISTORY OF "NATURAL CHILDBIRTH"

The reality is this: birth is a biological process involving two parties, a mother and a child. But the *how* of birth has come to feel just as important as the end result. No wonder. Unlike, say, a bar mitzvah, birth is both a life event and a physical event. In a sense, the discussion about natural versus unnatural birth—the whole notion that there is a moral vector to the process—is a privilege of the modern age. These conversations were simply not had prior to the 1950s. Consider the experience of one woman in the 1800s, who wrote of birth that "between oceans of pain, there stretched continents of fear; fear of death and a dread of suffering beyond bearing."[4]

Before the 1900s, there was no such thing as medicalized births in the United States. Birth occurred at home, either in the matrimonial bed or on a slab in the dining room. Women were attended to by experienced matriarchs, midwives, and husbands. It's a long-standing dramatic trope that men were told to go boil water, but it was an important job—the boiling water was meant to sterilize cloths in an era preceding antibiotics and effective infection control. Birth was a family affair, and it was statistically unlikely that any woman giving birth had not done so (or witnessed someone else doing so) before.

This kind of birth was later called "natural childbirth" by British obstetrician and sadomasochist Grantly Dick Read, who coined the term in his 1933 book of the same name. Dick Read was a World War I veteran who believed, based on a battlefield incident, that "God intended" women to give birth undisturbed by medical interventions or niceties. The story goes like this: Dick Read, then a medical officer, is wandering through the Flemish countryside, at least to the degree that it's possible amid the trenches and tunnels of the front. He sees a pregnant peasant woman in a field "drop a quick one," as he would later write, before gathering up her newborn and returning happily to her work. He spends a lot of time thinking about this and decides, after being taught a form of yoga-like stress-relief by an Indian soldier, that the pain of labor is largely caused by fear. Dick Read returns to England and, at the very dawn of medicalized birth, suggests the whole thing is a miscarriage of morality.[5]

Dick Read was a product of his time, which is a nice way of saying he was a racist and a misogynist. He concluded that "primitive" women did not feel pain in childbirth compared to women who were "civilized" because they were more in tune with their essential nature (becoming "factories" of life in Dick Read's formulation). Females, Dick Read suggested, just needed to focus on their prime directive.[6]

It's at least a little ironic that Dick Read's conclusions about the immorality of medical intervention at birth are now shared largely by people who would have wanted to punch his mustache off. But once sterile hospital births became standard, expecting mothers found that they were losing agency to doctors (overwhelmingly male) who took a paternalistic approach to their care and also sucked at their jobs. Shockingly, data suggests that the maternal mortality rate in America remained largely the same for home and hospital births until the 1950s, when maternal mortality rates finally began falling, thanks to better prenatal care, better antibiotics, and an increased understanding of what made a pregnancy high risk, like high blood pressure, diabetes, or carrying twins and triplets.[7]

Part of the reason for the lagging mortality rates was because doctors were increasingly enchanted with new tools meant to make the job of birth easier—whether they were helping or not. So much was the admiration for new technology and procedures that they became used in every birth regardless of need. Case in point: many physicians started using forceps to extract babies during any birth, whether they were called for or not. This led to a steep increase in vaginal trauma during birth as well as infant injuries and deaths.[8]

In the 1910s, the dissociative anesthetic scopolamine was found to cause women to "forget" the pain of birth experiences. As word got out, early feminists like Charlotte Carmody sought out what they considered a right to "pain free" births that resulted from scopolamine's so-called twilight sleep. At twilight sleep rallies organized by Carmody, she would tell the assembled, "If you women want twilight sleep you will have to fight for it."[9]

Sadly, Carmody would die in a twilight sleep during the birth of her fourth child in 1915. But scopolamine stuck around, and by the 1930s many doctors would administer the sedative in analgesic drug cocktails by default. The drug would essentially remove women mentally and emotionally from the birth process. There was still pain—so much so that women had to be tied to their beds while giving birth and neighbors living beside twilight-sleep birth centers complained of the screaming—it was just that the birthing mothers didn't remember it.

Doctors had tools, but they didn't have relevant tools—such as antibiotics for infection control. Still, even when hospital mortality rates began to fall, mothers felt burned by the doctors they were obliged to trust.

NEED TO KNOW

Birth Methods:
From Assisted to Water Birth

The birth plan covers just about everything leading up to delivery–from who will be allowed in the delivery room to pain management. But the heart of the document is what a couple expects from the delivery itself. If you're seeking more from the birth experience than simply delivering a healthy baby no matter how it happens, then there are a raft of birth options to choose from–none of which actually include giving birth on a raft, but you do you.

Assisted Vaginal Delivery

With assisted vaginal delivery, the baby emerges from the birth canal as one might expect, but mom and baby are receiving the equivalent of a Scott Skiles no-look bounce pass by way of medical intervention. Those interventions include episiotomy (surgical incision between the anus and the vagina), vacuum extraction (literally suckin' the baby out by the head), and forceps extraction (think salad tongs). Other methods of assistance are related to getting the process going (called induction) by introducing the hormone Pitocin or rupturing the membrane of the amniotic sack.

Bonapace Method

Bonapace is a method of delivery meant to reduce the need for doctors to use medical pain relief like epidurals (see below). The technique involves a partner providing targeted massage to a delivering mother while she engages in visualization and meditation. It requires agile, tireless, and strong fingers and an ability to mediate. There's no real reason a virtual reality headset can't be used in place of meditation and visualization. So, you now have an excuse to buy one . . . it's for her!

Cesarean Section

A cesarean section, or C-section, is a surgical delivery of a baby through the uterine and abdominal wall. It can either be an emergency procedure done when there are signs of fetal distress during delivery or be an elective scheduled procedure. Either way it's done, mothers generally require more recovery time. For fathers, that means more time with the newborn and some crucial skin-to-skin contact. Cesarean sections are weirdly controversial, particularly in "natural birth" circles, but they also give men a ton of infant time up-front.

Epidural

An epidural is an injection to the base of the spine that essentially blocks pain from the waist down. When they go perfectly, birth is a relatively painless process. But if they are administered too late or improperly, they can actually lead to a more painful birth. If your partner wants one or is on the fence, it might be better to plan ahead. There is a point of no return in labor when an epidural can no longer be administered. Epidurals are not harmful to babies and do not lead to less bonding or poor outcomes for women and babies.

Free Birth

Practiced by folks who are extremely averse to medical intervention, free birthers give birth without any kind of assistance whatsoever. There is some virtue signaling around this practice, for sure, and some women have died while free birthing. It's not recommended.

Home Birth

Home birth is exactly what it sounds like. Women, assisted by a midwife, give birth in their homes. There are some risks, should the birth suddenly become complicated, but most home births, particularly for women who are having typical pregnancies, turn out just fine. The best part is that it eliminates the nerve-racking drive home from the hospital, and the cost is significantly cheaper.

Hypnobirthing

The term *hypnobirthing* is directly related to a specific birth program but, like calling all soda Coke, it's also the common term for hypnosis-assisted delivery. The technique has celeb appeal, having been used by Jessica Alba and Kate Middleton, but it's also pretty effective for nonfamous women who'd prefer to have less medical intervention during birth. The technique basically involves breathing and self-hypnosis techniques that help women feel less fearful and more relaxed during birth. According to an analysis of five studies, women using hypnobirthing techniques were 50 percent less likely to need painkiller drugs during labor and 33 percent less likely to use an epidural. If this is the goal of the birth, this is certainly not a bad thing.

Natural Vaginal Birth

Plain Jane, vanilla vaginal birth with no fancy bells, whistles, pain medications, or interventions. One could argue that any vaginal birth is "natural," but some mothers and midwives are sticklers about what natural means. Generally the idea is that medical interventions are kept to the barest minimum so that women can feel and experience every single moment of the process. More power to them.

Water Birth

The point of water birth is to reduce the effects of gravity of the body while delivering. When a woman is submerged in water, there is less pressure on her spine, and there is a calming feeling of weightlessness that allows for less fear and anxiety. Water births can happen at birth centers or hospitals in specially appointed rooms, or couples can invest in renting a tub for home births. Water birth works mainly because when an infant is still attached to the umbilical cord, they are getting all the oxygen they need while submerged. Yes, you are giving birth in a bathysphere. Congratulations.

Though it's tempting—especially for the male beneficiaries of progress—to remember the second wave of the feminist movement as coincidental to the rise of birth control, birth control can have two meanings. "Giving birth naturally in the era of the women's movement became seen by some as an opportunity for consciousness-raising, spiritual fulfillment, and female empowerment," explains Jessica Martucci in her history of the medicalized versus natural birth debate published in the *American Medical Association Journal of Ethics*.[10] Or, as poet Adrienne

Rich put it differently in her 1976 book, *Of Woman Born*: "The female body has been both territory and machine, virgin wilderness to be exploited and assembly-line turning out life. We need to imagine a world in which every woman is the presiding genius of her own body."[11]

This idea sank in. In 2002, a survey showed 45 percent of women agreed that "birth is a natural process that should not be interfered with unless medically necessary." But this sounds very much like something Dick Read would say.

The most modern wave of feminism has come to level heavy critiques on natural childbirth as well, namely that the term "natural" paints women into the corner of their own homes where they would "naturally" be engaged in homemaking. Critics suggest this gender-normative bias is reinforced by the natural birth movement's push to have home births.

And then there's the seemingly bizarre insistence that women *should* feel pain. In her 1999 *New York Times* column "Pay On Delivery," Margaret Talbot notes that moralizers long considered it necessary for women to feel the pain of birth as a way to acknowledge Eve's original sin.

"Today's natural childbirth purists don't see moral punishment in pain but they do see moral superiority in refusing pain relief," Talbot writes. "They do see labor as a kind of performance, for which a woman can and should rehearse, and in which she can comfort herself more or less admirably."[12]

CHOOSING PAIN AND THE PAIN OF CHOOSING

For some women the pressure to choose pain during birth is like asking someone to forgo anesthetic during gallbladder surgery. The choice was clear for thirty-nine-year-old mother of three Annie Murray, a marketing copywriter from Youngstown, Ohio. She delivered her first child, Iris, as a twenty-six-year-old in Poole, England, through the National Health System, where maternity care is provided predominantly by midwives. She remembers that prenatal classes stressed the importance of having an unmedicated natural birth. But the thought of the pain terrified her.

"I felt very strongly that it's also a natural thing to embrace science and the human mind and how we've invented these things that make this process easier for women," Annie says. "I think that it's natural to want things as easy and enjoyable as possible."

She insisted on an epidural, but it was administered poorly and the pain remained—enough so that she was given a form of fentanyl that, she says, made her feel removed and out of it. Her second child, Henry, was born in the United States, and her epidural was, basically, delightful. Her husband, Lee, remembers that three hours into labor his wife looked to be struggling. He left the room for about twenty minutes and when he came back, she was sitting up, relaxed, cracking jokes and eating sorbet.

"I was having a wonderful time," Annie remembers. "The entire rest of that labor was . . . fun. I remember being disappointed when it was time to push."

The experience of pain of her first birth had certainly not made her feel stronger or better as a mother. Moreover, the painless experience of her second child had made the process joyful.

Importantly, studies show no real difference in the long-term outcomes of birth methods, whether they be considered natural or medical. For instance, a small 2016 study from the University of Wisconsin, published in the journal *Developmental Psychology*, compared the quality of mother–infant bonding in 167 mother–infant pairs in regard to their mode of delivery. The quality of bonding was measured at four and twelve months after delivery. At both intervals, researchers found the quality of bonding between mothers who had vaginal deliveries versus planned or unplanned cesarean deliveries to be the same. Authors concluded, "Results indicate little cause for concern about the quality of mother–infant interactions following cesarean deliveries."[13]

Most studies that look into the natural versus medicalized dichotomy note that, at least in the short term, satisfaction with birth regardless of intervention is largely dependent on whether parents feel heard and included in the decision-making processes.

NOW IT'S PERSONAL

In her study called The Good Birth Project, medical ethicist Anne Lyerly and her team interviewed a diverse group of 101 women who'd had a total of 201 birth experiences, from cesarean to natural. What she found was that women often felt guilty because what they expected and wanted from a birth was different from what they actually experienced. Lyerly identified five factors that made a good birth: agency, knowledge, respect, connectedness, and personal security.[14]

In many respects, a birth plan helps focus parents on these exact issues. It offers them a chance to have agency in their birth; it requires that they gain knowledge about the process; it demands respect for the parents' wishes from the medical staff that will use it as a road map to care; it offers a sense of security; and it brings couples together as they focus on the plan.

"This is a great time to be open about that and have free-flowing information," explains anthropologist Richard K. Reed. That's because the qualities that will make a birth good for a mother are not necessarily the same qualities that will make it good for a father. Working on a birth plan lays the groundwork for fathers to decide what they want to get out of the actual event—aside from a child to raise—which is not something that ought to be taken for granted.

"That's something that a birth plan can do: open up communication and legitimize communication, which is really important, verging on magical," Reed says.

To create the birth plan, couples need to orient themselves to the details of the birth of their child. In doing so, expectant parents are placed in a position to study procedures and options. A birth plan forces couples to learn, and that learning can and does increase confidence and readiness. When built as a couple, a birth plan also allows fathers to more clearly understand their role in birth. It allows a conversation to occur, meaning there is a chance for fathers to honestly interrogate their desire to be in the room during delivery and just how involved they want to be.

NEED TO KNOW

The Unlikely Controversy of
Fetal Monitoring

Notably, birth plans are generally used by parents who want a drug-free birth. That makes sense. By default, most hospital births will proceed in the manner deemed necessary for infant and mother safety. And when it comes to safety, hospitals generally default to more interventions rather than fewer. So women in labor will be given intravenous fluids, kept in bed and hooked up to a continuous fetal monitor. All of this despite the fact that studies do not show there are better outcomes with these interventions.

For instance, consider the case of continuous electronic fetal monitoring. The procedure, which includes outfitting the mother with a band to detect heart rate and oxygen flow to the fetus, was initially suggested in order to recognize fetal asphyxiation that could lead to cerebral palsy. As was the case for the use of forceps in the 1900s, fetal monitoring became a ubiquitous practice for every pregnancy, despite not being subjected to clinical trials.

Meanwhile, research began to mount that fetal monitoring in otherwise healthy women was leading to poor birth outcomes. Studies found that the practice was linked to a significant increase in unnecessary cesarean sections, and its widespread use did not decrease instances of cerebral palsy, infant death, or any other health indicators that would suggest it was a valuable intervention. Instead, it seemed to simply add more stress and uncertainty. Even to this day, fetal monitoring in America is the standard of care despite evidence that led researchers to call it "junk science" in a study published in 2017 in the journal *Medical Law International.*[15]

The issue of fetal monitoring points to the real benefit and promise of a birth plan, which is ultimately supposed to give you the birth experience you truly want—no wires attached.

In the best circumstances, birth plans help parents manage their expectations by learning what, exactly, the birth process looks like. But it's important to point out that every delivery is unique and there can be complications. In those cases, it's important for parents to respect the knowledge of nurses and doctors. That doesn't mean that your birth plan needs to go out the window. It simply means that the birth plan needs to bend a bit. Just because one intervention is required does not mean that other parts of the birth plan are lost. Just because the birthing position needs to change, for instance, doesn't mean that the baby can't be immediately breastfed.

In its *Planning* document, the Marine Corps stresses that plans need to be flexible:

"Planning is a process that should build upon itself—each step should create a new understanding of the situation which becomes the point of departure for new plans. Planning for a particular action only stops with execution, and even then, adaptation continues during execution."[16]

Eric Raszewski learned that what's true on the battlefield is true in the delivery room. His daughter Penny arrived after sixty-five hours of labor, which is about three times the average of twenty hours of early and active labor combined.

"We pushed off a lot of the different mechanisms that we could use for a while," Raszewski remembers. But once we got around the forty-hour mark, they came in and said, 'Here's the birth plan. It's just not gonna happen,' and we started to adjust from there."

Towards the end of labor, a doctor worried about the baby's heart rate suggested they would have to do a C-section within an hour. Raszewski says that at the mention of a C-section everyone went into "hulk mode," and Penny was born fifteen minutes later.

So, what kind of childbirth experience do you want?

The answer might be "research based" or "natural" or some combination thereof. Fundamentally, it's personal. For Raszewski, the process of creating a birth plan helped him connect with his wife. "It was the best experience we've had from a communications standpoint, understanding, togetherness. I relate it a little bit to the military, when you go through bad experiences but have a good result. It's a lot of that type of feeling. It wasn't a good time. But it was a meaningful time."

The result? A beautiful daughter. And that's really all the Raszewskis ever really wanted.

CHAPTER 4

Fathers in the Delivery Room

Andrea's water broke five days past her due date. It was a Sunday, October 15. Andrea's husband, thirty-year-old KeyBank social customer care manager Ian McCormick, called the doctor, who told him to sit tight, and the doula, who told Andrea to breathe. The next morning, contractions started in earnest, and Ian drove Andrea to the Fairview Hospital in East Cleveland on the leafy autumnal border of the Rocky River's metro park. Both were optimistic. Both expected a calm, uncomplicated birth.

But the water-birthing room was booked. That had been the whole reason they'd picked the center in the first place. Shaking off their disappointment, they settled into their less-than-optimal birthing suite. Then, nothing happened.

And nothing proceeded to happen at regular cycles until, twenty-four hours later, doctors decided to give nature a kick in the ass. They administered a synthetic hormone called Pitocin, which some women report causes labor to be more painful, to move Andrea's labor along. Still, despite moving into active labor, marked by regular contractions meant to push the baby out of the womb, Andrea's cervix remained resolutely undilated. No open. No sesame.

Ian struggled to keep midwives and doctors focused on the birthing plan. "There were times I had to really enforce it," he says. "But I was watching my wife go through a horrendous amount of pain. On one hand, I was hearing nurses say we needed to stick with the Pitocin, but on the other hand, I have my wife saying, 'Stop the Pitocin!' Our goal was to have our baby without epidurals or C-sections."

Two days after Andrea's initial contractions, midwives informed the McCormicks that their baby's heart rate was dropping. Andrea relented and accepted an epidural. Moments later they were told that an emergency C-section was necessary. It was the exact opposite of everything the couple had wanted.

Ian felt awful. He felt like he'd failed in the one part of birth that was his job to do.

Birth is lonely for dads. Global research on fathers' experience in the birthing room between 1999 and 2012—a scant twenty-three studies over a thirteen-year period—indicates remarkable consistencies and general disappointment. Common emotional themes include uncertainty, fear, and frustration. Men feel lost, and that's no wonder. Their role is ambiguous at best and counterproductive at worst. Though some men do wind up providing their partners with meaningful support and relief, they often do so at some personal cost—experiencing a degree of trauma or emotional discomfort.

Stress is certainly more manageable than nine months of carrying a child, hours of labor, a ripped taint, ice packs, frozen maxi pads, squirt bottles, doughnut pillows, and weeks of recovery. Still, men would do well to engage in some pregame expectation management for themselves or at least to consider why they are there to begin with.

Here's a question that soon-to-be parents don't hear: "Does the father want to be at the birth?" The presumption is that any expecting father planning on being a part of his child's life will show up. This is nice in the sense that it empowers fathers to participate and obligates them to engage with the visceral fact of the thing. You're about to have a child—you should be prepared to engage. But there is one thing having a father in the delivery room is not: necessary. It's hardly a given that fathers who attend their children's births are useful to their partners. On a medical, human, and biological level, it's all a bit sloppy, according to OB/GYN and member of the HealthyWomen Women's Health Advisory Council, Rashmi Kudesia.

"There's always that dad that is forced to be there," Kudesia says of the hundreds of births she's attended. "He's there but he's checked out. They put the woman in a situation where she feels self-conscious about her partner at a time when there are already enough things to be thinking and worrying about."

Kudesia acknowledges that those men are extreme variations of the dads-to-be who show up in the delivery room. After all, no one is ever "prepared" for the first birth experience—men or women. It's a wild ride that could go in any number of directions. But planning is necessary, as is having some sense of what you're doing there. Still, some men will show up, regardless of preparation or lack thereof, just because peer pressure is hard to ignore.

INTO THE PRESSURE COOKER

In 2008, foul-mouthed British celebrity chef Gordon Ramsay admitted to tabloid reporters at the *Sun* that he'd sat out the birth of four of his five children. During one of the births (he hasn't said which) he was fly-fishing.

"I don't want to see a skinned rabbit or skinned pigeon coming out of your ninny and then get excited and hold it," he explained.[1]

The inevitable backlash came fast for Ramsay—he complained in a 2019 Australian *Women's Weekly* interview that he'd been characterized as an "oaf." So, by the time his fifth child, Oscar, was due in 2020, Ramsay decided that, yes, on second thought, he would be there. He passed out.

Anthropologist Richard K. Reed, who spent years interviewing some fifty-three men about their birth experiences for his 2005 academic work, *Birthing Fathers*, describes the geometry of the inevitable hospital birthing room clusterfuck in triangular terms. Dad wants to soothe and protect mom. The doctor wants a successful birth. Mom wants to feel connected to a fundamental rite of womanhood. This is the "birthing triad," and it's a disaster waiting to happen.

Not all members of the birthing triad carry the same authority. Hospitals and birthing centers, for instance, require processes that aren't particularly flexible. Medical care needs to have rules, not just so medical procedures are successful but also to limit liability risk. That gives them a tremendous amount of power. Doctors aren't huge fans of patient opinion.

"That puts a father at an extreme disadvantage and peripheralizes them. When the doctor and the father enter into that tension, it's an excruciating moment for the mother. That's when the woman's voice is completely lost," writes Reed.[2]

When a father is trying to advocate for his wife, who is often in pain, his attempt to manage and control that pain puts him in conflict with the medical staff. When this happens, "you'll see a physician ratchet up the medical authority that they wield," Reed explains.

"For some men birth can be incredibly discomfiting to see all of these people messing with your wife's body in this medical way," Kudesia says. "They may not understand all the things that need to go on. I've had a lot of fathers, where the fetal heart rate drops, and a lot of people come in and Dad is really freaking out, understandably, because now he's trying to protect his wife."

"I was talking with Andrea, holding her hand, and then suddenly I heard all of this slicing and dicing," Ian McCormick remembers of his wife's C-section operation. "It was almost like hearing Wolverine pop his claws, except this was real life and you have these two people you love more than anything on the line."

Not all men—hell, not all people—react well to having their power taken away. Chef Ramsey credited his brief foray into unconsciousness to panic in the face of his own powerlessness. Unable to upbraid the staff, he simply switched off. Many men switch into more aggressive roles and wind up antagonizing, well, everyone, and starting fatherhood on the wrong foot.

"I've talked to some men for whom it was a horrible experience. They walk out angry at their partners, and their partners end up feeling let down and disaffected. And I've talked to women who've said they couldn't do it without their partner and their partners say it was a moving experience," Reed says. "These people have really different relationships. When you look at the variation in relationships between partners, you realize that when you subject people to one of the most stressful times of their lives, they are going to live out the incredible strengths in that relationship and the most tragic weaknesses."

"I've had situations where Dad says to his partner, 'Try doing it this way,' or 'You can do it. Just do it a little bit harder,'" says OB/GYN Rashmi Kudesia. "And sometimes in the incredible stress of birth people wind up fighting. Sometimes I think it would be better if Dad hit the brakes."

Unfortunately, birth has stakes beyond the well-being of the child. Of course, infant health should be prioritized over Dad's feelings. But a man's experience of birth can have a tremendous impact on everyone's emotional well-being in the first months of his child's life. A bad experience can increase the chances of men experiencing paternal postpartum depression and stress, which affects a child's quality of care. Moreover, stress can affect the support they can provide for their partner. This is particularly true for men with a past history of depression spectrum disorders.

A 2009 City University of London surveyed twenty-six fathers who had attended a traumatic or difficult birth and found that 12 percent had experienced symptoms fitting the diagnostic criteria for PTSD.[3]

While full-blown PTSD can occur in men after witnessing a complicated or traumatic birth, it's not common after normal births. But it's also not unusual for some PTSD-related symptoms to pop up. In 2010, a researcher at Derbyshire Children's Hospital had 199 fathers complete a PTSD questionnaire six weeks after attending the birth of their child. While none of the men had all three PTSD dimensions—hyperarousal, intrusive thoughts, and avoidance—12 percent of the new fathers reported "clinically significant symptoms" in at least one PTSD dimension, most often hyperarousal. More important, researchers found that developing a PTSD symptom was most likely to happen in men who had few children, who felt less prepared and less confident about coping, and who felt distress during the actual delivery.[4]

While all modern men may face the expectation that they attend the birth of their child, it's clear enough that when a man is a medical, logistical, and emotional liability—and his partner agrees with this assessment—not all men should be present. A conversation about the upside is probably in order. Doing something potentially problematic simply because that's the way it's done doesn't make much sense.

COOKING WITH YOUR OWN TOOLS

Suggesting a father should have the right to opt out of attending the birth of his child feels deeply subversive. But there isn't any research suggesting that a dad who attends the birth of his child is somehow a better father. To that point, women aren't better mothers for just having given birth.

There is no special magic in catching a baby from between your partner's thighs or snipping the rubbery umbilical cord like a grand-opening ribbon. Having a hands-on birth experience does not seem to matter for a father's long-term bond to his child.

It's hard to talk about expectations around major life events. And the birth conversation can be difficult to navigate, says Rashmi Kudesia. She would know. She had the talk with her husband before the birth of her daughter and discovered that he had a number of specific fears. He was particularly worried that his squeamishness would cause him to feel uncomfortable watching the birth. He had absolutely no interest in being front and center. Hearing this honest feedback, Kudesia opted to hire a doula to be a birth attendant, taking pressure off her husband.

"People have these different ideals. It requires a little bit of introspection about how those ideals line up between two people in a couple," Kudesia says. "It's not going to look the same for every couple. Ours didn't line up the same, and it was good to know ahead of time."

Richard K. Reed notes that bringing a fourth party into the birthing room can be a good strategy because it breaks up the devilish birthing triad that's so full of tension. "The fourth member breaks up the triad and allows the father to be there for himself, while the other person is there to assist the mother," Reed says. "You need to break that triad with someone who can absorb the heat, stand up to the establishment, and knows how to work it."

Given that there are professionals available who can take on coaching, attending, and medical liaison roles, dads-to-be have a bit more leeway to examine their birthing desires. There's room to consider the experience they want, including whether they want to be in the delivery room at all.

Of course the only way to understand whether you want to be in the room where it happens is to know what will happen there. That's why birth classes are an important part of preparation for dads. Many of these classes will be linked with pain and labor management techniques like Lamaze, which focuses on breath control, and the Bradley Method, which centers fathers in the role of birth coach. But there are dad-specific classes too.

The best classes will help dads understand how to manage their own feelings while providing support. They will also give a glimpse into what birth looks like via eye-opening documentary videos. These are particularly helpful so you don't freak out when your kid is crowning.

It's true that the popular story of fathers in the delivery room is that a man is immediately transformed when they are handed a child. The popular notion is that the birthing room is the crucible in which the identity of fatherhood is formed. But, in fact, the experiences of fathers who have been in the room are as diverse as the fathers who experienced them. Some dads will feel the transformation; some may not feel the bond until weeks after they have brought their child home. It's not always love at first sight, and there's no real reason to believe that matters.

Unfortunately there is no real data on how often fathers fail at immediately bonding with their infant. The stories are anecdotal, told like guilty confessions over beers. There's a void in the empirical data about why bonding may or may not occur between fathers and infants in the delivery room. The reason for this is simple: until the 1970s few, including dads, really cared about their presence at birth. And in the fifty years since fathers become a fixture in the delivery room, researchers have failed to produce a significant body of research that delves into the experience of fathers. Thus the conclusion of a 2017 study titled "Integrative Review of Factors and Interventions that Influence Early Father-Infant

Bonding," published in the *Journal of Obstetric, Gynecologic & Neonatal Nursing*:

"There is an immediate need to perform studies on specific interventions aimed at the promotion of early father-infant bonding in the United States," the authors wrote. "More research is needed to better understand the timing of early father-infant bonding and how this bonding influences a provider's role, attitude, and priority for establishing successful bonding interventions for fathers."

In other words, on this point, expecting fathers will best be served by talking to other dads than looking to science.

Jay Dorscher is a father of two boys, one his genetic offspring and one a product of his wife's previous marriage. He feels a deep bond with both. "When I got to know my eventually adopted son, I loved him as much as anyone I had ever loved before," Dorscher says. He adds that he's happy he was at the birth of his second kid. "I was changed again," he says. But he acknowledges he would have been no less the kid's dad if he'd been fly-fishing during the actual moment of birth.

For Ian McCormick, the change took longer. It might have been the chaos of the birth process or the fact that everything seemed to go wrong, but he didn't feel an immediate bond with his baby daughter.

"I felt a little guilty when she was first born," McCormick says. "I didn't automatically feel that connection to her like I thought I would when she was first born. It came with time, tending to her and being with her and having silent moments. I knew I was a father the day she was born, but I didn't feel like a father until a couple of months after."

But that's not to say that a decision to stay out of the delivery room should be made cavalierly. Many women feel a deep sense of support and comfort from having their partners by their sides during birth. And if lack of a father's presence, or conflict over a father's presence, causes acute stress, chances of complications like preterm birth can be higher.

For all of these reasons it's likely that most expectant fathers, like Dorscher and McCormick, will bundle their partners into the car and drive them to the hospital with the intention of being present for the whole business. And it's clear that the possibilities of what comes between checking in and childbirth are truly endless. But for every birth there are constants: waiting, punctuated by ferocious activity, nervousness, hand-holding, and plenty of encouragement. You will be sent out to retrieve ice chips. You inevitably get in someone's way. But in the end, you will have a child. And that kid will be the best thing you ever waited nine months to receive.

NEED TO KNOW

All the Words You'll Hear in the Delivery Room and What They Mean

The hospital delivery room or birth center can be a place where abject boredom turns into a high-stakes episode of *Grey's Anatomy* in a matter of moments. And like any good medical drama, the room will be filled with jargon and shorthand that might leave you guessing as to what's going on. From APGAR to Vernix, these are the words and phrases you'll need to decipher in the delivery room.

Abruption

When the placenta shears off the uterine wall, it can cause what's known as a placental abruption. This can require immediate cesarean delivery to save both mom and baby from the risk of massive blood loss. Rest easy, though. It occurs in only 1 percent of pregnancies.

APGAR

The first test you kid will ever take, the acronym stands for Appearance, Pulse, Grimace, Activity, and Respiration, all of which will be measured on your baby minutes after it is born. Each aspect of the APGAR is scored on a scale from zero to two–zero being not good and two being great–added together for a total score up to ten. Any score of seven and higher is normal. Babies rarely score a perfect ten.

Amniotic Sac

This is the bag your kid has been hanging in for the last nine months. Aside from your baby, it's also filled with amniotic fluid. When your partner's water "breaks," the amniotic sac has been ruptured, allowing the fluid to escape (it may not gush like the movies suggest). This often means labor is on the way. Sometimes, an obstetrician might manually rupture the membrane of the amniotic sac to get things going. This is called rupturing membranes.

Bloody Show

This is not a euphemism for *Game of Thrones*; it's a good sign that labor is progressing. Essentially, the term is used when the cervix starts to dilate and a mucus plug passes through the birth canal, with slight bleeding.

Bradycardia

This means the fetal heartbeat is too low.

Breech

When a baby is not in a head-down position, it is considered in a breech position. Doctors can attempt to turn the baby manually or they may suggest a C-section be performed.

CS

Shorthand for cesarean section or C-section. This is the term for delivering a baby via surgical incision in the mother's lower abdomen.

Cervidil, Cytotec, Misoprostol, or Pitocin

These are drugs and hormones that can help move labor along. Some, like Cervidil, can be inserted close to the cervix to help it soften and dilate. Others, like Pitocin, are usually administered via IV.

Cervix

This is a muscular structure that divides the uterus from the birth canal. It keeps the baby in place for the nine-month baking period, but it has to soften and open, or dilate, in order for birth to occur. When the cervix opens to six centimeters, as measured by the delivery doctor feeling the cervix with their finger, a woman is considered in active labor. The cervix must open to ten centimeters to allow the baby to pass through.

Contractions

The muscles of the uterus contract during labor to help push the baby through the cervix and into the birth canal. As a woman enters labor, the time between contractions gets shorter. This is why parents are asked to time the contractions.

Crowning

When a baby's head begins to emerge from the birth canal, it's called crowning. If your kid has a good head of hair, you'll generally see its fuzzy noggin as it crowns, if you happen to be in view.

Colostrum

The first breast milk a mother produces is called colostrum. It's full of all the good stuff a baby needs, including probiotics and immune-boosting antibodies. In a perfect world, a baby will be breastfeed immediately. In some rare circumstances, babies struggle to latch and some mothers have physical barriers to breastfeeding. In most cases, however, babies should be placed on the breast right away.

Cord Blood

This is blood from the umbilical cord and can be saved for banking. Some experts suggest that the stem cell–rich blood can be therapeutic in cases when a child might develop genetic conditions or early childhood cancers.

Effacement

The cervix is shaped like a long, muscular cylinder. For the baby to arrive, the cervix has to shorten so that it's flush with the uterus, which is called effacement. Doctors measure this by percentages. A cervix is fully effaced at 100 percent. This means good things are happening.

Engaged

You thought you'd wait decades for your kid to be engaged. Not so! When it moves downward in the uterus so that there is no more room between its head and the pelvic bones, the baby is considered fully engaged. Apparently "locked and loaded" was already taken.

Epidural

A common method of pain control used in labor, the epidural is administered via a catheter introduced near the spinal cord on the lower back. Once an epidural is administered, mothers can't walk until well after delivery. If a C-section is required, surgical anesthesia can be given through the epidural. This is known as a "spinal." Resist the urge to sing "Stonehenge."

Episiotomy

This is the increasingly rare practice of making a cut on the perineum (see definition below) to ease a baby's delivery.

Fetal Monitoring

Fetal monitoring measures a baby's heartbeat during labor. A device is often strapped around the abdomen, but there are also wireless versions. It should be noted that there is some controversy over whether fetal monitoring is ultimately helpful. Some researchers suggest that the use of fetal monitoring has led to increased assisted-birth interventions in otherwise normal pregnancies.

Fontanel

The fontanel is the "soft spot" on a baby's head. The spot is formed by a small gap between skull bones that allow a baby's head to mold itself to the birth canal for easier delivery. You're not going to poke your finger through it, so take a breath. The fontanel closes as the bones fuse together in infancy.

Forceps or Vacuum

Forceps look a bit like salad tongs, and a vacuum operates essentially the same way the vacuum at home does. Both instruments may be used to extricate an infant in dire circumstances, but they are rare.

GBS

Short for Group B streptococcus. Women can normally have this bacteria among their vaginal flora. Docs will test for it and administer antibiotics during labor, if necessary, to prevent a baby from developing a GBS infection.

Induction

Labor is "induced" when not happening spontaneously. The typical methods of induction are through medications (see Cervidil above) or through manual means like rupturing membranes or, a move only Pennywise could get excited about, inflating a specialized balloon in the lower uterus to help dilate the cervix.

Labor

The process often begins when the amniotic sac breaks and continues as the cervix dilates and uterine contractions push the baby through the birth canal. It's labor because it's hard, sweaty, painful, and exhausting damn work.

Meconium

This is the scientific name for your baby's first poop. It's usually green or dark brown. But if your baby poops before it's delivered, things can get dicey, sometimes resulting in the rare meconium aspiration syndrome, in which the baby breathes in the meconium.

Mucus Plug

A mucus plug is created by the cervix during pregnancy to keep infection from the uterus. Gross, but helpful, it will often be passed early in labor.

NICU (pronounced Nick-yoo)

Shorthand for the neonatal intensive care unit. Babies who are premature, or who are experiencing other health issues, will spend time here after delivery.

Nuchal Cord

A rare complication when the umbilical cord is wrapped around the baby's neck, a nuchal cord can cause fetal distress during labor.

Occiput Anterior and Occiput Posterior

This is when the position of the baby is head down, facing the mother's back, also called occiput anterior (OA). Less ideal is occiput posterior (OP), where a baby is head down but facing forwards. You might call this sunny-side up. This can cause more pain and slower labor progression and may be cause for a C-section.

Perineum

You probably know it as the taint. Located on women between the labia and the anus, the perineum will stretch during labor. Sometimes it may also tear. These tears will be repaired right after delivery, but they require painful and inconvenient aftercare that you need to be aware of and super cool about.

Placenta

A temporary organ that keeps your baby healthy during pregnancy. It's delivered after the baby is out. Please do not eat it. There is no reason to—no matter what your hippie friend told you. But if you want to plant it under a tree or whatever, go ahead.

Shoulder Dystocia

You might hear this if your baby's shoulders get stuck after its head emerges. The doc will help the baby maneuver to get free quickly.

Tachycardia

The opposite of bradycardia, tachycardia is when a heart rate goes too high.

Vernix

The vernix is the waxy residue on your baby's skin after birth. It's weird but totally normal and protects your kid's new skin.

Vertex/Cephalic

When your baby is head down for labor, like it should be, it is vertex or cephalic.

Vitamin K, Hepatitis B

Your child needs a couple of interventions right after birth. Vitamin K will help ensure a baby does not bleed too much. Antibiotic eye drops will prevent any eye infections. A hepatitis B vaccination will prevent Hep B.

CHAPTER 5

The Case for a Cigar

Before the 1970s, anyone in an American hospital could mark a father-to-be. He was the lonely fella who'd shed his suit jacket like an uncomfortable skin—leaving it draped limp, wrinkled, and forgotten over the arm of a nearby chair. Shirtsleeves rolled to the elbows, he paced back and forth, soliciting doctor and nurse for news. His wife was back there somewhere, going through God-only-knows-what, and there was really no one to share his anxiety except for the other expectant fathers in the "Stork Club," the labor-ward waiting room, lost in their own anxious, pacing thoughts.

Until the doctor came through those double doors marked "Authorized Personnel Only" to inform him he was now a father, that guy didn't know what to do with himself. But after that clap on his back, he did. He'd stride to that forsaken suit jacket and reach into the inside breast pocket to produce a package of Robert Burns cigars, their printed cellophane slips proclaiming "It's a Boy" or "It's a Girl." Then he'd pass them around to all the other men-in-waiting. With pride.

But Stork Clubs are no longer. America's modern dads are expected to be bedside when their wives deliver, and an overwhelming majority are right there.[1] For many men, meeting their new child "at the door," so to speak, is an undeniably essential part of the experience of fatherhood. But even as men move closer to the moment of birth, they've grown further apart from one another.

Parenthood is increasingly isolating. Men start fatherhood locked away with their partner during birth, far from broader male support groups. After that, if dads are lucky, they may score a few weeks of leave, the length of which requires a kind of immersive power-bonding that is necessarily focused on the family but further isolating from other men. Infancy requires fathers removing themselves from work friends and even close friends in order to focus on their new role. That's not to say that the time a father spends with his child isn't incredibly valuable for him, his partner, and his kid. But it is to say that loneliness—something that many American fathers struggle with—is all but imposed on day one. But loneliness is standard operating procedure for American masculinity. Consider John Wayne, the standard bearer for "real men" who wandered the lonesome West with only his horse and gun for company. He never asked for help. People asked him for help. New fathers in the United States, out West or not, hew pretty close to that rugged symbol of individualism, and at their own peril.

The new father cigar ritual has a history as long as tobacco cultivation and use in the Americas, according to cigar manufacturer lore. Though the stories are likely apocryphal: if you squint through the smoke rings of time, you'll see that cigar giving at birth has the hazy outlines of a Native American tribal ceremony during which high-status members gave away valuable items, like tobacco, to mark important events. These potlatch ceremonies occurred in Pacific Northwest tribes like the Tlingit and Makah to commemorate deaths, treaty signings, and, there's reason to believe, births. As tobacco grew popular with colonials and then with Americans, the (notably phallic) cigar became a token of maleness. Cigar rooms proliferated as male spaces for celebrating wealth and power.[2]

Stork Clubs came to resemble those rooms, allowing men to celebrate fatherhood and friendship in an atmosphere that reinforced maleness and social status. In a sense, the cigar became a way for men to celebrate fatherhood without being all femme about it. Overcompensatory as this may have been, it wasn't all bad.

In lighting up, a father wasn't just focusing on himself. By necessity, a cigar requires a certain time commitment, and so, as the ash lengthened, a father could ruminate on and talk through thoughts of the new family he was separated from whether he liked it or not. After all, his wife was sequestered in a recovery room, and his baby was in a nursery, unreachable behind a wall of glass. The cigar mandated his recognition of this transition.

Cigars were a rite of passage for mid-twentieth-century men. President John F. Kennedy was photographed with a Cuban cigar at John Jr.'s birth (this was before he smuggled twelve hundred H. Upmann Petit Coronas into the states on the eve of his embargo). Baseball legend Yogi "If the world were perfect, it wouldn't be" Berra passed out cigars in the Yankees clubhouse. Even Disney's Goofy came in contact with a birth cigar in his 1951 short *No Smoking*, which presaged the decline and fall of the stogie.

The peak of the nation's cigar smoking occurred pretty much in sync with the peak year of the baby boom: 1957. Between 1955 and 1957, twelve pounds of tobacco per capita per year was consumed via cigar smokers. Today, only about 12 percent of adult men admit to smoking cigars at all, and tobacco consumption has fallen to about a pound per capita.[3] And while public opinion about smoking aided in the decline of the birth cigar, it was only partially to blame for the decline in the ritual.

In the 1960s, expectant mothers began to demand a say in who could be present in the delivery room during labor and birth. Fathers were finally let in—only for labor at first. But as demand grew for birth partners and men started taking an active role in birth-coaching techniques like Lamaze and the Bradley Method, it became increasingly common for men to be present at the actual birth—closer to the action but further from the ritual of the cigar.

Much of this is, obviously, for the better. Smoking isn't good for you. Oh, and the aforementioned boys' club that spanned decades was deeply misogynistic and drew men away from their responsibilities as partners and parents. But by putting the Stork Club in the rearview mirror, something important has been lost. A community is missing.

Modern American fathers largely lack robust nonreligious rituals to mark the moment they transform from men into dads. In contrast, for much of human history, fathers in a diverse array of world cultures focused on their shifting roles through the ritual of couvade. Essentially, fathers who engage in couvade are placed in isolation in order to orient themselves towards the birth of their child and their new role. In isolation, they may be deprived of food or deprived of the use of edged weapons, according to Frank L. Williams, professor of anthropology at Georgia State University. He suggests that fathers could be helped in their transition by looking to a more connected past.

"We have a lack of contact between people, and this leads to depression and suicide and drug abuse and violence, and fatherhood is no different. So can we invent new cultural mechanisms to bring back the couvade?" Williams asks. "Looking back to these rituals of the past can help us invent rituals for our American context."

Williams details several rituals. Fathers might be feasted for a time, or be required to stay in bed, or simulate the pangs of birth while their mothers comfort them. Couvade rites were observed in New World cultures, African cultures, and Asian cultures. A couvade ritual was even practiced in Scotland, birthplace of the free market, as recently as the first decade of the twentieth century. But the practice became rare as nations industrialized. Couvade, like so many rituals, was easier to integrate with the demands of agrarian work.

It's worth noting that many of these rituals were required of fathers by their community, much the way baby showers are foisted on mothers-to-be whether they like it or not. Not only was couvade a way for men to symbolically pass into fatherhood, it was also a way for a man to earn higher standing. Fathers who refused to engage in couvade were shunned, becoming social outcasts among their peers—proto–deadbeat dads of their day. Fathers who participated were celebrated. For them, becoming a father meant also becoming a more engaged member of their communities. So couvaded men would be baffled by this more recent phenomenon of the paternal disappearance, where modern fathers socially withdraw during and following the birth of a child.

NEED TO KNOW

Notable Couvade:
Why Becoming a Huichol Father
Takes Serious Balls

In Mexico's Sierra Madre range, the indigenous Huichol people have abided for some fifteen thousand years–based on the carbon dating from their oldest ceremonial sites. They are a shamanistic society known for their peyote rituals and their bright, psychedelic "yarn paintings" depicting their rich animistic belief system. These popular yarn paintings are a valuable craft for the Huichol and are made by pressing brightly dyed string or yarn onto a wooden panel covered in beeswax and pine resin. They're commonly bought by tourists who prize both the primitive imagery and the brilliant colors.

Among images depicted in Huichol yarn paintings is a birth scene. A nude female figure is shown, legs akimbo, with an infant emerging from her birth canal into the world. But above this figure is a male figure, also nude, with penis and testicles exposed. In these images two lines extend from the testicles to the female figure's hands. What's going on here?

The most cited explanation comes from Spanish researcher Adele Getty, who lived with the Huichol for several years, exploring their shamanistic ways (and their peyote), which she detailed in a hard-to-find book published in 1990 titled *Goddess: Mother of Living Nature.* Getty explains that the image illustrates an extreme couvade birth ritual that allows the father to feel some of the "pain and joy" of labor.

Apparently, during the birth of their child, Huichol women would tie strings to the father's testicles–one string for each hand–and then pull on the strings during contractions so that the fathers would feel some semblance of the pain of delivery. Getty neglects to say more about how forceful or prolonged these nut pulls would be, but it's safe to assume that any stringed abuse of one's jewels at the hands of a delivering mother would be excruciating.

"In the end, the husband feels as much joy at the birth of the child as the wife–or even more!" Getty contends. And that makes some sense, because the best thing about someone furiously tugging at your testicles is when they stop.

It's important to note that there's an outside chance the description of Huichol couvade ritual is apocryphal. Aside from Getty and the occasional yarn painting, there are no modern anthropological descriptions of the practice. Still, it's not beyond the realm of plausibility considering there is a modern analogue. Many an expectant father has given his partner his hand to squeeze as she bares down during labor only to walk away duly impressed by her superhuman, bone-crushing grip strength. Sure, the pain of a hand squeeze is no match for the pain of serious sack pulling, but it's something of a shared discomfort.

Interestingly, there are no contemporary rules that suggest birth plans can't include some testicle pulling during delivery. So maybe keep this one to yourself and offer your partner your hand instead.

For modern dads, the isolation formerly associated with couvade rituals occurs after birth rather than before. While this modern brand of isolation is an incredible way to orient a father to his family, it leaves him estranged from the community that can support him. There's no balance. Instead, what develops is his perceived association between fatherhood and loneliness—as well as actual loneliness for this new father too.

Research conducted in 2019 by the nonprofit Movember Foundation (which raises awareness of men's health issues via the annual mustache growing fundraiser, Movember) found that one of every five men stop meeting with friends in the first twelve months of fatherhood.[4]

That stat is backed up by a University of Singapore metasynthesis of thirteen studies that probed the experiences of new fathers from around the world. Researchers found that new fathers universally reported sacrificing "their personal, social, and leisure time for family time." But it could be that they are also giving up important social support.[5]

A 2006 study looking into the causes of postnatal depression in fathers found that lack of social support and higher rates of depression appeared to be linked. Similarly, researchers from the University of Lodz Institute of Psychology in Poland looked at the depressive symptoms in thirty-seven first-time fathers and discovered that a father's sense of depression was correlated with a perceived lack of social support.

"With no previous experience of being a father...a man might become uncertain about how to fulfill the requirements of his task," the researchers reasoned. "Therefore he might look for a lot of support." But given the need to be supportive of his family, he might not be able to find people who can, in turn, support him.[6]

And that's what makes bringing back a ceremony like the birth cigar so appealing. It's nondenominational and secular so that people both inside and outside the parents' religious traditions can participate. And it allows a father to draw his community near while keeping his focus on his family.

But these ritualized celebrations of fatherhood don't have to include cigars. In fact, as men have children in the waning years of the birth cigar, they've started finding their own traditions and rituals. "These days cigars are text messages," says new father and writer Chad R. MacDonald. Besides, there would have been no time for a cigar for MacDonald anyway. His son, Liam, arrived via emergency C-section while he was still attempting to get into scrubs.

"My father is far away," MacDonald says. "Her mother is far away, so there were a lot of text messages." Still, he and his partner weren't content with commemorating the birth of their child via text. Who would be? They wanted a more public event that would allow them to connect with their community. "We're atheists. We see why religious rituals have value. But our rituals were personal," MacDonald says. So instead, the two had an event two weeks after their son's arrival. "We had a reception, I guess you'd call it, where friends and family came to meet our son. We had brunch and bagels. It was like saying, 'Everybody, meet Liam. Liam, meet everybody.' It was incredibly nice. We felt a sense of community from our friends and family."

If we look back to the fella pacing in the Stork Club, waiting for his own chance to hand out his cigars, it's not a stretch to see the echo of a couvade ritual here. Just as the cigar is linked through tobacco to the potlatch ceremony, this father's separation from his family in the labor-ward waiting room is linked to couvade by this isolation. Imperfect as it was, he had a kind of ritualized gestation and labor too. It was public, marking him as a father-to-be by his community.

Happily, fathers are no longer separated from the experience of birth, left to pace the floor in their anxiety and fear of what was happening behind those closed doors. Entering fatherhood as a partner is important. But that doesn't mean we can't look back into the smoke and atta-boy back slaps of the Stork Club and take the best of this new dad's experience here—the public pride and the invitation for others to share in the moment.

Yes, sometimes a cigar is just a cigar. But sometimes, it's also a way to make meaningful connections that will be important to a father's future.

Skills

How to Have a Baby

SKILL:
How to Have Sex with a Pregnant Lady

I have always heard that women are extra horny when they're pregnant, but for me it's been interesting.

—Khloe Kardashian

Let's begin with the most salient point: You're not going to poke your baby during sex. There are, in fact, few physical reasons that you and your partner can't get busy right up until birth.

Here's another, more crucial, point: Sex while you're pregnant is . . . different. Physically, sure (see below), but also in every other possible way. What went down with much fanfare between the sheets before may no longer be a crowd pleaser. Moods may have fundamentally changed. Does your partner want to have sex? You don't know anymore. Don't try to read the signs—talk about it. It's a whole new world. But when you both are feeling in the mood, here's how to physically hop to:

+ **A history of preterm labor and birth:** The science is far from settled on this subject, but while there is no conclusive evidence that sex triggers preterm labor in women with a history of preterm delivery, doctors frequently recommend abstinence.

+ **Placenta previa:** This condition occurs when the placenta covers the uterus side of the cervix. Doctors examining the cervix with their fingers can cause women with this condition to hemorrhage, so penetrative sex feels like a bad bet even though there are no studies of sex-induced hemorrhaging.

- **Premature rupture of the membrane:** This is the term for when the amniotic sack breaks, also known as "water breaking," prior to a baby's due date. If this occurs just before the due date, sex isn't advised because labor is looming. If this occurs before thirty-four weeks, sex isn't advised because there is a higher risk of infection via the introduction of outside bacteria transported by the penis.

- **Incompetent cervix:** A woman's cervix can be weakened for any number of reasons, including damage from past births. When a cervix is not strong enough to keep a baby in for the duration of a pregnancy, it's crudely referred to as "incompetent." Depending on how weak a woman's cervix is, a doctor may advise against sex.

Ways to Have Sex by Trimester

First Trimester: From a sexual standpoint, plenty is likely to change during the first trimester, but nothing has to change. Hormonal surges and bouts of morning sickness are likely to interfere with whatever normal intimacy looks like, but there are unlikely to be physical obstacle to sex—no matter how acrobatic. Weirdly, you may want to prioritize missionary as face-to-face will become impractical as the fetus develops.

Second Trimester: As your partner's pregnancy progresses, the angle between you during sex will need to become less acute. Which is to say you'll need more room between your two bodies to get it on. Consider sex while spooning, or hit a straight-up 90-degree angle by standing and entering her with her bottom at the edge of the bed. Many pregnant couples embrace the lotus position, which allows the pregnant partner to control how close she is and the depth of penetration. (Essentially, she lowers herself onto her partner's lap while he sits upright, legs extended or crossed.) Stretch beforehand as this can trigger a bit of pain in the lower back.

Third Trimester: It's not uncommon for pregnant women to experience a sexual resurgence in the third trimester. The problem is that pregnant bodies are unwieldy, especially for those occupying them. Communication and creativity are key. Many couples spend more time engaged in hand and mouth stuff, but sex from behind works well. So-called doggystyle sex is a practical solution as it allows the pregnant partner to keep weight off their stomach. Playing Snoop's early work is not necessary, but strongly recommended.

SKILL:
How to Doula

Asking for help isn't a sign of weakness, it's a sign of strength.

—Barack Obama

A doula, specifically a birth doula, is an individual meant to act as a support, coach, and advocate for birthing parents as they work through labor and delivery. Studies routinely show that the presence of a doula is associated with better birth outcomes. That's particularly true for women of color and marginalized women, for whom birth outcomes are relatively poor in the United States.

Consider the 2019 doula study by Alabama-based researchers published in the *Journal of Interprofessional Education & Practice*. The researchers found that when doula-supported birth outcomes were compared to all Medicaid-funded births in Jefferson County over the course of a year, mothers who used a doula were less likely to receive cesareans and epidurals and saw a tenfold increase in the adoption of breastfeeding. A similar study out of the University of Minnesota found that the odds of cesarean delivery were a whopping 40.9 percent lower for Medicaid-funded births with doula support than for Medicaid-funded births generally.[1]

Part of the reason that the presence of a doula leads to more successful birth outcomes is that they provide continuous labor support. The key word is "continuous." That kind of support is uncommon in many hospitals and birthing centers, simply due to staffing issues.

Can expecting fathers provide continuous support? Possibly. But the high stakes of welcoming a child into the world can heighten their emotions and stress, which can cloud their ability to act calmly and reasonably. This is especially true with a first child, in which case a dad's experience is nonexistent.

Doulas are that calm advocate and guide that so many births need. If a birth goes off-script, the parents-to-be can rest easy knowing they have an expert present who can guide them through the unknown. This creates a less stressful environment and boosts the confidence of the person giving birth. The upshot, as borne out in studies, is less need for interventions, including labor-inducing drugs like oxytocin, that can make labor more painful.

But having another person in the room can sometimes cause men to feel as if they are being removed from the process. Territoriality may ensue, which will help no one during the birth. With that in mind, a few rules of engagement will make the relationship easier for fathers who may feel like a doula could crowd them out.

INTERVIEW AS A TEAM

Yes, the doula will be largely focused on the woman giving birth, but if their personality clashes with yours and makes you tense the entire time, it's not going to be a good fit. Ask questions about how they work with fathers. Offer honest opinions as you talk over who to hire with your partner.

Use the Doula as a Resource

Doulas don't have the medical training of midwives or doctors, but they do have tremendous experience and are well versed in the birthing process. So it's a good idea to use them for expectation management. They can also act as mediators when communication with the hospital staff gets tense.

Make Expectations Clear

If your doula doesn't know how you want to be involved in the birth, they won't be able to help you. Do you want to just be a witness? Do you just want to offer encouragement and support? Do you want to catch the baby or coach breathing? Make your intentions clear. It's not a doula's job to guess.

But when a doula does understand your desires, they can help fathers-to-be have an experience that is more rich. When there is someone else in the room providing continuous support, fathers can be more emotionally invested with their partner.

Get the Most out of Your Doula

When your doula is on the clock, you can have them run the communication show between your partner and the hospital staff so you can be free to just hold her hand and be as present as possible. A doula should also be available to your partner if and when you can't be. The point is total coverage.

Consider a Postpartum Doula

Postpartum doulas are able to provide support after your baby arrives. They can act as breastfeeding coaches, help with the grueling postpartum recovery, and provide space for new moms and dads to bond with their baby. They can even run interference with visitors and provide infant care when parents are just too tired.

A doula can be an incredible resource. They not only can improve birth outcomes for mother and child but also can make a father's birth experience more meaningful. With thoughtful questions and clearly communicated expectations, a doula makes an excellent guide into parenthood.

SKILL:
How to Catch the Baby
(If You're into That Kind of Thing)

You gotta catch the sauce. Move with me . . . I'm dripping sauce.

—Future

When obstetricians and midwives talk about delivery, they often use the phrase *catching the baby*. And while newborns don't emerge from the vagina at velocity, they do need someone with soft hands to ensure the completion of their emergence into this world.

Being a baby catcher does not require practice or skill. It does, however, require nerves. In order to catch your baby, you have to be in the thick of the action—and you can't blink. And boy, if you thought making the baby was intimate, just know that sex has nothing on full dilation.

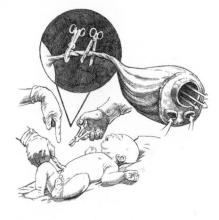

Why to Do It: Catching the baby is a nice way for a new father to be involved without interfering in best medical practices. Participation demonstrates solidarity with mom. Also . . . curiosity?

Why Not To: There's no need to add anxiety to an already fraught experience, and catching a baby is absolutely not necessary. There are no style points awarded in the delivery room.

Baby Catching 101

+ Be communicative. To catch your baby, you have to communicate to the doctor that you are interested in catching said baby. The coach ain't going to put you on the field if you don't ask to play.

+ Listen up. Midwives and doctors may be brusque. That's because there's precious little time for coddling communication. Do what they say.

- Be prepared. You'll see some things you may not expect. Your wife might poop a little while pushing. You may find the sight of a furry head emerging from between her legs disconcerting. And, channeling Daniel Day Lewis, "There may be blood." There will definitely be amniotic fluids and afterbirth.

- Have good hands. When your baby hits your hands, he or she may be lighter than you expect. And slippery. Cradle gently and quickly take in the immensity of the moment before passing the child to mom (who did all the actual heavy lifting, after all).

SKILL:
How to Comfort a Crying Baby

When we are born we cry, that we are come to this great state of fools.

—Bill Shakespeare

The first few months of life aren't called the "fourth trimester" for nothing. Remember, your kid would prefer to crawl back in the womb for a nice, long nap. (You probably would too, in this early stage of fatherhood.) Giving them a womblike experience when they're distressed is often the best way to offer comfort. Happily, you don't have to have a womb to simulate one successfully.

Sound

Your baby was able to hear while in the womb. They heard your partner's voice. They heard your voice. And yes, they heard you listening to RapCaviar and Enya. But those sounds were muffled and swishy and sublimated by the ambient noise of mom (intestinal gurgling, the aortal backbeat). It was an aural chowder, which is why babies are primed to like white noise.

To be clear, you don't need a special baby sound device or white noise machine to spin a suitable playlist. You can actually make white noise with your own mouth by making "sh" sounds repeatedly.

Importantly, whether you're using your own lips, a specialized machine, or radio static between stations, the white noise will need to be pretty loud. How loud? Well, the baby should be able to hear it over their own crying or else it's not effective. So the best bet is to very loudly shush your child. Just keep it under fifty decibels—this means quieter than a washing machine, electric toothbrush, or conversation at home—which is the threshold set in most hospital nurseries.

Space

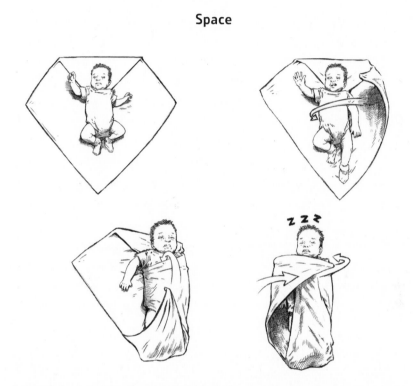

A womb is a cramped space. Babies feel comforted when their limbs are close to their bodies and lightly constrained. Newborns also tend to wake themselves because they lack control of their limbs. Known as Moro reflex, this dynamic is when babies naturally spread their limbs and flinch (it's the same thing as when you wake up just after falling asleep and feel like you're falling; thank your tree-dwelling ancestors). This is why swaddles are so effective in comforting a baby.

The comfort of close limbs can be witnessed firsthand in videos of Santa Monica pediatrician Robert Hamilton, who developed his own specialized infant hold, which he imaginatively calls "The Hold." The foundation of his hold is crossing the infant's arms over its chest and holding it up, facedown at a forty-five-degree angle with head up, one palm of a parent's hand under the baby's bottom, and the baby's chin settled snug on the meat between the thumb and pointer finger of the other hand.

Position

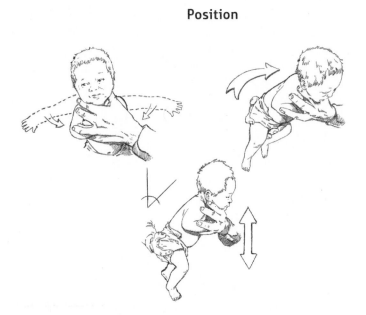

Babies are more easily soothed if held on their sides or positioned so there is pressure against their bellies. Researchers aren't totally sure why but hypothesize that crying causes discomfort in the digestive tract, which is relieved by this pressure.

Movement

A mother's womb isn't particularly still. As she moves, there's plenty of swaying, swinging, and rocking. Newborns are used to constant movement, which is why rockers and bassinets work so incredibly well. There's nothing like a gentle sway while holding a baby to bring a sense of calm. You don't need to be particularly coordinated—just shift your weight from foot to foot. Imagine you're on the gently swaying deck of a schooner. Wear boat shoes if you want, skipper. Just don't get seasick.

A Note on Pacifying

One of the first abilities babies develop is sucking. This soothes them. In the absence of something to suck on, they will opt for their own fingers. During ultrasounds, it's not uncommon for babies to be seen sucking their thumbs in utero.

Your baby may be fine finding its own thumb to suck, but it's usually not the go-to midcry outside the womb. If it's feeding time, a nipple or a bottle will do the trick. Other times, feel free to use a pacifier. Don't worry about long-term effects or pacifier dependency. There are a lot of internet forums in which pacifier use is decried as tantamount to abuse. (There are also a lot of internet forums in which Stanley Kubrick is lauded for his work for the CIA.) Ignore this shit posting. In most circumstances, children grow out of pacifier use long before there's a chance for the devices to cause any abnormal tooth development or lifelong dependency issues guaranteeing they'll be back in your basement in adulthood.

Skill:
How to Navigate the Baby Bureaucracy

Bureaucracy gives birth to itself and then expects maternity benefits.

—Dale Dauten

A baby is born into a world of bureaucracy. From the moment babies enter the world, they are required to be on the books—at least if they want to receive the benefits of the society they're born into. As a parent, part of your job from the outset is to make sure your kid's paperwork is completed. And it's best to get used to it quickly because until the kid is filling out their Free Application for Federal Student Aid, you'll be signing on the dotted lines.

One Document to Rule Them All

The most important form you will see in the hospital is the Certification of Live Birth. This is a standardized government form, created by the Centers for Disease Control for the purpose of collecting information on births in the United States. The two-page form, broken into four distinct sections, is designed to act as a birth certificate application, a Social Security number application, and a data collection tool. Because some of the sections require discreet information that parents may not be able to provide, completing the form is generally a collaborative endeavor. It looks like this:

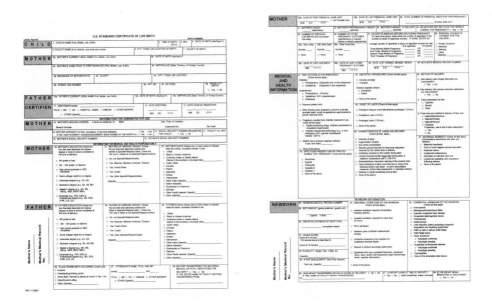

US standard certificate of live birth

Source: Centers for Disease Control

(https://www.cdc.gov/nchs/data/dvs/birth11-03final-acc.pdf)

Because of its outsized importance in our national bureaucracy, it's almost guaranteed that a nurse or midwife will provide you with a birth certificate application in the hospital. Even in birth centers and home births, midwives will have these forms on hand.

Getting Your Baby a Birth Certificate

The birth certificate is not the same as the Certificate of Live Birth, but the two are related. The Certificate of Live Birth acts as the first documentation of your child's existence. It is a legal document that is first entered into the hospital or birthing center's database before being sent to your state's office of vital statistics. The office of vital statistics will then use the form to generate your child's official birth certificate.

As a document, your child's official state-issued birth certificate will look different according to the standards of the issuing state. The birth certificate is the gateway document to all of the necessary paperwork your child may need for the rest of his or her life—including a passport, public school enrollment and, eventually, driver's license. All of the information required for your baby's birth certificate is collected in the top third of the first page of the Certificate of Live Birth.

As a dad, you will likely have the privilege of filling this section out, particularly if your partner is recovering from a C-section or busy breast-feeding or sleeping. Also, nobody wants to do paperwork after giving birth. Luckily, the vast majority of midwives and nurses will be able to help you fill out the application. They've seen their fair share of dads chagrined to be doing paperwork in a delivery room. Your confusion and questions will not be new.

If you fail to fill out a certificate of live birth at the hospital, you'll need to get in touch with your state's vital records office. The reason? The government doesn't actually keep vital records like births and mar-riages. Instead, states collect the information and then report it to the government at regular intervals. So if the hospital, birth center staff, or midwife isn't walking you through the process, the state vital records office will be able to help. But take note, it's not a bureaucrat's place to show the kind of nurturing care common to the maternity ward staff.

Information required for states to issue a birth certificate include:

+ Time, date, and county of birth, including facility name and address

+ Mother's name (including maiden name), date of birth, birthplace, and current address

+ Father's name, date of birth, and birthplace

The person certifying the document will ask you and your partner to provide identification, which means that your delivery go bag absolutely needs room for your and your partner's driver's licenses or passports.

What you don't need on your birth certificate application is your ba-by's final name. You can give your kid a placeholder name and then make changes later if you happen to be stymied for a name at birth. This will add an additional step to the process of securing a birth certificate. A parent will need to request a name change with their state vital statistics office within six months of applying for the birth certificate.

Some hospitals are willing to mail off the Certificate of Live Birth to the state vital records office for you. But you can always mail it yourself. Either way, there will be an application fee that will cost somewhere be-tween $15 and $30.

Your baby's birth certificate should arrive in the mail after its infor-mation has been processed by the vital records office. How long will that take? Honestly, it depends on your state. But, on average, it will likely take over a month.

Keep in mind that some hospitals may also give parents a souvenir birth certificate. After all, official birth certificates aren't the most sentimental of documents. These sweet, filigreed commemorative documents will generally look like a diploma and may include details like gold seals and your baby's footprints. They are not an official document in any respect and most will have fine print explaining just that.

Getting Your Baby a Social Security Number

Here's an interesting little fact: getting your child a Social Security number is not mandatory. But while that's fine in theory, it's a practical misrepresentation of what it requires to live a normal life in America. If you want to claim your kid on your taxes as a dependent, for instance, they will need a Social Security number. They will also need it to collect social security—should the program manage to survive long enough to benefit them.

US standard certificate of live birth

Source: Centers for Disease Control

(https://www.cdc.gov/nchs/data/dvs/birth11-03final-acc.pdf)

If you happened to be dead set on not getting your child a Social Security number, nobody would come busting down your door. It would, however, make your kid's life way harder should they want one in the future. Anyone over the age of twelve who applies for an original Social Security number is required to submit to an in-person interview at their local Social Security office.

With all of this in mind, most parents opt to apply for their child's Social Security number at the same time as they apply for their birth certificate. The Certificate of Live Birth makes this particularly easy. All parents have to do is check a box saying they'd like their child to have a Social Security number and then provide their own Social Security number on the document.

Getting Your Baby a Passport

Once your child is officially blessed with a state-issued birth certificate, you can apply for a passport. Unlike applying for a birth certificate and Social Security number, a passport is far more complicated and difficult to acquire. As annoying as that is, it does make sense. A passport is the primary document for travel in and out of the country. The rules and regulations for acquiring one for a child are a pretty good deterrent for people who might otherwise traffic children out of the country.

Source: US Department of State, Bureau of Consular Affairs
(https://tsg.phototool.state.gov/photo)

To get your baby a passport, you must apply in person with your spouse and baby at a passport application center. Happily, many publicly funded facilities like libraries, courts, or post offices double as passport application centers. There is usually no appointment necessary to apply; just make sure you check the hours before heading in. There are also fourteen regional passport offices scattered across the country, but applying in these locations requires an appointment.

Considering that doing anything with a baby can be a chore, it will help to download the passport application from travel.state.gov and fill it out before your visit. If you do fill out the application ahead of time, remember to keep the signature blank. Part of the point of applying in person is so and official can witness your signature.

You will need a few crucial documents when you apply. Chief among these is your child's certified, government-issued birth certificate. Importantly, the names of both parents need to be on the birth certificate. Parents should also have their current passports or driver's licenses handy for proof of identification.

Like adult passports, your baby's passport will require a photo, and it's important to stress that the State Department doesn't loosen up its picture requirements for babies. The photo must be 2 by 2 inches, and within that frame your child's head must be between 1 and 1 3/8 inches from the bottom of the chin to the top of the head. That makes the picture one of the most difficult parts of the process. Though there are a few tips to getting it done right:

Keep the baby in a baby carrier. Parents are allowed to drape a white sheet over a baby carrier and place their baby in it for the photograph, though there are caveats. The carrier should not cast any kind of shadow on the baby's face.

Lay the baby on its back. You can also lay your child flat on its back on a white sheet and take the photograph from above. The trouble is that taking a picture of your child from above can lead to shadows, which are a no-no.

Don't worry about the eyes. If you're taking a picture of an infant for a passport photo, the State Department allows a baby's eyes to be closed or partially open.

There are a few issues that are sure to get your baby's photo rejected.

+ Blurriness

+ Baby not looking straight ahead

+ Headwear

+ Pacifiers

+ A tongue sticking out

+ Unnatural or washed-out color

Passports are the priciest of all the documents you'll encounter. The processing center will generally charge around thirty dollars. The State Department requires sixty-five dollars with an additional sixty dollars for expedited service.

SKILL:
How to Leave the Hospital

Going home must be like going to render an account.

—Joseph Conrad, *Lord Jim*

You shouldn't stay at the hospital any longer than is absolutely necessary after your kid is born. It is a stressful, uncomfortable place wholly inconducive to nurturing a newborn. But you can't just bundle up your baby, pack a bag, and split. That'd be as chaotic and unfruitful as leaving the Saigon embassy via rooftop helicopter. Learn from Henry Kissinger and have an exit strategy in place before the time comes to head home.

Fathers have a unique role in leaving the hospital, largely thanks to the fact that their genitals haven't been traumatized and they don't have a newborn to breastfeed. Generally speaking, fathers are better rested and more mobile, so they are better positioned to manage paperwork and run essential errands that will make getting the baby home that much easier.

Get Trained Up

While a hospital isn't anyone's idea of a good time, it is where helpful people tend to congregate—the pros who can coach you in essential skills like swaddling, caring for an umbilical stump, giving a bath, and changing a diaper. So while you do want to get out fast, you also want to take advantage of the vast knowledge at your disposal. If you have questions about baby care, the hospital is the place to ask them. Better to get it down now than realize you wish you'd asked how to burp a baby at 2:00 a.m. in the inky, inexplicably heavy solitude of your own home.

Act as the Advance Team

You'll be leaving the hospital with a lot more stuff than you arrived with. Yes, one of those things is the baby, but there will also be a lot on nonessential crap that babies tend to attract like weird crap magnets. There will be swag like diapers and bottles and binkies and blankets and whatever other courtesy items the hospital wants to throw at you. (Don't get excited—they'll bill you for it.) There will also likely be flowers and stuffed animals and cards and teeny tiny baby socks. Finally, there will be folders and binders full of information and important documents.

You will not want to carry this stuff out of the hospital when you leave with your baby—it's simply too much to manage and think about. The better idea is to make a quick trip home with a load of stuff before being discharged. That way, you only have to think about the essentials when leaving the hospital. Namely: your partner and your baby.

If you do make an advance trip home, take the time to do a bit of prep. Make sure there are enough supplies, that the temperature is set appropriately, and that the home has a general cozy, uncluttered vibe. This is a fine time for a bit of meditative tidying in silence before everything in the environment changes for good.

Cross the T's, Dot the I's, and Ask for the Bill

There is some important paperwork to get done before you can leave the hospital with your baby. These are the documents to be aware of:

Birth Certificate
As mentioned previously, getting this document in order is a requirement, although putting a name on it isn't. So fill it out thoroughly, and how about you leave the name blank and take a beat with Dandelion? Really sit with it.

Discharge Plan
At some point, your partner will be given a discharge plan consisting of instructions for her continued healing and caring for your baby once you've arrived home. This information will be directed at the mother, but fathers should take note and take notes. Some portions of the discharge plan will be best managed by mom because the directives relate to her body. But it's best to have two sets of eyes and ears around for information related to the baby. That's particularly important if your baby was born prematurely, experienced complications or medical procedures, or has common issues like jaundice.

Itemized Bill
Before you leave, make sure you ask the billing department for an itemized bill. This bill will include only charges currently entered in the system, but it will give you a better idea of what you're being charged for and help you spot discrepancies. Asking for an itemized bill may prompt hospital billing departments to scratch costs that don't make sense right away, lowering your bill. Also, be sure to check for information that

hasn't been entered correctly, like your name and address. Flag weird-looking charges to discuss with the billing department later.

Get Phone Numbers

Finally, before you leave with your brand-new family, make sure to get the contact information for any helpful professionals. It will help to have numbers for lactation consultants, nurses, and any doctors who might be helpful in the future for follow-up information.

Tipping the Hospital Staff

This used to be a thing. It's really not anymore. Nurses who accept tips are violating the law and can lose their jobs. Exceptions are made for new parents of Chinese descent, who traditionally offer *hongbao*, or "red en-velopes," to those involved in the birth of a child. No more than five dollars can be placed in those envelopes.

All that said, it's classy to make a gesture if you feel your partner and child have been looked after properly. No one hates flowers.

Get the Car

One of the more nerve-racking parts about being a father at discharge is leaving your wife and baby at the entrance to the hospital while you get the car out of the parking garage. This is a very good moment to take a beat and a calming, centering breath before turning the key in the ignition.

The trip home won't be fast (or furious, hopefully), but it will be mo-mentous. More than any road trip you've ever taken, driving your kid home from the hospital will stick with you forever.

SECTION II

GOING NUCLEAR

Having a baby is a bit like splitting the atom: once it's done, there's no undoing it and everything after is forever changed. Now you are Dad, creator of families.

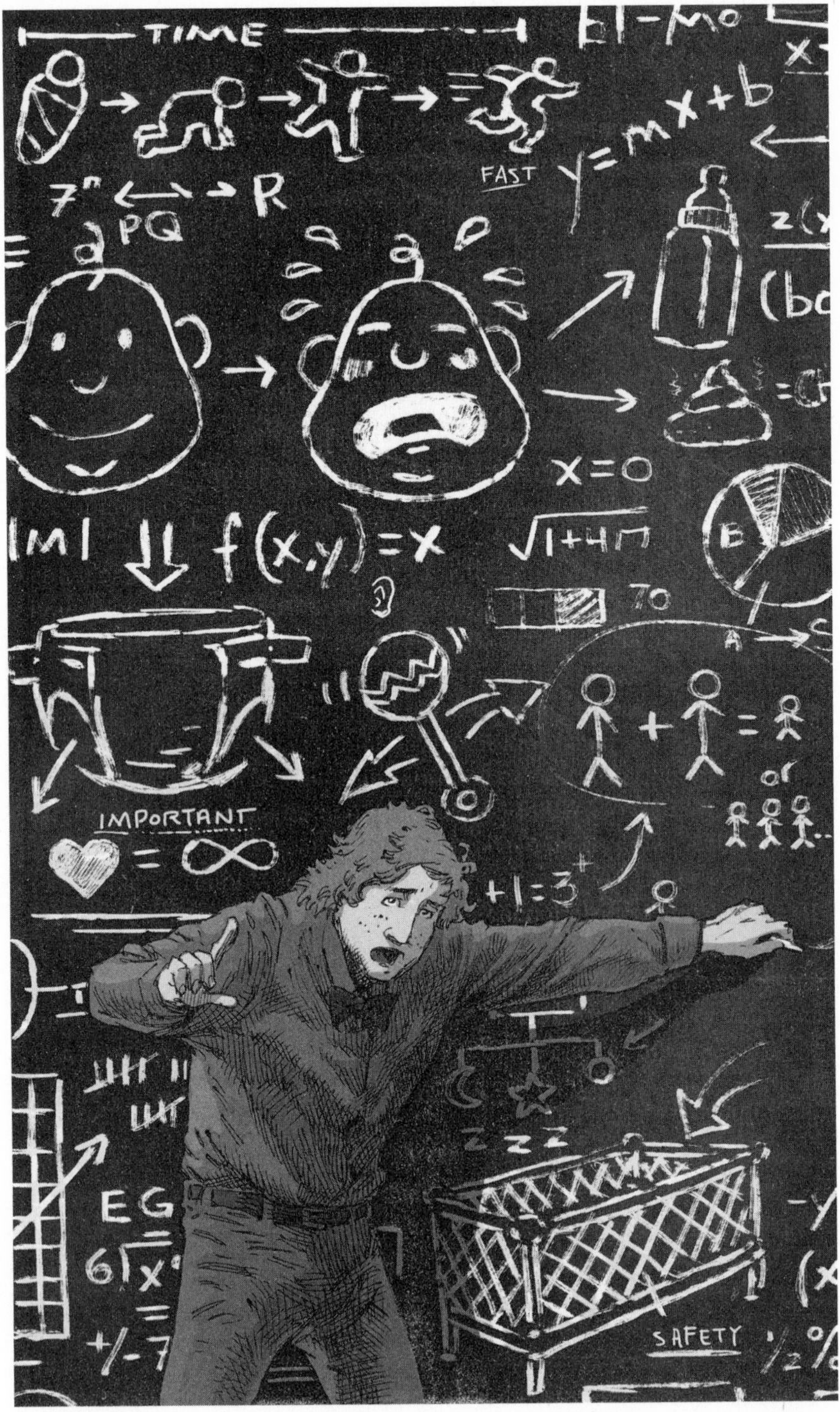
TIME
FAST
y=mx+b
x=0
f(x,y)=x
or
IMPORTANT
zzz
SAFETY

The Case Against Taking Baby Advice Seriously

Parents have been subjected to advice on how to raise children since the beginning of recorded history and probably well before that. Most of that advice has disappeared over the millennia, removed from cliff sides and cave walls by heavy rains and itchy bears. But certain ideas persist. Consider, for instance, the wisdom of the authors of the Book of Proverbs, who offer fathers the following bit of guidance: "He that spareth his rod hateth his son: but he that loveth him chasteneth him betimes." This bit of received wisdom has survived three thousand years, countless wars, endless religious incursions, and the Beanie Baby boom, morphing into a sentence familiar to every parent in America. But that sentence, "spare the rod and spoil the child," is worth dwelling on for a minute.

As is the case with so much parenting advice, it doesn't mean what you think it means.

The Book of Proverbs, the so-called collection of collections, is notable for a number of reasons, but the big one is that it represents the collective wisdom of ancient Middle Eastern cultures. It is a crowdsourced collection of accepted premises and received wisdom on everything from proper communication to how much honey a person should eat ("eat only enough for you, lest you have your fill of it and vomit it." Proverbs 25:16).

A modern corollary might be WikiHow, which is a bit light on the philosophical but offers tips on how to wallpaper your living room, remove blood stains, sell baseball memorabilia, and—because time is apparently an illusion—not spare the rod. WikiHow's step-by-step guide to spanking a child is a tribute to the unique problem of parenting advice.

Above the vector illustrations depicting a splayed hand striking a pained-looking child's blue-jean covered bottom, bullet points indicate that spanking is not recommended by "most child psychologists." The page goes on to urge parents to "be sure to use an open hand and use limited force. . . . The focus should be on teaching your child better behavior, not hurting him/her."

This sort of "don't do this, but if you're going to do it here's how" style of parenting advice remains common even in the age of big data, behavioral economics, and feelings. Parenting can be understood in scientific and social scientific terms (X parenting behavior correlates to Y child behavior) and in cultural and traditional terms (X parenting behavior is critical for continuing Y community's traditions). As such, almost every parental impulse possible is validated by some book somewhere authored by someone with questionable credentials (keep in mind that both Jenny McCarthy and New England Patriots tight end Benjamin Watson have published parenting books). So why not just follow the data? Well, it's far from complete. The history of scientific parenting advice is nearly as full of fuck-ups as the history of cultural parenting advice, which is saying quite a lot.

Let's return for a second to Judah, where that advice about rods originally emerged. The interpretation of the rod of discipline has long meant "loving" corporal punishment to conservative Christians. But it's likely that interpretation is due to a poor translation. In Hebrew, the word for the rod is *shabat*—a tool for shepherds to tend sheep. Historical records show that sheep weren't struck by the *shabat*. Instead, it was used to count them, to provide veterinary care by helping examine beneath the wool for pests and infection, and to ward off predators as a weapon. Sometimes shepherds would throw it ahead of the sheep like a spear to get them to stop and prevent them from straying.

This is all to say that many well-meaning religious people may be laboring under a misapprehension about what they've been called to do for their children. They're thinking in terms of a firm open-palmed slap on the ass when the Bible is suggesting greener pastures. Or not. Let's be real: three thousand years is a long time. Who knows what Arabian Peninsula shepherds would make of the number one Google search result (out of 2,350,000) for "How to Spank a Toddler"—a blog entry by a "wife, mom, nurse, and organizer" who suggests "a quick pop on the mouth if they're in a rage you can't snap them out of." Even a parched, hardscrabble shepherd would probably call that child abuse—and likely register confusion if it was suggested the whole thing had been his idea to begin with.

THE HISTORY OF WESTERN CHILD-REARING ADVICE:
From Greeks to Gurus

This passage on discipline from the Book of Proverbs exemplifies how the earliest parenting advice was handed down via religious dogma. The suggestions lacked ambiguity. The advice was meant to strengthen your offspring's relationship to God, and for that reason, parents followed it. The first documented secular child-rearing advice was authored in the second century CE by Soranus of Ephesus. Soranus was a Greek physician and student of Hypocrites who looked a bit like Mickey Rourke post–boxing career. His book *Gynecology* offered the followers of Artemis a survey of the science of reproductive health and infant care. Was it parenting advice? Not exactly. Ephesian kids were raised by slightly older Ephesian kids, slaves, and servants. Many did not survive this care. Soranus had precious little to say on that issue, but he did manage the first recorded instance of wishy-washy baby advice: "One (must) not always give the child (the) breast because it cries. . . . But one should not let it cry too long."[1] Naturally, the book was a hit.

But Soranus's early adventures in parenting advice did not rise to cultural phenomenon status. For that kind of parenting advice, it's necessary to jump roughly two thousand years, fast forwarding through the Dark Ages, the UFO landing at Giza, and the Renaissance, to early modern Europe, where the dissociation between parents and children was ultimately challenged by the rock star philosophers John Locke and Jean-Jacques Rousseau—born eighty years apart, in 1632 and 1712, respectively. Both men shared a belief that parents should be the ones giving care and taking special interest in childhood.

Locke, in "An Essay Concerning Human Understanding," suggested children entered the world like a blank piece of paper on which the rules of humanity and morality had to be written. And because the tiniest experience could be hugely influential, Locke argued parents should not leave the job to strangers. In fact, careful care had to be taken to raise a kid, because from the moment they were born children's minds were "as easily turned this or that way as water itself."[2]

For his part, Rousseau felt children were completely free of the ability to reason. Based on this conclusion, he insisted parents should engage in a protean free-range parenting style. He said children should be raised by parents who would let them grow in natural rural settings where they could learn through the experience of roaming around the countryside.

"Love childhood," wrote Rousseau, who would later quietly convince his baby mama to dump his infant son in an orphanage. "Look with friendly eyes on its games, its pleasures, its amiable dispositions."[3]

What Locke and Rousseau did was introduce parenting (read: the behavior of parents toward their children) as a valid topic for serious study. They also paved the way for parental anxiety by suggesting that children's outcomes were derivative of parental behavior. And where anxiety arises so too does a market opportunity. Plenty of physicians were happy to offer some reassurance, at a price.

The first notable doctor to suggest a best way to raise children was William Cadogan. In 1740, he made waves suggesting that men were better equipped to raise children because mothers brought to parenting a host of "superstitions."[4] Then came William Buchanan, whose 1804 book, *Advice for Mothers*, blamed moms for dwarfism and deformities.[5] But hold on. If you think that's bad: in 1962, pediatrician Walter W. Sackett Jr. went viral with the claim in his book, *Bringing Up Babies,* that night feedings would turn babies into socialists.[6]

NEED TO KNOW

Better Baby Contests:
How Eugenics Crept into Pediatrics

During America's progressive era in the early twentieth century, a cultural movement to improve the country through social controls flourished. The idea was that humanity could improve itself through genetic parentage and behavioral choices. This was the foundation of eugenics, which posited that weakness and ill health could be bred out of populations with careful consideration.

Eugenics' most egregious practices included forced sterilization of individuals with low IQ and the support of racist policies banning the intermarriage of ethnic groups. But the eugenicists also left their mark on parenting advice through their influence on pediatrics. To this day many of the standards that are still used to measure the well-being of children were developed in what were known as "Better Baby Contests." The events, taking place at state fairgrounds across the country starting in the 1920s, were essentially livestock competitions but for children.

The idea was to encourage mothers to improve their offspring by pitting babies against one another in a dizzying array of tests and measurements that examined a child's temperament, physical development, and intelligence.

Why would a mother be keen to put their baby to the test? It didn't hurt that the tests and measurements took hours and were required to be administered away from a mother who might distract or coach their kid. That meant parents received a few hours free to enjoy the fair on their own.

Of course, the results of Better Baby Contests were largely meaningless. Science has evolved to understand that all babies develop at their own unique pace and in their own time. Not to mention the standards for the eugenicists perfection were most often strapping Caucasian farm babies of European descent.

Despite this strange history you might still be asked on modern pediatric forms if your baby can draw a straight line–a question pulled directly from the Better Baby Contest years. But thankfully, these are becoming rare hints pointing to pediatrics' complicated past and America's motives for making babies better.

In 1946, parenting arrived in the modern era as Benjamin Spock published *The Common Sense Book of Baby and Child Care*, which assured mothers they knew more than they thought they did and encouraged them to be attentive and trust their instincts. Spock's work, supported by observations he made in his practice as a pediatrician, became hugely popular. With over fifty million copies sold in eighty years, the book was a publishing sensation second only to the Bible.

And like the Bible, Spock's book was littered with headscratchers. In early editions he argued that mothers should always stay at home to care for children. In later additions he advocated for giving babies a plant-based diet.[7] More seriously, Spock advocated for mothers to place their children to sleep on their stomachs. His reasoning was that babies appeared to sleep better when placed face down. But we now know that placing a baby face down to sleep greatly increases the risk of SIDS. It's estimated that some sixty thousand babies died because of parents following this advice.[8]

Today, the dominant strain of parenting advice is derivative of the work of the famous pediatrician William Sears, who developed "attachment parenting" in the 1990s. Attachment parenting is a method of child-rearing that encourages mothers to have nearly constant contact with infants. Breastfeeding is required, as is "baby wearing" and cosleeping. The idea is to form a complete bond of trusting attachment between a baby and parents.

The concept was developed from observing "traditional cultures" in places like Bali and Africa where mothers constantly carry and care for their babies. Because these cultures were considered more "natural," it followed that attachment parenting was the more natural way to raise babies. Unfortunately, this is both pretty racist and extremely wrong. As any primatologist will tell you, there's no such thing as parental instincts. Primates, including humans, learn to parent in the context of the culture in which they live.

The traditional cultures that Sears based his work on are largely collectivist, which makes their wisdom singularly irrelevant in the hyperindividualist context of modern American suburbs. Moreover, Sears' attachment parenting dismisses the possibility of fathers being primary caregivers, but research into the outcomes of babies raised by homosexual couples has dismantled that argument pretty thoroughly.

The point is that when someone starts to give you advice on how to raise a child, it's extremely likely that what they are actually doing is equivalent to giving advice on how best to incorporate fictionalized communal agricultural practices into the indigenous cultures of Papua, New Guinea, while paying homage to the pleasures of rural France.

This is not to say all parenting advice is bad or wrong, just that the shepherds would do well to distrust shepherding theorists.

EVIDENCE VERSUS ADVICE

Evidence can be a tricky thing. Even parents who eschew experts-in-name-only for scientifically valid guidelines can have a hard time finding the best advice. There's just so much of it. And every new study related to raising kids is breathlessly amplified as the new best practice. Even when the coverage is cautious, the sheer fact the study is given ink lends a sense of importance and gravitas to often trivial or inapplicable findings.

Consider the ever-present struggle with screen-time guidelines. At present, the most authoritative recommendations come from the American Academy of Pediatrics (AAP). The organization urges parents to keep toddlers younger than two years old from engaging with digital media. After that, the AAP recommends children between the ages of two and five limit screen use to a single hour per day of what they call "high-quality programming,"[9] which is doctorspeak for *Mister Rogers' Neighborhood.*

NEED TO KNOW

Breast Is Best. So, What Does Dad Do?

Breastfeeding is the gold standard of infant feeding because it is beneficial to both babies and mothers. It helps regulate hormonal levels, provides beneficial probiotics and antigens to the baby, and promotes bonding. Breastfeeding is also a quasi-brand thanks to the "breast is best" campaign that began in earnest in 1991 when the WHO and UNICEF launched the Baby-Friendly Hospital Initiative. The initiative is a massively successful global effort to promote and support breastfeeding.

This campaign, which has successfully encouraged a healthy behavior, has happened to coincide with a generational movement toward more engaged fatherhood. Unfortunately, the reality is that breasts are not necessarily best for dad. Research shows that fathers of breastfeeding infants often feel helpless and inadequate. In a 2010 study published in the *American Journal of Men's Health*, men whose partners breastfed reported lower measures of health quality of life scores compared to men whose infants were bottle-fed. That remained true even controlling for confounding factors like employment and income.[10]

Why is this?

A 2019 study review found, rather predictably, that fathers often feel fenced off from opportunities to bond when their partner breastfeeds exclusively. The lack of connection to feeding can also cause fathers to doubt their abilities or feel helpless to provide the care they'd like to their newborn. All of this corroborates the common findings that fathers who feed their infants also bond with them more easily.

None of this is to suggest that new parents should skip breastfeeding for the sake of dad's feelings. There is simply an emotional tax paid by men locked out of the feeding process. The most obvious solution is to talk with your spouse or your therapist and, frankly, deal with it.

A more extreme measure could include the purchase of wearable synthetic breasts manufactured by the Japanese design company Dentsu and marketed as a "Father's Nursing Assistant." Practical? Not really. But if you're mixing bottle and breast anyway, it can make you feel a bit more part of the show. And don't worry–those puppies are smartphone compatible.

The problem is that these recommendations are made out of an abundance of caution, not because studies have found that children suffer long-term adverse effects from exposure to screens. In fact, to date, there are no results from long-term studies examining whether and how children's brains might change in relation to screen time. And any study currently being run is unlikely to have results on effects until today's children are grown. So what is a time-poor parent to do? There's not a good answer to that question as suggested by the data. The only answer that seems to be consistently true is . . . have more money and time. That's great advice, but far from easy to follow.

And none of this is to conclude that screen time doesn't affect children or that parents shouldn't care. There are countless studies on the issue, but conclusions are contradictory. In a 2018 study published in the journal *Child Development*, researchers surveyed nearly twenty thousand families of two- to five-year-olds and found no correlation between AAP technology-use guidelines and children's caregiver attachment, resilience, curiosity, and positive affect in the thirty-day period before the interviews. In fact, after a statistical analysis of parental response, researchers concluded, "Taken together, findings suggested that there is little or no support for harmful links between digital screen use and young children's psychological well-being."

Even the researchers behind the major study that found links between measured screen time use and developmental outcomes of 2,441 children between two and five years old were loath to suggest causation. After looking at their data, the Canadian researchers posited that the negative outcomes could be related to screen time getting in the way of activities like imaginative play or interacting in positive ways with parents.[11] In other words, the issue might not be the actual screen but a parent's interaction with children.

Try writing that in a headline.

So, if parents want to follow evidence-based, data-backed parenting advice, questions follow: Which evidence? What data? After all, it's the nature of scientific inquiry that theories are tested repeatedly and either upheld or disproved and replaced with a new theory. The only real scientific fact is that the scientific facts have a half-life, and that can make parenting via data maddening for moms and dads desperate for absolutes.

Talk to the leading researchers on child development about how they parent, and the common thread becomes self-deprecating jokes. Many times they don't follow their own advice and behave contrary to suggestions derived from their own findings. They shrug off received wisdom as superstition, then follow it anyway, because it's easier to go with the flow—and no one likes a know-it-all. They recognize that there is no accepted standard to which they can hold themselves. To understand whether what they do is working, they do the same as all parents and look for cues from their kids.

PARENTING ADVICE'S RACIAL ASTERIX

In the mid-1960s, developmental psychologist Diana Baumrind built a parenting "typology" that described three distinct parenting styles: authoritarian, authoritative, and permissive. The differences among the three styles were defined by a parent's responsiveness (or lack thereof) to their children and what they did or did not demand from them.[12]

What Baumrind found was that children's outcomes appeared to be most optimal when parents adopted an authoritative style. That is, one in which they were both highly responsive to children's needs while setting clearly defined and communicated expectations and limits.

Baumrind's styles became part of the developmental psychology bedrock. But there was a glaring problem: Baumrind's research relied on the observation of families connected to the largely white and affluent University of California, Berkeley, where she worked. Her implicit biases were not an aberration in the study of child development.

In 2020, psychology researchers from Stanford University's Center for Comparative Studies in Race and Ethnicity looked at the prevalence of race within five decades of psychological research. They examined over 26,000 publications and found that representation of people of color was embarrassingly underwhelming. That was as true for developmental psychology as any other field.[13]

The study authors found that from the 1970s to the 2010s only 8 percent of research published in child development journals highlighted race. During that period, 83 percent of the editors-in-chief of developmental psychology journals were white. When authors did focus on race, 73 percent were white. White authors of race-related child development research were likely to have more white participants than were researchers of color.

The Stanford researchers note that the issue of white bias in psychological research seems to rest in the belief that psychological issues are universal and race-agnostic. The presumption is that the way a white child develops is no different than the way a child of color develops.

"Racialized experiences shape how people think, develop, and behave," the authors write. "To dedicate no attention to this . . . in our view, is a disservice to psychological science, especially in the face of increasing racial diversity, segregation, and inequality." It also can be a massive disservice to parents seeking science-backed guidance.

Take Baumrind's study. She found that among her described parenting styles, the authoritarian parents—unilateral decision-making with less responsiveness—were more likely to raise children with poor outcomes. That might be true for middle-class white kids, but in the introduction to a 2016 study published in the *Journal of Child and Family Studies*, researchers cite a half-dozen studies that show better outcomes for authoritarian parenting in black families relative to white families. Those outcomes include better self-regulation in three-year-olds, reduced suicidal behavior in depressed kids, and higher academic achievement in adolescence.[14]

There always seems to be at least two sets of data, whether you're looking at psychological, sociological, or statistical research. Consider the birth statistics presented in chapter 3. While only 35 percent of deliveries in the United States were cesarean, data also shows that black women are 24 percent more likely to have cesareans. Yes, 90 percent of babies arrive full term, but black women are twice as likely to have a preterm birth. And while in 2018, there were only 14 maternal deaths for every 100,000 live births, the Centers for Disease Control report that "Black, American Indian, and Alaska Native (AI/AN) women are two to three times more likely to die from pregnancy-related causes than white women."

The tremendous danger in race-specific data is that it is extrapolated to reinforce bias—it's okay to punish black kids, nonwhite mothers are medically challenging. But what different sets of data should point to are not conclusions but questions: Are the relatively better outcomes from authoritarian parenting for black kids due to cultural expectations? Why do nonwhite women die more often in the delivery room?

It is very hard to answer this in a scientific way, with a single, conclusive study. Racism is pervasive and varied in its machinations. And science is by no means immune to it. But it's the nature of science to constantly challenge itself. So emerging racial and cultural understandings of how kids develop has the potential to incite change.

In the meantime, the fundamental suggestion on how to take parenting advice doesn't change. There is still only so much parents can control, and kids are resilient, no matter where they grow up or who raises them. It's good to be thoughtful. It's good to listen to science, and it's good to be skeptical.

But it's best to love your child. Plain and simple. That advice is universal.

HOW TO TAKE BAD ADVICE

If a parent were to attempt to follow all the most vetted, most up-to-date advice available, he or she would go broke in a month and insane in two. The art of processing parenting advice is the art of understanding the impossible in the context of the plausible and the likely.

Plausibility bounds what a parent can reasonably be expected to do. Likelihood bounds who a child can reasonably be expected to become. Emerging research suggests that, in fact, the person a child becomes is most likely a mix of genetic, social, and environmental factors. On the nurture side, the person a child becomes is understood as primarily influenced by the unique environments in which they live. On the nature side, the person a child becomes is essentially predetermined by genetics. Either way, there's only so much a parent can do.

In other words, parenting advice is calibration, not strategy.

Consider how babies learn to walk. There's a great deal of pride when it happens early and a great deal of stress when it happens late. This is largely because pediatricians and parenting experts treat the ability to walk as a fixed point in child development. American parents expect walking to occur at twelve months, which is about average. The problem is that an average is not an absolute. Advice about when children walk and how they should start walking is, like most received parenting wisdom, based on trends and observations being communicated as clear best practices. In fact, how babies walk is largely a product of cultural influences.

A study from 1976 found that babies in some tribes in Kenya learned to walk a month earlier than peers in industrialized nations (somewhere around ten to eleven months) largely because they are taught to do so by their parents.[15] On the other hand, babies in rural areas of Tajikistan, who are often bound in cradles called *gahvoras* for the first twenty-four months of life, do not learn to walk until much later, compared to their Western counterparts.[16]

At the end of the day, Tajikistani kids walk just as well—though perhaps not as far—as Kenyan tribespeople. Not that this matters much anyway. A 2013 study from Zurich found that early or late walking was a poor predictor of outcomes.[17]

What is a good predictor of outcomes? Love. Care. Money. Beyond that, things get fuzzy. When Princeton University researchers built an artificial intelligence to predict the outcomes of children and families based on fifteen years of data, the machine utterly failed.

"Despite using a rich dataset and applying machine-learning methods optimized for prediction, the best predictions were not very accurate and were only slightly better than those from a simple benchmark model," researchers wrote. "Social scientists studying the life course must find a way to reconcile a widespread belief that understanding has been generated by these data with the fact that the very same data could not yield accurate predictions of these important outcomes."[18]

That's programmerspeak for "piss off."

Which brings us to the one study that—take this with a Dead Sea worth of salt—may best explain how to react to parenting advice.

In a 2019 study, Susan Woodhouse, of the Lehigh University Child Attachment, Relationships and Emotions (CARE) Laboratory in Pennsylvania, examined whether the way parents respond to their baby's needs correlated with measurements of the baby's attachment to their parent. She was looking for the baby behaviors that showed developmentally appropriate and secure orientation to the parent. These behaviors were typified by a baby being able to explore independently without completely ignoring a parent, returning back to the parent occasionally for check-ins, crying appropriately should a parent leave, and showing happiness at their return. Together these behaviors are known as "secure base attachment."[19]

What Woodhouse found was that babies were able to develop this attachment as long as the parent responded to their cues correctly at least half of the time. That means parents could put in a F-level performance, and the babies were essentially fine.

Why? Babies are resilient. They don't come with instructions because instructions aren't needed.

So, following advice doesn't guarantee an outcome. Not following advice doesn't guarantee an outcome. The best bet is to pay attention to research and a *lot* more attention to the child. Good enough is good enough. And if there's ever a need for clarity, for God's sake, don't read WikiHow.

CHAPTER 7

Dad Depression

Geoff Lott remembers the gridlocked freeway, the slate-grey sky over Seattle, and the feeling that something was off. He was heading home from his new gig to his newborn (and his wife and his two-year-old) and thinking about his bed. "I had this weird thought," Lott, a forty-six-year-old IT project manager remembers. "Instead of wanting to get in bed, I wanted to get under it. I didn't want to interact with anybody. I didn't want to see my wife. I didn't want to see my kids. I just wanted to hide and completely disappear. It was the first time in my life I'd ever had that kind of thought."

The thought was so clear and strange and disturbing to Geoff that he decided to track it to its source. He was exhausted—earlier that week he'd booked a conference room just to take a nap—but this thought wasn't just about being tired. He called a friend who was a mental health counselor and explained what was going on. The friend directed him to an online depression screening tool, and thirteen questions into a fifteen-question test, Geoff knew what was going on.

What he did not know, sitting in traffic in his gold 2000 Honda Accord, was just how common among new fathers the thoughts he was having actually are.

According to a 2010 study in the *Journal of the American Medical Association*, depression afflicts some 14 percent of new fathers after the birth of a child.[1] But that figure is likely low. According to a 2017 Swedish study surveying 447 new fathers, a full 27 percent reported depression.[2] Of those afflicted, more than 75 percent said they kept the feelings to themselves. So there are, in short, many men like Geoff who suffer in silence—a biological problem being amplified by cultural norms.

The cultural reasons are at least understandable. Birth is a momcentric life event and much has rightly been linked to the issue of postpartum depression, which affects some 15 percent of new mothers. Postpartum depression seems to garner so much coverage because it feels so antithetical to the cultural narrative we inherit about women and motherhood as the ultimate fulfillment of their womanly potential.

The rhetorical battle over who can and should be depressed after birth, and what that depression should look like, has led to scholarly discussion of whether postpartum depression in men should be recognized as a specific condition. Some say yes because there seem to be a surfeit of cases. Some say no because, unlike postpartum depression in women, the emotional dysregulation in men does not seem to be the result of estradiol and progesterone withdrawal.

To help clear things up, some researchers have begun testing emotionally dysregulated new fathers against the Edinburgh Postnatal Depression Scale (EPDS), developed in the United Kingdom in 1987 to screen mothers. The ten-question survey queries the frequency of emotional states with questions like "I have been so unhappy that I have been crying." The problem is that men experience depression differently than women. For instance, men are less likely than women to be weepy and far more likely to simply stop experiencing meaningful emotions altogether. Depressed men often engage in risky behavior in an effort to feel something. Depressed women— and this is a broad generalization—are *already* feeling something.

MONGOLIAN GERBIL TESTICLES AND YOU

The numbness of male depression can be exacerbated by the specific conditions of new fatherhood. Being congratulated all the time is a significantly less lovely experience when you don't feel joy. Interactions are suddenly at odds with feelings. Dad dutifully goes through the motions and winds up wedging himself under the Tempur-Pedic for another troubled night's sleep.

As mental healthcare has been very slowly normalized over the last few decades and more fathers have come forward about their mental health issues, more researchers have sought biological triggers.

The result? A public dialogue about testosterone (and the lack thereof). Research shows that male testosterone levels drop and estrogen levels increase over the course of pregnancy and the first months of a child's life. A drop in testosterone has well-established links to depression.[3]

A 2015 study from Florida's H. Lee Moffitt Cancer Center and Research Institute showed that when men are deprived of testosterone to treat prostate cancer, they experience a distinct uptick in depressive symptoms and diagnoses.[4] While the reason for the shift is different for dads, it's still likely that the dip in a dad's testosterone does increase the risk of depression. The problem is that the cure—all those pills hawked onscreen by beefy men—treats depression as an ailment rather than a *symptom* of fatherhood. In fact, the unmarketable truth is that Dad is sad because Dad evolved to be sad so that Dad's baby could survive.

Emory University professor of anthropology, psychiatry, and behavioral sciences James K. Rilling has spent the last seven years of his career looking into the biological shifts men experience in the transition to fatherhood. Using a combination of magnetic imaging, hormone testing, and interviews, he has worked to develop a snapshot of the male body after fatherhood.

"When men become involved fathers, their testosterone decreases," Rilling explains. "That has a lot of different consequences. Part of that is being able to interact with an infant in a more sensitive and empathic way—in a way that you're less likely to be frustrated and lose your temper."

In other words, the testosterone shift could be adaptive. One clue is that this dynamic also tends to occur in the small number of mammalian species that develop coparenting relationships. Researchers studying creatures like the male Mongolian gerbil, for instance, believe that the shift in hormones that occurs after the birth of the monogamous rodent's pups allow it to engage in nurturing behaviors.[5] That's important, because parenting baby gerbils requires a different set of skills than tracking down the perfect lady gerbil with whom to make the babies. Whereas coupling may require strength and sometimes aggression, those traits can be dangerous when raising young.

The downside, of course, is that sometimes the Mongolian gerbil just wants to watch *Seinfeld* reruns and not talk to anyone, which is pretty alienating to both his gerbil family and his gerbil friends, who were hoping that he'd still be part of their lives postbaby. Also, his testicles shrink.

So just like life itself, dad depression goes back to the balls.

In 2013, Rilling (who is unfortunately not available for kids' birthday parties) ran a study to see whether new fathers' testicle size was correlated with their reported parenting ability. Using an MRI and some serious pick-up artist skills, Rilling was able to demonstrate that, as hypothesized, the smaller-testicled man had partners who described them as an involved father. Moreover, their heads lit up like those of involved fathers should.

"We scanned the brains of these men while they were looking at pictures of their toddlers, and we found men with smaller testes had stronger responses to viewing a picture of their child within neural systems we know are associated with parental motivation and reward," Rilling notes.

The reason? Animals invested in mating produce more testosterone, which in turn increases the amount of semen produced, resulting in larger testicles. Animals investing in caring for young rather than producing them tend to save energy by limiting hormonal production.[6] Smaller balls don't cause better parenting, but strangely enough one can say that parenting—at least in the evolutionary sense—causes smaller balls.

But it's not always helpful to compare human males to animals. For one thing, gerbils are even less fazed by cultural norms than your average suburban dad. For another, human behavior is far less hormonally determined. We might not be totally free, but the leash is long. Which is why all this focus on testosterone is more instructive than it is helpful. Most men don't know the status of their testosterone without some sort of test (and, no, you can't just measure your balls), which is the last thing on anyone's mind during the first weeks of parenthood. And even if a new father does know his testosterone level, he's accounted for only one factor—and very few doctors will recommend taking supplements.

WELCOME TO THE SHIT SHOW

It's important to put hormonal antecedents in their social contexts. That means engaging with the idea that while being a dad is fantastic, it is other things as well. Stressful. Disorienting. Sleep destroying. Time consuming. World eating. Wife stealing. There are any number of reasons, ranging from financial pressure to marital discontent in the wake of attention splitting, that a new dad might be upset. Loss of testosterone doesn't help, but it shouldn't be shocking to anyone that fatherhood, which delivers a host of long-term benefits—the least of which is the opportunity to play catch again—is less emotionally rewarding in the very, very short term.

Geoff Lott was facing a laundry list of depression risks, shrinkage or nah.

"We were out of our element, out of our routine," Geoff says. "We not only have a new baby to take care of, but I was trying to help my wife get around. I was trying to take care of three other people in the house at the same time."

On top of that, he was contending with starting his new work role and was unable to take any leave time. He was back at work within a week of his child being born. Plus, between the demands of his work and home life, the bulk of his self-care amounted to walking from the parking lot to work in the morning and then back to the parking lot at the end of the day.

NEED TO KNOW

That's Why They Call It the Baby Blues

Having a baby is hard. Taking care of yourself and your partner will help make it better in a matter of time.

For a smaller percentage of parents, however, baby blues may progress into clinical depression. When that happens, the ability to live a normal life is significantly affected, and there may be a need for medical intervention either through therapy or medication.

The problem is, how do you know whether you or your partner have crossed the line between feeling crappy because of a significant life change and requiring medical intervention? Luckily the line is pretty stark.

Postpartum (or perinatal) depression symptoms tend to be more debilitating than the baby blues, and they stick around for much longer. Please note that the list below is meant to be a rough diagnostic guide.

It's important for partners to check in with each other over the first month of parenthood and be honest about mental health concerns. If new parents suspect they are slipping past the baby blues, seeking help early might make all the difference.

The baby blues:

- Physical discomfort
- Fatigue
- Mild anxiety
- Feeling overwhelmed
- Feeling "let down"
- Feeling uncertain about parenting role

- Feeling sensitive and irritable
- Generally resolves within two weeks

Postpartum depression:

- Loss of enjoyment
- Isolation
- A sense of detachment from the baby
- Violent or intrusive thoughts
- Mood swings
- Sorrow
- Anger
- Anxiety
- Loss of appetite
- Trouble sleeping
- Generally persists past the first month of parenthood

Researchers have found that some of these types of difficulties can be ameliorated by the creation of strong familial bonds. But, like Geoff, most American men have to get back to work very quickly after the birth of their children. This lack of institutional support leads to a disconnect at home and at work. New dads wind up in a daze, feeling every bit the depressed Mongolian gerbil they've become.

"Most men have the capacity to be involved in direct caregiving," Rilling says. "But how society is structured determines whether or not that's realized."

The trouble is, strong bonds don't always help. At forty-nine years old, janitorial supply distributor and salesman Brian Benson had developed incredibly strong bonds with his wife and two-year-old daughter, in their small home in Hudson, Ohio. In fact, he felt his life was perfect. Everything was just right. He was the happiest he'd ever been. But his wife wanted another child, and after some back and forth, he relented. Unexpectedly, they conceived twins.

"There were so many things that became difficult, overnight," Brian says of the birth of his twin sons. "We had three kids in diapers instantly. Everything that had been so easy and so great instantly became not easy and not great."

Despite being incredibly involved in parenting the twins, Brian remembers that after about three months, he and his wife started fighting. They had never fought before. He started to withdraw. He became sullen.

He had the occasional fantasy about leaving his family and working on a fishing boat in Alaska. "I thought of myself as an optimistic person, but no amount of positivity was going to make it any different," he says.

Brian knew he was depressed. Moreover, he was mourning what had been. "I felt a sense of loss for that life, and it's not coming back. I have to deal with this new life. I don't think anyone really understood what I was going through."

Like many men, Brian didn't seek any real help. After two sessions he decided therapy wasn't for him. He never sought medication. This tracks with information from the CDC's National Center for Health Statistics: while one in ten men experience depression, fewer than half seek treatment.[7] A lot of dads who struggle with postpartum depression may recognize it but decide to grit their teeth and power through.

Brian was lucky to stumble upon a solution. "Time," he says. "As kids are getting older, they slowly become more independent, and that's given me a break. I'm able to have some of my own thoughts and time to myself."

For most men, the depression simply fades. Babies turn into toddlers and dads begin to find their parenting groove. When men adjust to their new role here, many of the stressors that mark parenting in infancy diminish.

Also, for what it's worth, testosterone returns. Not entirely, but a little. A 2018 study from Northwestern University found that as dependent children grew older there was a small hormonal rebound in a father's testosterone. Similar to the dip, the rebound of testosterone is likely tied to a shift in biological priorities. As kids get older there's less need for direct care, and a man's biological system can focus again on making another kid.[8]

Kids growing up may also help dads find time to engage in naturally testosterone-boosting activities. Getting more sleep helps. Exercise and weightlifting help. Getting outside for some sun to help the body produce vitamin D helps too.

With his twins now five years old, Brian Benson has found that he has more time to crack an IPA on his deck in the afternoon and go on hikes with the family. These activities weren't prescribed, but they absolutely help.

Not all problems have clear and easy solutions. Dad depression will remain common. The only real comfort there is that it's unlikely to become chronic. It's an undersung sacrifice men make for their families, but it's far from the last.

CHAPTER 8

Mommy Maintenance and Maternal Gatekeeping

I n a comfortable living room somewhere in the middle of Ohio, a young woman approaches a couple with a bundle in her arms. The couple sit side by side in front of a fireplace, incongruous in red-canvas folding camp chairs. The man wears a white polo, his broad forehead gleaming above a patient smile. The woman beside him smiles too. She has long dark hair and a tight black turtleneck that stretches over her pregnant belly.

The young woman reveals that she's cradling a floppy cloth baby doll. It looks like a collection of bean bags sewn together into a baby shape and dressed in a white onesie. It's genderless and featureless, but the young woman speaks to it softly, as if it were the real thing.

"Hi, baby, aren't you cute?" the young woman coos. It isn't, but she continues anyway. "I bet your mommy and daddy are so excited to meet you!"

She plops the doll into a basket in front of the "parents." The woman picks it up with awkward enthusiasm and coos to it as the dad watches and lovingly strokes her leg. This is not their baby, but the woman is pregnant, so the game of social science make-believe feels weirdly high stakes. The couple pass the baby doll back and forth, argue playfully about its gender, then lay it down for a nap.

The whole interaction is recorded for a study about maternal gate-keeping designed by Sara Schoppe-Sullivan, and that recording is a weird watch. The members of Schoppe-Sullivan's team are used to it. They've seen a lot of videos and have specific criteria by which they analyze the footage, coding specific behaviors. The process is called pre-natal Lausanne Trilogue Play, and Schoppe-Sullivan believes the technique can be used to predict the behavior of future mothers and fathers, specifically whether mothers will attempt to keep fathers at arm's length, a common behavior social scientists refer to as "maternal gate-keeping," an unfortunate term that puts way too much blame on mom from the start.[1]

"We looked at the mother's encouragement or discouragement of their interaction with the doll during the procedure and found that it was predictive of father perceptions of their coparenting relationship after the birth of their child," explains Schoppe-Sullivan.

In other words, if a mother-to-be keeps a father from playing with the faceless baby doll, she is also likely to keep a father from providing meaningful care to the child. Many women naturally engage in this behavior. And it's worth noting up top that Schoppe-Sullivan isn't judgmental about it, and no one else should be either. "Maternal gatekeeping" may sound like a men's rights fever dream, but it's a common phenomenon when it comes to childcare. The term was introduced in 1999 by Brigham Young University researchers Sarah M. Allen and Alan J. Hawkins in their groundbreaking study "Maternal Gatekeeping: Mothers' Beliefs and Behaviors that Inhibit Greater Father Involvement in Family Work." It's not the breeziest read, but it explains a lot.

GATE BUILDING 101

Maternal gatekeeping is a thoroughly modern phenomenon. And that makes sense. Up until the late 1960s and early 1970s, the areas of family life controlled by mothers and fathers were thoroughly fenced off from one another. If *Mad Men* has anything to say about history, Dad went to work and made lewd comments to his underpaid secretary. Mom stayed home and took uppers while vacuuming the ceiling and taking care of the babies. There was no gate in her fence to keep because Dad wasn't trying to get in. Then Dad's job got shipped to China.

Globalization led to a decline in skilled union jobs and an increase in low-paid service labor. Soon, a single wage was not enough to keep a family solvent, particularly while said family was putting aside money for college so the kids didn't have to take said low-paid service jobs. At the same time, second-wave feminism was empowering women to enter the workforce and earn for themselves in order to establish financial independence. In effect, women joined the workforce just in time to ensure that employers could pay workers unsustainable wages without forcing them into poverty—poverty being inconvenient because it leads to tardiness. It became relatively common for both parents to be in the workforce. With the paid labor burden shared, the unpaid labor burden got shared too.

Well, almost.

A 2016 Pew Research study found that since 1965, the amount of time men spend on childcare duties has more than tripled, and time spent on household chores has doubled.[2] So the gate between gendered responsibilities looks like it's wide open. But that thing still swings closed.

The truth is, while fathers are engaged in more childcare and household duties, women are still doing a majority of the family work. Explanations for this can be found elsewhere in this book, but the data is the data, and many fathers report they want to do more with and for their children than their spouses allow. There's a lot to unpack in that claim, which is sexist in about five directions, but social scientists accept that there's a reason eight out of ten fathers report spending too little time with their kids.

The reason—and, again, there's no moral judgment here—is moms.

For their groundbreaking study, Allen and Hawkins surveyed 622 wives and mothers from around the United States and found that when women strongly identified as mothers, believed in gendered marital roles, and had high standards of household work, their husbands were forcibly excused from childcare.[3] Those three behavioral factors, the researchers claimed, made up the basis for maternal gatekeeping. And since 1999, a mix of psychological and social research, including Schoppe-Sullivan's prenatal Lausanne Trilogue Play experiments, has confirmed the importance of gatekeeping as a significant barrier to more equitable childcare and household work between mothers and fathers.

Importantly, the barrier isn't always glaringly obvious. Maternal gatekeeping is often disguised as behaviors that feel normal for those sliding into more traditionally gendered parenting roles. Fathers concede to mothers who want to own responsibility for nurturing activities like diapering or feeding without realizing that they are being frozen out of important duties. They then find themselves in a support role, which feels natural but also triggers some resentment. They don't want to hear "you're doing it wrong" even though they're open to the message. Even so, this dynamic reinforces a discouraging thought: aren't women just better at this stuff?

For their part, mothers may not even be aware that the behaviors they are engaged in constitute gatekeeping or have negative side effects—not even if they are specifically trained and paid to look for those behaviors in others. Such was the case for New Jersey–based licensed mental health counselor Sheina Schochet. Despite helping couples resolve gatekeeping behaviors in her role as a family therapist, she discovered that she was engaging in her own gatekeeping behaviors with her husband. But not until her second child was born.

"I like to get bath time done quickly, whereas my husband liked to pull out all the toys and make it into a whole fun event with our older daughter," Schochet says. "I would criticize the way he went about it, which obviously made him not want to do bath time, which led to me doing it more than I wanted to."

Schochet hadn't set out to make her life more difficult or put a strain on her marriage, but there it was. How did Schochet solve the problem? She didn't. Not really. She had a second kid and, shortly thereafter, no choice but to let her husband bathe her daughter any way he saw fit. "It was a win for both of us," she says.

BLAME-GATE

Maternal gatekeeping is not going well for women either. According to the annual American Time Use Survey conducted by the US Bureau of Labor Statistics, married mothers who were employed full time spent about an hour more per day than fathers employed full time on household chores and childcare combined.[4] A 2017 study from the Ohio State University based on the BLS data set found that during nonworking hours, fathers spent about half their time in leisure activities. Mothers spent, at most, 20 percent of their time enjoying leisure activities.[5]

No surprise, gates are also no picnic for kids.

"We know that when mothers close the gate to fathers, either by criticizing them or thwarting opportunities for fathers to spend time alone with their children, it can dampen involvement in child-rearing later on," explains Schoppe-Sullivan. "Also, the observed quality of fathers' interaction with their infant went down when mothers were more critical of their parenting."

From a child development perspective, Schoppe-Sullivan says, parents' interactions with a child should be more about quality than quantity. So if the quality of children's relationships with their fathers declines because of maternal gatekeeping, it could have a serious effect on a development.

But being a dad doesn't mean they have no part in constructing the gate. The bond that oxytocin helps create between mother and child can feel intimidating and impenetrable to fathers. Physiologically, Mom has a more significant role through birth. And, unlike fathers, during pregnancy and at birth women are flooded with oxytocin, a hormone that helps strengthen bonding between mother and baby, promoting feelings of love and closeness. Oxytocin also triggers the breast milk let-down reflex, enabling babies to breastfeed. So fathers often feel that women are "naturally" closer to their newborns than men will be. And often that sets a precedent for what comes next.

NEED TO KNOW

A Little of that Human Touch

In the 1950s psychologist Harry Harlow discovered that touch was essential for normal primate development. Early in his career, Harlow had bred a captive troop of rhesus macaques for his experiments. Some were raised with mothers; others were not. He noticed that motherless macaques developed odd behaviors and clung to their cloth diapers. He wondered why it seemed the cloth was so important.[6]

Harlow's experiments, which were undeniably cruel, exposed baby monkeys to two sets of mother surrogates. One was made of wire with a false monkey head. It provided nourishment via milk. The other surrogate was the cloth mother: same head, a body covered in a soft fabric, but no nourishment. Harlow observed that the baby monkeys would always choose to spend time with the cloth mother rather than the wire mother that provided food. Only intense hunger would drive them to the uncomforting mother, and even then only long enough to feed before scampering back to the soft mother. Later experiments showed that when baby monkeys were raised in a socially isolating "pit of despair" (as Harlow dubbed it) they would develop "severe deficits in virtually every aspect of social behavior."

The lesson, as laid out in Harlow's 1958 address to the American Psychological Association, titled "The Nature of Love," was that touch was far more important for baby development than anyone realized. The conclusion ran counter to the infant-rearing advice at the time, which suggested that, apart from nursing, mothers should limit contact with their infants to avoid spoiling. It was a revolutionary insight, later confirmed by studies of infants raised in Eastern European orphanages, where babies were provided adequate nutrition and physical care but lacked touch and social-emotional care. Like their primate cousins, these human babies raised in isolating conditions suffered behavioral issues and delayed physical development, resulting in stunted growth. The bottom line is this: babies and children need physical contact. They need touch. Both are necessary for both physical and social development and should come equally from mothers and fathers. But maternal gatekeeping can hamper contact by keeping dads at a distance.

It's time for dads to open the gate and make with the cuddles.

But Dad doesn't get to complain if he doesn't communicate his desire to be more involved. Studies show that a mother's gatekeeping behavior can be influenced by a father's attitude about his future parenting duties during pregnancy. "What we found was that when the father was more confident about their parenting skills before the baby was born, mothers were less likely to close the gate, criticize or curtail their involvement," says Schoppe-Sullivan.[7]

Schoppe-Sullivan says that gatekeeping behaviors can also be influenced by how committed a mother perceives her partner to be. Mothers who see fathers as emotionally detached or not in it for the long term are more likely to keep those fathers from childcare and household responsibilities. If the causes of maternal gatekeeping—a product of millennia of ingrained sexism and certain biological realities—are hard to fully comprehend, the solution is far clearer. Dad needs to speak up. The goal here is not to dictate but to facilitate a change in Mom's attitudes, which threaten to make her own life much harder.

Still, obstacles remain. Some mothers put parenthood at the core of their personal identities and relegate Dad to a secondary role in order to become the ideal parent they wish to be.

None of this makes these women bad partners or bad mothers. It makes them people in need of material help from understanding coparents. The truth is that even if couples have progressive ideas about gender roles, feel confident in their parenting abilities, and want to evenly split parenting duties, there are strong social and biological influences that promote gatekeeping. In fact, the prominent institutions that define and interact with modern families almost force women into gatekeeping whether they have an inclination toward that behavior or not.

Before couples even start a family, women are often established as the center of the family. The wedding-industrial complex largely caters to the bride. Her experience is central while the groom often takes on a supporting role (the "it's not about you" talk is a ritual for grooms). Given the fact that 61 percent of babies are born to married mothers, it's important to consider how early this pattern that continues during pregnancy is established.[8] Mothers handle registries. They host the showers. They take parental leave. Then, as the kid gets a bit older, they function as the default point of contact for pediatricians, caregivers, and educators.

Being the primary contact serves to reinforce the role. Soon enough all of the information about the children is collected and controlled by mothers, who may never have wanted it in the first place. This creates a kind of bureaucratic barrier for dads who, without the required insight, show up to appointments and parent–teacher conferences looking ill-informed—reinforcing bias in the professionals who struggle to deal with them.

Even the media places mothers at the center of housework and child-care. Moms still star in commercials for cleaning and childcare products, and many businesses advertising to parents have big marketing budgets explicitly devoted to mothers.

Given all that—the enforcement of the behavior that wrong-foots so many dads—it's no wonder that even progressive couples struggle to find balance, and it's unlikely that anything will change anytime soon. But that doesn't mean that gatekeeping is inevitable. Schoppe-Sullivan says that her research points to practices gatekeeping-resistant couples have in common. And it seems those traits can be developed well before a baby arrives.[9]

- *Communication:* A couple that can speak freely about their needs are more likely to be successful when they feel overburdened.

- *Confidence:* Parents who feel confident of their skill set are far less likely to be reticent to take duties that help reset balance.

- *Negotiation:* Couples that negotiate with each other tend to be more successful when it comes time to negotiate complicated issues and circumstances.

- *Practice:* There's no room for Allen Iverson–style gameday focus ("Practice!" "Practice?" Yes. Practice.) Dads who expect Mom to mentor in the moment and neglect their training tend to wind up in secondary caregiving roles.

When it comes to balance, couples thrive when they are explicit in their expectations. Importantly, this doesn't mean dividing up the work fifty-fifty. In some cases—breastfeeding being a prime example—that's impossible or ill considered. What's more important is that couples agree that the division of labor makes sense to them as a family. Some couples may, in fact, skew to more traditional gender roles. If it works, great.

CHAPTER 9

Meet the Grandparents

Marie Barlow lives in Chicago. She has eleven children, sixty-five grandchildren, and two great-grandchildren. Most American school buses seat seventy-eight kids, and if Marie Barlow ever decided to take her family on a field trip, there would be only one seat left—two if she took the driver's seat. And she probably would. Barlow is like that.

Barlow lives in a house that's probably more than she needs but is really the only practical way to cope with the slings and arrows of outrageous hereditary fecundity. She donates her licensed caregiving services (she's still working!) to her children, so her home/workplace is always full of a rotating cast of children, both her own grandchildren and those she cares for. That's eight kids all in, every day. It's more than enough, and she's happy with the situation. But there is one asterisk levitating just above her Calumet Heights row-house-turned-childcare-center.

"I tell my kids if you don't like what I do, then keep them at home," Marie says. "You know how I live. You know how I am. I am going to cook and make cookies and cake. If you can't accept that then I'm not the one you want."

With day care costing an arm and a leg and threatening to take another limb, this might sound like a no-brainer, but there have been confrontations. Of course there have. Kids don't choose their parents and parents don't choose their kids. Many if not most young adults see eye-to-eye with their parents only when squaring off. People mature, but resentments don't. They hang around the house, playing video games in the basement and waiting to get called up for dinner.

So there was a fight when one of Barlow's children heard a new word slipping from the lips of their ankle biter: chocolate.

"They didn't know he was eating chocolate until he started talking well," laughs Barlow, unrepentant as Hannibal Lecter at a tapas flesh bar. "He knew where I kept the chocolate and would point to the cabinet and say, 'chocolate.'"

To speak to Marie Barlow is to like Marie Barlow and to come to happy terms with the proliferation of Barlows in the great Chicago metroplex. But insomuch as Barlow is an advertisement for the human species, it doesn't take long before she fails to resist the oldest of canards. She says her parenting was good enough for her eleven children, so her grandparenting ought to be good enough as well. It's an entirely understandable sentiment but fundamentally wrongheaded. And she seems to know this. She admits that some of her kids want to raise their children differently and that she's understanding of that fact.

But is she? Are grandparents trustworthy or is even the best grandmother likely to go rogue? Conflicts between children and parents are inevitable, especially in an age of drastic cultural shifts, but these problems are too often couched in human terms or articulated in the language of offense. In truth, there's a structural issue at play. Time passes and there's no white picket fence high enough to keep out entropy.

Researchers are learning more about childhood development and the importance of parenting. More informed parents raise children intentionally and do so with a set of values that informs their decision-making. That, as you may recall, is the premise of this book. But the accepted narrative around parenthood is that it's a timeless experience and that the once applicable can always be usefully reapplied. Unfortunately, like Scotch Tape or Big League Chew, parenting best practices lose their stickiness and freshness over time.

And who wants to go to their parents and have that discussion? Who wants to tell their parents that what they knew—the very premises on which they staked their children's lives—was complete horseshit? That conversation always ends badly. So, instead, modern parents end up in diplomatic talks with Grammy and Pops, leading to either détente (but the Russian word *razryadka,* meaning "relief of tension" more fully captures the stress of it all) or further conflict.

These concerns and tensions are relatively new, historically speaking. Americans used to have more kids—with just more than eight kids per family, the Pilgrims made the Irish look like the Trojan Man—but they also had the good manners to die young of now-preventable diseases. Grandparents today live longer, live farther from their children, and, somewhat paradoxically, they live to serve, providing more care for their grandchildren than ever before. They are somewhat media savvy and act as an economic driver considering how many of them there are. Today, there are an estimated 70 million grandparents alive in the United States, which is a 25 percent increase since 2001.[1] Fox News doesn't watch itself.

NEED TO KNOW

Portrait of an American Grandparent

It's easy to consider "grandparents" a monolithic brand. They are easily stereotyped as kind, gray-haired elders who have a penchant for baking and passing down war stories and life lessons. Sometimes they are presumed to be out of touch with a larger world that tolerates their doddering ways  because they carry around hard candies and call people "Sweetie."

 The truth is that grandparents are wildly diverse and far more adept at navigating the modern world than the broad brushstrokes of Western popular culture would have you believe. There are more grandparents now than ever before, and they are as crucial to the modern American economy as they are to the modern American family.

The grandparent demographic has long been captured and represented by the American Association for Retired Persons, or AARP. The organization regularly checks in on its membership, offering a deep demographic dive into the State of Grandparenting. Their last big survey was completed in 2018, and the insight from their "Grandparents Today" report offers a reality check about what American grandparents really look like:[2]

There Are More Grandparents than Ever Before

One of the most startling things about grandparents is that they are growing in numbers. The AARP found that 70 percent of eight-year-olds will have a living grandparent by the year 2030. In fact, most parents become grandparents by the age of sixty-five. Of the generation currently in grandparent territory, the Baby Boomers, most have, on average, four grandchildren, while emerging X-er grandparents have only two grandchildren on average.

Grandparents Buy a Lot of Stuff

The AARP study notes that grandparents are pretty much aligned on dropping some money for grandkids' gifts, intergenerational vacations, and higher education–in that order. As a whole, spending by grandparents is significant, reaching about $179 billion in 2018. Yearly, the amount of money a grandparent spends on their grandkids is around $2,500.

Grandparents Aren't into Your "Newfangled" Parenting Styles

Most grandparents prefer being called Grandma or Grandpa instead of some cutesy sobriquet like Gammy or Pawpaw. Along with the traditional handle, grandparents are pretty sure their traditional methods of child-rearing were better. In response to AARP questioning on current parenting styles, a majority of grandparents felt that spanking was okay and that modern parents are too lax with their kids. Additionally, grandparents overwhelmingly report feeling that discipline and parenting were better "back in the day" compared to modern styles.

Grandma Really Does Wish You Would Call More Often

Because just over half of grandparents live at least two hundred miles away from their grandkids, communication is a crucial concern, according to the AARP poll. And while 46 percent will use the phone to talk with grandkids every couple of weeks, grandparents are increasingly tech-savvy. Just over a quarter of grandparents surveyed will use text messaging and video chats to connect with their grandkids every couple of weeks.

Grandkids Are the Key to Staying Young

Perhaps the best motivation for keeping grandkids connected with grandparents is the fact that elders report the kids keep them spry. Nearly 90 percent of grandparents polled by the AARP said that their grandchildren keep them mentally healthy, and nearly 70 percent reported that grandkids help keep them physically active.

Though it often doesn't seem like it, Americans are generally happier for having their parents around. A 2016 Boston College study published in the journal *Gerontology* found that postadolescent children and young adults who report having good relationships with their grandparents are likely to have fewer depressive symptoms.[3] And that effect goes both ways. Grandparents who report good relationships with adult grandchildren have fewer depressive symptoms too.

Grandparents benefit children in other ways too. A 2011 study from Brigham Young University looking at 408 families found a particular benefit in grandparent emotional involvement.[4] When grandparents were emotionally involved with grandchildren, those grandchildren were more likely to display prosocial behaviors (like sharing and honesty) both at the time of the initial measurement and a year later.

Children who have regular contact with grandparents are also less likely to have ageist views, according to a 2017 study out of Belgium. Researchers found that a prejudiced view against elderly adults expressed by grade-school aged children declined significantly when the children reported they were happy to hang out and spend time with their grandparents.[5]

More than that, grandparents can help children connect with and understand their ethnic and social roots. They pass down family lore through stories and often remain in family homes that provide a place to gather. This connection to the past can help children feel part of a larger story and imbue them with pride in who they are.

Finally, grandparents can act as guardrails in times of economic or family insecurity. It's not uncommon for grandparents to enter roles as caregivers if parents are debilitated and unable to care for kids. Grandparents can and do provide financial support in times of crisis. Maria Barlow, the youngest of the Barlow kids, says knowing her mother is around gives her a sense of profound security.

"If I have an issue at work, I know my mom will talk a billion dollars' worth of trash but she'll help me," Maria says. "She's always there if I need her. My son also knows that."

These benefits of grandparents, however, rely on children reporting that they have "good relationships." In her work in family court, Maria sees what can happen when those relationships break down between parents and grandparents. She has seen the pain of grandparents who are becoming estranged from their grandchildren because of a divorce or death. That's because parents are the gatekeepers of grandparent relationships with children. In the best circumstances parents keep that gate open. But that's largely dependent on the strength of the relationship in the first place. The stronger the relationship between expecting parents and soon-to-be grandparents, the more likely it is that a child will reap the benefits of having a grandparent around.

"I have found that many families do have clear and concise conversations about their expectations with the grandparents," Maria says. "It helps."

In her work, Maria deals with the most explosive conflicts between parents and grandparents—generally battles around access to a grandchild. She notes that it's rare for her to recommend anything other than some kind of reconciliation. She notes that at the heart of the matter, grandparents interfere not out of self-interest but because they truly want to give their love to a child.

"Listen, for everything you don't like about grandma, or grandad, who are they as a grandparent to your child," Maria tells the parents she represents. "Take yourself out of it and determine who is this person and how do they treat your child."

Of course that's sometimes easier said than done. Whether it's family history or a clash of personalities, some parents still struggle to work through conflicts with grandparents. Maria has advice for them too: fake it till you make it.

"Deal with them as if you like them," she says. "If you come at it that way and you talk with them like it's someone you like, then it won't be so hostile."

NEED TO KNOW

When Grandparents Aren't So Grand

Parents should be willing and ready to support a child's relationship with grandparents. This especially goes for grandparents with physical or cognitive disabilities related to age. The fact is that it's important for children to be exposed to aging adults regardless of age-related struggles they face. And it's just as important for aging adults to be exposed to the boundless optimism and joy of children.

Frail grandparents, or those who are affected by cognitive decline, should be able to enjoy supervised contact with their grandchildren. Parents should consider the unique gifts that grandparents can offer children outside of direct care. Those gifts might include storytelling or teaching unique hands-on skills. Simple companionship is important too. For instance, children can benefit from talking with grandparents about books they read or watching television programs together. Exposure to diverse perspectives helps kids expand their understanding of the world–up to a point.

Some grandparents might refuse to moderate views, such as those promoting misogyny or homophobia, that challenge core parental values. Some grandparents might refuse to change risky behavior, like drinking and driving, that could have serious consequences for a child's well-being. And while every attempt should be made to support grandparent relationships as best as parents can, parents absolutely have the right to draw a line.

The most important person in these family relationships is the child. If there are issues that feel difficult but fixable, you might want to try family counseling. If the issues create too much tension and stress and result in fighting or regular bad feelings, the relationship may simply be too toxic to salvage.

As sad as it might be, there is no shame in walking away from a grandparent relationship for the health and safety of your child.

Grandparents are people too, and like so many people, sometimes they're toxic. Yes, you can cut grandparents out of your kid's life—but it's not something to be taken lightly. If salvageable, grandparent relationships can be greatly beneficial to childhood development. But if the relationship is detrimental to the kid, a parent can and should cut ties. You owe your kids this. Your parents? Not so much.

There are some obvious grandparents who should be avoided. It is okay not to see a grandparent who's an addict. It's okay to ditch a grandparent who is racist or homophobic. It's okay to limit or restrict time with grandparents who were abusive or neglectful as parents.

These conversations tend to be most effective if they take place before a child is even born. According to child psychologist Chad Brandt, family members often slip into new roles in the wake of a birth without having explicit conversations about intergenerational expectations. Brandt, the father of three sons his in-laws care for daily, says that what worked for him was having the philosophical conversation well in advance of the first behavior-specific confrontation. When he had the conversation, he did so respectfully. Brandt respected his in-laws and also understood that his family would suffer without their support—a reality for many millennial parents.

"When we had our first son, I was in graduate school—there was no way I was running a family on my salary," he remembers. "We knew my wife would have to work. Her parents said that they would be happy to help."

Pumped for advice, Brandt says the word *routine* a lot. He bends and folds sentences around it. He takes the path taken every day at precisely the same time and it has made all the difference.

"A schedule is really important," he says. "The kids are up around the same time every day; they're eating around the same time every day. We swim at the same time, and we don't have sugar after a certain time."

But he notes that the schedule is more than just for his kids. It also eliminates ambiguity for him and his wife. Part of routine is consistency, which is to say, a clear understanding of what goes where, both organizationally and behaviorally speaking. Barlow's children understand that rules are contextual. Grandma and Grandpa have different rules, and that's fine. Those are their rules, and they are to be respected. Mom and Dad's rules are also to be respected; they're just enforced in a different home.

This is a critical point as many intergenerational conflicts are born of the idea that kids need just one set of rules. But life is not like that. Ask ex-pole vaulters, dancers, or explorers working office jobs. Context is king and kids totally get that. The issue isn't with the complication that presents but with the hypocrisy and unfairness children perceive when rules are poorly rather than harshly enforced.

And harsh enforcement often becomes an issue between parents and grandparents. Even ex-hippies tend to be more liberal with corporal punishment than their children, and if parents aren't aware of harsh discipline tactics, or make no effort to change the tactics, kids will likely come to view them as complicit in their pain and stress. Those children may act out, creating a damaging and vicious cycle. So when it comes to communicating around punishment, it's critical to be extremely explicit and unwavering.

Brandt admits he had to have a serious chat with his father-in-law about discipline. It's not that anyone was being unreasonable but that new information had come to light. Eventually they agreed upon shared standards. Brandt is wildly appreciative of this because his in-laws taking care of his kids is, well, work. Compromise is hard, and caregiving is even harder.

"We try to be appreciative. Watching kids is a lot of work. My in-laws are happy to do it, but we try to give them a lot of notice and days off if they need them," Brandt says, adding that the system has been effective.

It's worth noting, however, that said system does not extend to Brandt's parents. Brandt's mother has no desire to be a caregiver to his kids. She lives in Florida, and the distance definitely affects the tenor of the relationship; mostly she'd just prefer to be the "fun" grandma.

It also should be noted that Brandt's experience with his mother is not unusual for fathers. Paternal grandparents are generally not as involved with children as maternal grandparents. That's because women do a majority of "kinkeeping" in families—essentially managing relationships between relatives. Heterosexual couples, even before children, generally have more contact with the woman's family. That trend only continues when a baby arrives. Data backs this up. A 2010 study from State University of New York looked at 227 three-generational-families and found a distinct matrilinear bias in who keeps and transmits family information. Those patterns persisted even when couples divorced.[6] Fathers should prepare for the fact that the grandparents they are communicating with are most likely to be in-laws.

And all parents should internalize a harsh truth: those communications may go poorly or simply end. That's possible in America in a way that it's not in Europe, which guarantees visitation rights for grandparents, or China, where adults have a legal responsibility to visit their parents.

So if a grandparent's behavior is more damaging to a child than is their absence, American parents can pull the plug. And many do.

Parents need to put their child's health, safety, and development at the forefront of any relationship. If grandparents endanger any of those priorities, it's important for parents to consider putting limits on the relationship. For instance, parents probably shouldn't leave their children alone with a grandparent who is unable to properly supervise them for whatever reason, but that doesn't mean all contact has to be severed. Supervised play can be encouraged, or contact can be buffered by a parent's presence. That said, when relationships are deeply toxic because of a family history of neglect or abuse, it's okay for parents to keep their child isolated from a grandparent for the child's own safety.

But these considerations get trickier in instances in which conflict is due to personal or political ideology. Because the truth is that sometimes, specifically during holidays, it might be difficult to shield a child from a grandparent's clashing social or political views. Importantly, though, parents can buffer outdated or antisocial views by having open and age-appropriate conversation with their kids about what they might have seen or heard at the Thanksgiving dinner table.

That talk doesn't need to be complicated. It can be as simple as saying, "Grandpa/Grandma used some words about people that we don't use in our home because . . ." If those explanations are backed up by strong values in the home and good modeling from parents, there's little to worry about from the occasional awkward holiday celebration.

What doesn't help, however, is when parents have verbal fights with grandparents in front of their children or, even more damagingly, criticize grandparents behind their backs. Children look to parents to understand how to navigate their own relationships, and so when parents model behavior that is petty or aggressive, children will add that to the psychological operation manual they are continually building in their heads. Which is to say if you treat your parents like crap, you shouldn't be surprised when your kids grow up to treat you like crap too.

Maria Barlow loves her mother, who, again, is great. But there's some ambivalence there around certain types of messaging—when and where kids can eat Popsicles for instance. So rather than expecting her mother to change, Maria asked her son to moderate his behavior and not ask for Popsicles when he knows he's not supposed to. In doing so, she's teaching her son to be respectful and flexible while also demonstrating care for her mother and her mother's demonstrably good intentions.

"When the grandparent doesn't mind keeping their kids, it's because they love their kids and they're going to put the time in. They're not going to do anything wrong to the kids or teach them anything wrong," says Grandma Barlow.

That may not be precisely right, but it's not wrong either. Parents would do well to remind themselves consistently that Grandma and Grandpa are looking out for their best interests. They may not be doing so in precisely the way parents would hope or using the language they'd prefer, but most grandparents are happily doing what they can.

"I love them," adds Grandma Barlow. "That's basically it."

Yup.

A PRACTICAL GUIDE FOR ESTABLISHING EXPECTATIONS WITH NEW GRANDPARENTS

Establish Expectations Early

You can't expect grandparents to be mind readers. And you can't possibly intuit the type of grandparent your own parents want to be. It's important to have talks about the changing dynamics before the kid even arrives. There are some important questions to ask:

What level of support and care do the future grandparents want to provide?

What kind of access do grandparents expect, and is that realistic given geography and resources?

Are there specific parenting tactics that you plan on using, and do you expect grandparents to fall in line?

How is the way you plan to raise your children different from the way you were raised?

Are there deal breakers like swearing, alcohol and drug use, or open bigotry?

Be Practical from Day One

From the moment you bring your infant home, grandparents will likely want to visit and be involved. From simply a health and energy standpoint, it will help to talk about who will be visiting when.

Keep in mind that new babies are still working on their immune systems. Grandparent kisses and touches are unlikely to pass on pathogens like herpes or coronavirus, but it's not unheard of. So, baby touches and kisses are best relegated to knees and feet. Also, try to plan things in a way that an infant's contact with people outside the home is relatively limited. A schedule will help, and framing the schedule discussion around baby's health will help defuse unnecessary family politics.

Talk Travel and Holidays

Many families feel pressured to celebrate holidays with grandparents, and in many cases this will require a family to travel. When both sets of grandparents are alive and live far from the family, the logistics and feelings around holidays can get very complicated very quickly.

It's possible to delay holiday decisions when a child is a baby. After all, it's not always practical or cost-effective to pack up an infant for a flight or a long drive to spend a holiday with a grandparent. And, frankly, those excuses are usually enough to keep holiday wrangling at bay for a child's first year or so.

But it's better to establish a travel and holiday schedule as early as possible. Some grandparents may be okay splitting up Thanksgiving and Christmas on a rotating basis. Some may prefer to own a holiday. Others might want to corral off the warmer months so that they can enjoy outdoor activities with grandchildren as they grow. The important part is to have the talk early and erase any ambiguity.

Talk about Money

One common area of conflict comes from spending. Grandparents tend to enjoy shopping with children or buying them big toys. In a practical sense, if that spending is unchecked or too lavish, it could eat into a grandparents retirement fund or cause outspent parents to feel hurt and inadequate. But there are ways to help grandparents spend reasonably.

- Remind them that your kid would get a kick out of just spending some time with them.
- Offer suggestions of free or affordable activities for uncreative grandparents.
- Pool resources for one big gift that doesn't come from any one person during the holidays.
- If they insist they want to give more, ask them to secure a safe investment (savings bonds, tax-free college savings) in your kid's name that could help them in the future.

Know Everyone's Limits

A good relationship with grandparents will always require some amount of compromise, so it helps to know exactly what you're willing to compromise. Some parents may not mind a little extra screen time or sugar at a grandparent's house. Other parents may want to insist on keeping these rules consistent.

On the other hand, some grandparents may be fine with taking a kid on short notice or adhering to strict dietary restrictions. Other grandparents might want to have strict limits on how much time they'll give grandkids or what they will or will not prepare for food.

Relationship tendons will be relaxed when parents know what they intend to stand firm on and what they're willing not to fight.

CHAPTER 10

Communicating with Caregivers, Consultants, and Clinicians

The nuclear family was never supposed to be radioactive. The explosive term actually derives from stability, the Latin *nux*, or nut, from which it derives, denoting an essential core. The family and the atom, in our inherited linguistic formulation, are essential units. And like atoms, families do not exist in a vacuum. They gyrate and bounce among friends, loved ones, childcare professionals, and services providers. They have certain properties, but to observe one is to change it, and to split one is to court disaster.

Fission is what happens when a nucleus is split by a neutron. And in a social sense it's what happens when Mom takes the nanny's side in a fight with Dad. It's not a blast, but it's the prelude to a firestorm. It's also hard for parents to avoid because communicating with caregivers is inherently difficult. It's a unique relationship because it's the only common service relationship that precisely mirrors the structure of a kidnap and ransom plot.

Caregivers may wish the best for the children they look after, but it's important for parents that they have continued access and even control of those children. It's no wonder things get volatile.

In the last fifty years, parental concern for a child's economic future and the related explosion in highly involved "intensive parenting" has skyrocketed to secure that future. It helps that technology has made it easier for parents to be more involved in the care their children are receiving. Communicating with caregivers has become more of an issue as technology enables parents to check in, check up, and engage in research of topics they might have otherwise entrusted to an expert.

A constellation of caregivers revolve around our kids. These are nannies, day care workers, bus drivers, lunch ladies, school nurses, educators, crossing guards, and pediatricians whose livelihood depends on keeping kids safe and healthy. They derive their authority from experience and training—be it weeks or years—and do the jobs that parents can't do because they lack the expertise, time, or patience to do so.

This sounds like any other relationship in a free market economy. But unlike any other service transactions, caregivers are unique because what they offer parents is a happy, healthy, or educated child. Their goals for a kid are pretty narrow based on their occupation. They only look at a part of a child's life. Because of that, their perceptions of a child can be remarkably removed from a parents' perspective.

Communication with people who care for our children is fundamentally different because the kid is in the middle. They can't ask questions or report on their own condition. The kid is kind of like the proverbial elephant with the blind men. One feels a leg and says it's a tree. One feels the trunk and says it's a snake. It's the same with caregivers and parents: the pediatrician feels the legs, the nanny feels the tail, the teacher feels the tusk, and the parents feel the chest and the beating heart. Each has a different perspective of who the child is and what they need. Everything would be cleared up if the elephant could just say, "I'm a damn elephant, okay?"

THE PEDIATRIC TANGO

The baby had been crying, almost continually, for at least two months, and thirty-five-year-old Brooklyn comedian Evan Kaufman was the only person who could make it stop. Once the wailing would commence, he'd hoist his son into his arms and just walk. Evan imagined that part of what made the walking work was because he's tall, over six feet, and he figured his son Desmond must like being up high to see the world. On Christmas morning of 2019, he found himself trudging in circles around a water tower in the cold woods at 4:00 a.m., a kind of baby gulag that he had to endure because it was the only way that his son would sleep.

Evan and his wife, Kaitlyn, had established a relationship with a pediatrician with their first son, Rory. But despite the good working relationship, answers were hard to come by.

"People kept telling us, at four months he'll be better; at six months he'll be better," Evan remembers. "It was like going up for parole and being told the governor changed his mind."

Answers were floated, but a diagnosis was never clear. There were suggestions of silent reflux, colic (essentially prolonged crying for no apparent reason), and perhaps even an allergy. Nothing seemed to be right. The crying continued.

"When you have a kid who's so fussy you think, if something's really wrong with him, I'm going to feel terrible," Evan says. "The problem is that we'd go in and they'd say he's good on the growth chart."

The Kaufmans had run straight into the misalignment of perceptions. In terms of pain and discomfort, their pediatrician was treating it as one of many metrics. But in terms of a data point, it was not as important as the fact that the kid was growing well. For Evan and Kaitlyn, the crying was the most important data point because it meant their child's quality of life, and their own, was not as good as it should be. In fact, it was bad. The pediatrician saw a line on a growth chart saying everything was good. The Kaufmans saw a baby that would cry ceaselessly, robbing their nights of sleep and their Christmas morning of cheer.

"Nobody has colic for ten months," Kaitlyn says with deadpan disappointment.

In only a few instances, say temperature or the color, frequency, and consistency of excrement, do parents like the Kaufmans have discrete objective data points to share with a pediatrician about their baby's health. So parents and pediatricians are left to try and come to a shared understanding based on largely subjective reporting. This is the best system devised to date for the health of a child, but it isn't much to write home about. Maybe more often than not, pediatricians and parents end up on different pages of the board book.

Proof of the misalignment of perception between parents and physicians was brought into sharp relief by the recent obesity crisis. A study from the University of Rotterdam in 2012 looked at data from obesity studies covering some thirty-five thousand children globally to see how parents fared in perceiving children's weight problems. Of the 11,530 children identified as overweight, 67 percent were identified as having a normal weight by parents. The problem was particularly bad for parents of children between the ages of two and six, who were more likely to misperceive their child's weight issue compared to parents of older children.

But the misperception can happen on the part of pediatricians too, which can be a serious problem, particularly when children are chronically ill. A study from the Wilhelmina Children's Hospital, Netherlands, found that compared to parents, pediatricians tended to perceive less pain and discomfort in kids suffering from cystic fibrosis, leukemia, juvenile arthritis, or asthma. That trend was consistent throughout care and occurred regardless of how long the pediatrician had an established care relationship with the child.

Relationships with pediatricians can and do change. The initial contact between pediatricians and parents is often through the first rote well-child visits, where a kid is measured, weighed, vaccinated, and sent on their way. This is fundamentally a data-based exchange. Is my baby growing normally? Yes or no? But as a child grows and starts to communicate, the relationship with a pediatrician shifts. Now the parent is acting as mediator and interpreter, as well as being an interested stakeholder in their child's health. What results is a dance of child well-being. And sometimes the legs can get tangled up.

A 2010 Italian study of young headache sufferers and their parents illustrates how communication dynamics between families and pediatricians shift as kids get older. Researchers found that the parents and children in their study largely expected both to be reassured that the headaches weren't related to larger health concerns and to find out their cause. Pediatricians in the study, however, were unlikely to recognize those expectations, preferring instead to focus on treatment.

This kind of disconnect can lead to an erosion of trust and a pediatric shuffle. Parents can, and do, seek out providers who are better aligned with their children's and their own expectations.

But it's not always as simple as trust, says pediatrician Corey Fish. He worries that the biggest barrier of coming to shared understanding of a child's health is parents who are afraid of asking questions. It's hard to come to an agreement when parents are unwilling to ask clarifying questions.

NEED TO KNOW

Dads versus Pediatricians

Pediatrician Corey Fish notes that there is a running joke among pediatricians that when a dad comes into the office, doctors will have to call the mom. He acknowledges that it's a sexist generalization, although commonly held. But it's illustrative of the barriers fathers face when interacting with care professionals.

Yes, childcare professionals should recalibrate their unhelpful outdated notions. But fathers who want to be involved with childcare professionals need to acknowledge they are battling the bumbling, disconnected, and clueless dad stereotype. It helps to come into pediatric appointments prepared. That means making sure you and your partner are on the same page before the appointment. It means coming in with a cheat sheet of notes if necessary and not being afraid of taking notes and asking questions during an appointment.

Hopefully, as dads arrive more knowledgeable and prepared, pediatricians will start to consider them equal partners in a child's health care. Because fathers do matter to a child's health and need to show up to support that health whenever they can.

"It's almost like they don't want to waste our time," says Fish, the plainly spoken chief medical officer of Brave Care urgent pediatric care in Portland, Oregon. "You can tell when someone is not asking the question. You get done with the interview, and you can tell they're not feeling settled about it."

The thing is that parents are paying for the pediatrician's time as well as their expertise and, frankly, should feel emboldened to walk out of the office with all of their questions asked and answered. But that requires parents to know what to ask.

It's important that parents and pediatricians are on the same page from the beginning of their relationship. Asking questions from the outset can help a parent figure out whether the relationship with the pediatrician will be fruitful. Questions like:

- How much experience do you have as a pediatrician and how long have you been in your current practice?

- Do you have a strong opinion or philosophy on child health issues like potty training, immunizations, breastfeeding, or cosleeping?

- Do you have a policy related to prescribing antibiotics?

- Do you have a subspecialty that would be helpful in the future or salient to my child?

Once a relationship has been established with a pediatrician, parents will find it easier to ask questions during visits if their concerns are right in front of their faces. It helps to have a notebook handy in the weeks before a pediatric visit to jot down observations and concerns to address at the doctor's office. Then, of course, comes the trick of remembering to bring it to the appointment.

Once in the office when the poking, prodding, and measuring are complete, parents should have a set of a standard set of questions to end every visit.

- Is my child growing consistently and should I have any concerns about their development now?

- If my kid is sick, then how should I expect the illness to progress?

- At what point should I reach out if my kid is sick and does not seem to be getting better?

- If my kid needs over-the-counter medication, what are the doses and the correct timing?

- Can I safely delay a medical procedure or treatment with antibiotics without risking my child's health?

- What is the timeline for vaccinations, and can I receive the most recent copy of vaccination records?

Finally, before leaving, parents should repeat back care instructions as they understand them to verify they're correct and give the pediatrician a chance to catch any needed changes. But Fish says that parents should also do a gut check before heading out.

"Trust your instincts. I tell my family this all the time," says Fish. "Parental instincts to me are huge. If you pediatrician doesn't take that seriously then it's probably time to switch pediatricians."

NEED TO KNOW

Questions to Ask Before Choosing a Pediatrician

The best way to develop a good relationship with a good pediatrician is making sure he or she is a right fit for your family. Sure, you want a pediatrician who is conveniently located to your home and compatible with your insurance, but you're also going to want a pediatrician who is a good fit with the values in your home. That's because childhood wellness isn't like automotive repair. You can't plug a kid into a computer and have a part number pop out for the fix. Childhood wellness is about the body, the mind, and the way they develop in the context of a family. So a super-conservative pediatrician who is big on child discipline, for instance, won't be a good fit for a family leaning into discussion-based, punishment-free parenting.

The gist is that to find the right pediatrician, parents need to ask the right questions. Some are practical, others are a bit trickier.

How soon will they start seeing your kid?

A lot of pediatricians like to see the kid a few times before the family is discharged. This gives them a really good foundation on who your kid is (and enables them to start charging you right away!).

Are they associated with a certain hospital?

If so, make sure that facility takes your insurance and isn't too far from your home. You'll want to limit the amount of time your kid can spend projectile vomiting in your car.

When and how are they available?

Knowing how/whether you can reach them on a Saturday or late at night helps you understand how much they're putting into their practice and how much they're practicing their putting.

Do they have kids?

You don't have to have kids in order to be a pediatrician, but it helps build empathy. It's one thing to like kids. It's another thing entirely to know what it's like to be a parent staring down a 102-degree fever at 3:00 a.m. No fun. That's what it's like.

Are there same-day appointments?

Same-day appointments are crucial when your kid's yuck factor reaches a certain level. You'll want to follow up this question by asking whether the doc will be the one who'll see them at these times.

Who do you see when the doc's not there?

Doctors get sick (you would, too, if this was your job), so it's best to make sure the backup isn't an asshole.

How do they feel about (insert tricky subject here)?

Breastfeeding until five years old? Modified vaccination schedules? Alternative potty-training methods? There are plenty of tricky subjects you'll want to make sure that you and the doc are gelling on. Otherwise things are going to get super awkward.

It also might help to recognize medicine is not monolithic. Just because someone might have chosen to be a preschool teacher or pediatrician for a career does not erase the fact they bring unique perspectives to their job, according to Palo Alto, California, pediatric neurologist Sarah Cheyette.

"Pediatricians are people too," says the ADHD specialist. "We come to the evaluations with our own set of feelings and beliefs, and that can influence the evaluation. Some pediatricians are laid back, others are fanatical about nutrition, others judgmental about video games."

Cheyette says it's important for parents to understand these perspectives because they can color the subjective observations that pediatricians make when providing care. That said, she cautions parents about trying to find a pediatrician who shares their exact beliefs. The danger is that it could create dogmatic blind spots that aren't ultimately healthy for a child.

"Look for someone you can have a conversation about things with. Someone who is reasonable," Cheyette says. "You want to have some growth in your parenting, and someone who is the same as you and just reinforces your beliefs is not necessarily the best person for your child."

In fact, understanding when to cut ties with a pediatrician is an important part of the child well-being dance. If communication becomes intractable, it might be time to find a new pediatrician.

This is not to say that the customer is always right. Parents do need to acknowledge that they aren't the medical experts. At the same time, if they walk out of an office feeling guilty or blamed, it's not helpful. If a pediatrician is unengaged with a kid's care, or a child feels uncomfortable, or if parents feel the need to continually look elsewhere for additional advice, the relationship has likely stopped being beneficial for a child. And it's okay to make changes. It might feel like a hassle. It probably is a hassle. But sometimes making a change means better care for a child.

Despite the lack of resolution of their son Desmond's colicky behavior, the Kaufmans have stuck with their pediatrician. Evan doesn't blame the doctor. Though his baby isn't "fixed," Evan understands that there are some things that might not be solvable. What's more important for him is that his pediatrician has been receptive to every call and suggestion, regardless of how frequent those calls are. That responsiveness has helped the Kaufmans feel heard and supported despite having a normally developing baby boy who just can't seem to stop crying.

"Sometimes babies are just babies," says Evan. As Desmond has grown, things have gotten a little better. Being able to sit upright seems to help. But the mystery remains. "I'm sure he's not going to be crying like this when he's twenty. If he is, there are definitely bigger issues we'll need to address."

THE EARLY EDUCATION TWO-STEP

The caregiving back-and-forth shouldn't be considered unique to pediatricians. In lieu of objective measures, parents and professionals in all fields have to come to an agreement on the personal preferences and feelings. You might expect that a babysitter, day care worker, or teacher will not perceive your child's emotions and behaviors in the same way you do. So once again, a dance of child well-being. And again the legs can get tangled up.

Communication with day care centers and preschools can be particularly fraught for parents. Leaving a baby in someone else's care requires a great deal of trust, and parents are often asked to develop that trust inorganically and at speed. Emotions run high when what could be called the child onboarding process is out of sync with a parent's willingness to let go. A lake of tears is shed every year in preschool parking lots.

This is both sad and normal. According to US Census data some 61 percent of American children under five are in some form of nonparental care arrangement. Of those children, 32 percent are in the care of someone other than a relative. The majority of those children are in day care centers or preschool programs.

A 2002 study from Otterbein University in Ohio is slightly more damning, for parents. Researchers quizzed parents of children in day care about how their day care center worked. The quiz included questions about staff turnover rates, type and length of staff training, and adult-to-child ratios. On average, parents answered only 45 percent of the questions correctly. What's more, the score did not go up with the number of hours a child spent at the center or the level of parental educational achievements. Well-educated and not-so-well-educated parents scored similarly, as did parents of kids going to the center full time versus part time.[1]

For many parents of young children, the coronavirus exposed a fundamental ignorance of day care best practices and the degree to which they were unfamiliar with the inner workings of the institutions they'd previously relied on so heavily for caregiving work. When kids can't hug, touch, or interact, parents attempted to take a closer look at what, exactly, the day looked like—down to every hug, sneeze, and the proximity to them at group reading. In many cases they were refused. What became clear was that, like car mechanics, early education providers were being paid to do a job, not explain their process. And this left a lot of parents very uncomfortable.

Maybe that discomfort was for the best. Modern parents have been, in many cases, forced by the demands of their professional lives to seek solutions rather than care.

"Our system has a lot of problematic assumptions built in from the outset," explains Rebecca Parlakian, senior director of programs at early education and care advocacy group Zero to Three. "All of us are stuck with a suboptimal situation. If parents were in general more aware of the challenges and limitations of the current child care landscape, it would at least create a sense of empathy and manage expectations."

But when? The biggest touch point between day care centers and parents happens at the most tender part of the day—pickup and drop off.

The problem, says Parlakian, is that the transfer of children is not compatible with the transfer of information. It's the most emotionally and physically freighted part of the day. Kids are sad to leave their parents in the morning, and in the afternoon they simply want to get the hell out and go home. There's a reason that companies don't conduct quarterly reviews in the cafeteria. Discourse requires a forum, and there are precious few that serve either parents or early education providers. That can result in parents making assumptions, for better or worse, about the care their kid receives. Parents come to trust teachers they shouldn't and resent teachers they should lionize. They operate in an information-poor environment and provide nonsensical feedback or—and this is really the best-case scenario—fail to smartly advocate for their children.

"We're all different humans with different life experiences. There's always going to be points of conflict. When that happens it generates a lot of feelings in all of us, and those feelings get directed towards our child-care providers," explains Parlakian. "We need to stop and acknowledge that, because we need to manage and validate our own feelings before we go to resolve it or else the interaction just isn't as productive."

Parlakian points out that there are ways to hack the day care communication system for the benefit of all parties. It helps for parents to go out of their way, making sure the caregiver is part of the family's essential support group. How? She suggests:

+ Let caregivers know of any changes in family structure or routine that might affect a child's behavior.

+ Note significant changes in daily schedules, whether they be dropped naps or shifts in bedtimes.

* Inform caregivers of important events in the home: both triumphs and tragedies.

* Offer a brief weekend report at the opening of the week so caregivers have a chance to connect with a child on events outside of their classroom.

* Ask for validation or corroboration of a kids' issues at home and seek information on facility techniques caregivers use to deal with behavioral issues.

Parlakian draws this advice from firsthand experience with her son. "I had a work project where I had to travel to China a couple of weeks at a time, several times over a one-year period," she says. "I was working long hours too. During one two-week period when I was away, he fell apart. At school he was completely acting out. He turned into a little monster. It hadn't even occurred to me to give anyone a heads up about my work."

Preparing her son's teachers would likely have helped manage his stress, she says. But many parents fail to bring their stresses and struggles to their care providers, even though it clear those stresses affect a child's life.

But knowing what to communicate doesn't make the act of communicating itself any easier. Parlakian offers a loophole: nap time. Turns out that nap time is the point in the day when care providers are least busy. When kids are snoozing, caregivers have the breathing room to offer updates and insights. Parents also have time to ask questions that would create delays at the beginning or end of the day.

It's a creative solution, and it requires that parents step up and take control of the communication. Really, the need for parents to take control of the communication is consistent no matter who they might be dealing with—babysitters, teachers, day care workers, or pediatricians. These individuals each have their own set of rules and perspectives. Waiting for professionals to offer communication and then reacting creates a weird patchwork of expectations, assumptions, and mismatched perceptions.

If communicating with care professionals is a dance, then parents need to take an assertive lead. That might mean offering more information than would have otherwise been given in a service relationship. It might mean asking more questions, even if you think they are dumb. But by leading the communication, parents can push for consistency and work to tame ambiguity. The result will be professionals who will have a better understanding of the child they are caring for and, ultimately, better outcomes for the kid.

THE HELPERS POLKA

Doctors, caregivers, and teachers aren't the only professionals who will act as caregivers to a child. Over the course of any given day kids will interact with any number of adults whose job it is to see to their well-being, if only for a brief period of time. These individuals include bus drivers, crossing guards, "lunch ladies," librarians, and in rare circumstances, police or other first responders—those individuals who create the net of support Fred Rogers acknowledged when he encouraged kids to "look for the helpers."

Do all of these people need to be approached and addressed directly about the needs and expectations parents have for their child? No. Are there times when that might be appropriate? Yes, particularly in instances where a child might be affected by disabilities that act as barriers to accessing services. But parents should understand that when it comes to communicating with helpers, many are locked into a bureaucracy that might make it hard for them to address individual concerns.

Parents should always feel comfortable asking for a meeting or sending an email to a helper, but they should also ask about the chain of command. Is there someone better to address the issue? Is there someone who should have visibility to the conversation? Just like some school meetings might require both the teacher and the principal, communicating with a bus driver might be best accomplished with the transportation director knowing about it.

No matter what communication needs to occur, parents should approach helpers with an understanding that they are often unacknowledged and underpaid for the responsibility they take on for kids. A bus driver may be in contact with a kid for a scant half hour, but in that time, they are directly responsible for the health and well-being of that child. A little vocal understanding and empathy for a helper's role goes a long way.

NEED TO KNOW

The Babysitter Blues

Babysitters are one of the more crucial caregivers that parents communicate with. And for the record: yes, it is totally bizarre to entrust your offspring to a teenager just so you can feel like an adult for a couple of hours. Look, we've all seen the horror movies–teens aren't known for making the best decisions.

Be that as it may, thousands upon thousands of parents hire babysitters every day in America, and nightmare scenarios are incredibly rare. Keeping them rare is a matter of understanding who you're hiring and making expectations explicitly clear at the start of the working relationship. If all goes well, parents can potentially gain a long-term care partner that will ensure a few date nights and a whole bunch of sanity.

WHO TO HIRE

Friends

A parent's first babysitters are likely to be friends. That's because when babies are fresh, people don't mind hanging out with them. That changes when tots start developing those meddlesome things called "opinions" and "preferences" and the ability to express them. It's fun to chill with a baby. It's not as fun to spend time with a toddler that's learned to say no. And let's be honest, that's exactly what parents are trying to escape from for a few blissful hours at a local eatery.

The Word-of-Mouth Unicorn

In the best-case scenario, peers with kids will have already developed a relationship with a good sitter whom they can recommend. Babysitters who have a client base and get new jobs through word of mouth are the most coveted sitters. Another trusted parent's recommendation is essentially the best reference. And recommended sitters are generally the ones who perform professionally and thoughtfully. They do, after all, have a reputation to protect.

That said, a good babysitter discovered by word of mouth will also be in high demand. That means you'll have to be incredibly thoughtful about how far ahead you book them. Some parents might find themselves competing with friends and acquaintances on important nights like New Year's Eve.

Young Extended Family

Barring known babysitter pros in your circle of parenting acquaintances, parents may want to look to close, younger family members. Brother, sisters, and cousins are good options for babysitting–particularly if they are trying to get into the babysitting game. They also come with the added benefit that they are more familiar with the charges they will care for. That familiarity will help make everyone feel much more comfortable with the arrangement. Young, close relatives will also likely be more flexible with their payment rates. Consider it a family discount.

Online Pros

There are a handful of online services, chief among them Care.com, that act as a clearinghouse for caregivers of various stripes. For parents without options, local babysitters can be found on these types of services.

Looking for babysitters online is a bit fraught because the person parents hire is ultimately an unknown quantity. That's why websites are often the last place a parent will look for someone who can watch their kid for a couple hours.

The good news is that the most reputable sites make sure that their caregivers have references and background checks. They are usually certified in skills like infant first aid and CPR and have headshots, so you can look into their virtual eyes for signs of evil intent. Also, you can, and probably should, ask for a reference.

In truth, hiring a babysitter from an online service is safe, though it may feel pulse-quickeningly risky.

RULES FOR SITTERS (AND PARENTS)

There is obvious information that you'll want to give your sitter (allergies, diet restrictions, and health issues) and a few not-so-obvious guidelines. But the person caring for the kid while parents are out trying not to talk about the kid should have a set of house rules to ensure that things stay on the rails as much as could be expected. Likewise, parents should abide by their own set of rules to make the process as easy as possible for all involved.

Follow the Bedtime Routine

Bedtime routine mismanagement can derail otherwise good sleepers. It's important that sitters stick to both the time and the process for getting kids to bed, particularly for younger children. For new sitters this may necessitate parents putting the routine and time down on paper. It may also mean sending a text as a reminder.

No Administering Over-the-Counter Meds Without a Call

Kids get headaches and tummy aches. They get gassy and constipated. It makes sense that a well-meaning babysitter might want to jump in and help relieve a child's pain and discomfort with what's available in the medicine cabinet. But parents need to make it explicit that the sitter calls before giving any medication.

Heed Content Warnings

Television and streaming videos are often a good (and certainly easy) way for sitters to pass the time. But you'd be hard pressed to find a teen ready to sit through a couple hours of *Paw Patrol* or *Curious George*. They might try to sneak in entertainment that they can deal with, potentially exposing kids to images and information they're not ready to process. If you have strict rules on content your kids are allowed to watch, make it explicit and check out streaming histories when you get back to double check.

No Company Allowed

There's only so much a parent can control when they leave their home and family to a single person. Adding in another person, particularly when they are young and filled with raging hormones, can make an environment super unsafe super quick–not because a babysitter's company could be trouble, but because they are a huge distraction when all attention should be on the kids.

In Case of an Emergency Call 911 Before Parents

This may not seem obvious to sitters who might feel like their main obligation is to parents. But when there's an emergency, every second counts. And if things go sideways, far too much time could be wasted trying to check in with parents before calling emergency services.

Know Rates, Have Money, Make Payment

Parents need to know well in advance how much they'll be paying the sitter and in what manner. Cash is king, obviously, but if a sitter prefers to be paid via an app, you don't want to waste time trying to get it set up after you get home. And parents should not send a sitter away without payment–it's just bad form.

Any communication with helpers will be helped by making sure children are treating them with respect for their position too. While kids shouldn't be taught blind obedience to adults, they should be taught that helpers have authority related to their specific job. On the bus, you respect and listen to a bus driver. In an emergency, you listen to and respect first responders. In the crosswalk, you pay attention to the crossing guard. But kids should also note that beyond their area of expertise, a helper's authority ends and there are few, in any, instances in which a helper needs to be alone with a child.

The helper polka, like any dance with a caregiver, then, is about balance. There should be trust, boundaries, and a flow of information that goes both ways. It's the only way to ensure that the nuclear family remains stable.

Skills

Helping Your Baby Thrive

A GUIDE TO YOUR BABY'S WEIRD HEAD

I'm not kidding, that boy's head is like Sputnik; spherical but quite pointy at parts!

—Mike Meyers, *So I Married an Axe Murderer*

Of all the weirdness you're likely to see when your baby enters the world, the head and its shape may be one of the most shocking. But you shouldn't panic if your newborn's head looks strange, it's part of the miracle of nature that allows it to come into the world.

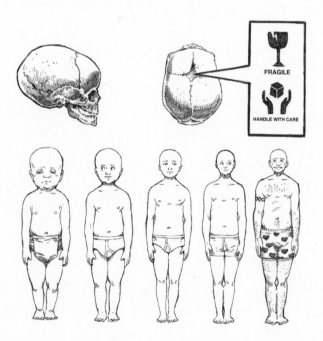

Human skulls are composed of several bones that come together at joints known as sutures. In adults the skull is a nice hard shell, but that's not how it starts. In newborns, the bones are malleable, or to be more accurate "loosey goosey." Babies are already born relatively helpless largely because their skulls need to get through the birth canal before their brain gets too big. If the skull in question were immovable and solid, it would be nigh impossible to squeeze through the birth canal and pelvic bones. Essentially, a baby's soft head is one of the reasons our species has been able to survive.

But that presents a bit of an aesthetic problem for new parents. The tremendous pressures that are applied by the pelvic muscles combined with the limited space a baby must pass through sometimes results in a weird-shaped noggin that may be pointy or elongated or flat in certain places.

The good news is that for many months after birth a child's bones remain relatively soft. They continue to shift and slip along the sutures and are separated by softs spots called fontanels where the bones have not yet fused. That means that it's relatively simple to mold an infant's skull into the proper shape. Many obstetricians and midwives are pretty adept at pushing things into shape after birth when the skull shape is extreme. But in most cases head shape will sort itself out without any big efforts on anyone's part. In rare and very specific cases, however, a doctor may prescribe that a newborn wear a helmet for a few months to help the skull become round.

Most importantly, if your baby's head looks weird, it's not usually a sign of any kind of cognitive disability. More likely it's a sign you've given birth to a human being, and that's a good thing.

HOW TO INTRODUCE YOUR BABY TO OTHER PEOPLE

One can begin so many things with a new person!—even begin to be a better man.

—George Eliot, *Middlemarch*

Your friends probably want to meet your baby. And you probably want to show off the wondrous creature your genes have wrought. Your baby? It couldn't care less, honestly.

Introducing your baby to the world is pretty much for the benefit of the parents and the community that the parents want to create. For that reason, it's a crucial consideration. After all, it pays to have people as excited about your new family as you are. The more invested your community is in your baby, the easier it will be to find help, perhaps even childcare, and maintain social ties.

The hard part is making the introduction in a way that is safe for the kid, and it all comes down to distance and time. Basically, the younger your baby is and the closer people are, the greater the likelihood that your child could get sick from visiting well-wishers. So when considering options for introducing your baby to other people, start with a birth announcement and then close the gap with in-person meets for individuals who are considered close family and friends.

The Baby Introduction Hierarchy

To maximize introducing your baby to the most people, the safest way possible, while saving yourself some hassle, tailor your announcement to your audience.

The Town, Village, or City
Local newspapers continue to be a vital source of information for highly regional news, and there's no harm in making your baby part of that news by paying for a birth announcement in the local rag. It is a slightly antiquated practice, but in contemporary times you get a bit more for your money as most print copy is also placed on regional newspaper websites. The bonus is that parents will have a website link for emails and social media posts. At the same time, the physical paper is a nice keepsake. Because rates and availability for birth announcements will vary, contact the publication for details.

The Neighborhood
There's nothing like a good old yard sign for neighborhood communication. But the humble wire-mounted placards don't need to be relegated to political endorsement or recognition of student athletes. Staking a sign in front of the house that announces the arrival of a new baby will put a smile on neighbors' faces as they drive by and might even lead to a casserole on your front porch.

Acquaintances
Social media was pretty much designed to inform acquaintances about important life events, like that good-looking salad you ate for lunch. Because a baby is more appealing than even the most beautiful salad, it

makes sense to announce the birth on the social platforms you have at your disposal. One caveat: when sharing news of your baby, take privacy considerations into account. Unlike newspapers, you can lock down who gets to see, share, and reply to news of the happy occasion.

Close Acquaintances and Coworkers

It's easy to send birth announcements to those individuals you have email addresses for. There are numerous websites that help parents create and send e-cards, it's just a matter of finding which site works best for you, uploading a photo, and adding the details. The nice part about sending an e-card birth announcement is that you can get it done in one shot, and it feels slightly more personal and pointed than a social media post. For coworkers, e-card birth announcements help them recognize your transition to parenthood and helps them understand why you're not in the office for however much parental leave you can take.

Friends and Distant Family

Hopefully, you or your partner have the address list you used to send wedding invitations lying around somewhere. If that's the case, then sending a physical birth announcement is super thoughtful. Friends, distant aunties, uncles, and cousins will be thrilled to learn of the new addition to the clan and appreciate the ability to place a physical memento on their mantle or bulletin board.

Close Friends and Immediate Family

There is really no way that you're going to be able to keep your closest friends and family out of your home for an in-person meeting. But that's okay. Close friends and family should have the luxury of getting some baby time if you're going to call on them for assistance in the near future. But it's important to know how to make that physical meeting occur safely.

How to Safely Introduce Your Baby in Person

The reason in-person meetings are such a concern is because a baby's immune system isn't really ready to rebuff a biological onslaught until they're about six months old. Given the recent history of the COVID-19 pandemic, protecting a baby from viral infections might be even more of a concern for parents. But a baby will be able to meet your closest friends and family with the following precautions:

- **Manage Traffic:** The more people come through your front door, the more exposed a baby will be to pathogens. It helps to schedule meetings carefully. But because new parents are often overwhelmed, it helps to designate a trusted and fastidious friend as a point of contact who can establish and maintain a visitation schedule.

- **Ask the Uncomfortable Questions:** You can't protect a baby from what you don't see coming. Before friends and family visit, ask about their recent health. Ask if they have had recent fevers, coughs, or other ailments. Ask if they have been around anyone who has been sick recently. Don't feel bad about begging off meetings if the answers don't meet your requirements. Your baby's health is more important than anyone's feelings.

- **Consider Masks:** By now, most of America has become familiar with the habit and practice of wearing masks to protect one another from infection. The bonus is that many people will have a homemade mask available. If you are at all concerned, there is no harm in asking that visitors wear masks when meeting your baby before they are six months old.

- **Handwashing:** Have guests wash hands or use a hand sanitizer the second they come into your home.

- **Keep Touching Minimal:** Everyone wants to get their grubby mitts on a baby. Touching is okay as long as it occurs from the tummy down. Happily, tummies and toes are the most coveted and touchable baby parts.

- **No Kisses:** This is a hard one to enforce, particularly when it comes to newly minted grandmothers. If kissing is necessary (it never is), keep the lips away from hands and heads. Instead, focus on the toes, knees, and tummy.

HOW TO DO SKIN-TO-SKIN BABY CONTACT

It's a sad man my friend who's livin' in his own skin and can't stand the company.

—Bruce Springsteen

Kangaroo care is the act of holding an unclothed but diapered newborn against the skin of a parent's chest for prolonged periods after birth. It's so named because the technique requires making a de facto pouch out of a blanket or a parent's clothing. Inside this pouch, the back of the baby is kept warm while the front is pressed against the parent.

The marsupial whimsy of the term *kangaroo care* is offset by its deeply tragic origins. The method was pioneered by accident in Columbia in the late 1970s in response to a 70 percent infant death rate for preterm babies in Bogota, largely due to the lack of resources like incubators and caregiving personnel. To combat the high preterm death rate, National University of Colombia professor of neonatology Edgar Rey Sanabria recommended that mothers of preterm babies have continuous skin-to-skin contact with their infants. The thought was that continuous contact would keep the low-birthweight babies warm while also increasing their access to breastfeeding. What doctors found after the implementation of the recommendations was that the preterm infants who received what Sanabria called kangaroo care survived at significantly higher rates.

Research has found that infant reactions to a father's skin-to-skin contact are pretty much the same as it is for a mother's.[2] Moreover, despite a father's lack of functioning breasts, infants who are given skin-to-skin contact with fathers after cesarean sections develop better sleeping and "prefeeding" behaviors like the rooting reflex, all of which improves the initiation of breastfeeding relative to babies who are placed into a cot after delivery.

Shirts versus Skins

Since the Bogota intervention, research has revealed a wealth of improved infant health outcomes from skin-to-skin contact. In the short term, they include:

- Improved infant caloric use

- Regulated heart rate and body temperature

- Higher oxygen concentrations

- Better breastfeeding

- Transfer of skin flora to boost the immune response

- Overall improvements in infant development

But there are long-term effects to skin-to-skin contact as well. A 2016 study published in the journal *Pediatrics* looked at individuals twenty years after receiving kangaroo care and found the continuing positive outcomes:

- Increased IQ

- Improved home environments

- Reduced school absenteeism

- Reduced hyperactivity

- Reduced aggressiveness

- Less sociodeviant conduct

Pediatricians recommend that skin-to-skin time lasts at least an hour. So be prepared to clear that time to focus on your baby and relax.

Benefits of Skin-to-Skin Contact for Dads

Becoming a father means entering a new world of physical intimacy. Having a kid automatically requires more touching and more being touched. Most men probably won't notice the increase in the amount of physical contact in their life—at least, not until they get an unexpected sticky cuddle from a messy toddler and reevaluate their life choices. Still, there's a biological benefit to increased touch.

Sensations of holding, cuddling, and caressing prompt the body to release the neurotransmitter dopamine and a neuropeptide called oxytocin. The reason babies can better regulate their heart rates, breathing, and feeding with the skin-to-skin contact is linked to the propagation of these and other hormones. But when contact is made, the flood of biochemicals occurs in baby and father simultaneously.

In adults, dopamine is crucial in activating reward centers of our brain while oxytocin influences feelings of connectedness and can regulate aggression. In the context of evolution, fathers having feelings of reward and connectedness toward their child increases the chances that a father will care for and protect their offspring, giving them an opportunity to develop in a safe and nurturing environment.

When the touch between a father and an infant is skin-to-skin contact, there appear to be additional positive outcomes for fathers. One study conducted by researchers at the National Taipei University of Nursing and Health Sciences found that fathers engaging in skin-to-skin contact with a newborn felt as if they were actively attaining the role of fatherhood. In a sense, they were experiencing a more gradual version of the surge of hormones mom got during birth.[3]

FEEDING A BABY

I've always had a bottle I could turn to
And lately I've been turnin' every day
But the wine don't take effect the way it used to
And I'm hurtin' in an old familiar way

—Merle Haggard

Sucking It Up

The first known precursors to modern baby bottles date back over four thousand years. The animal- and breast-shaped clay vessels, discovered by archeologists in the graves of ancient Bavarian children, featured a nipple-like protrusion. Archeologists posit that the vessels allowed mothers to wean children from the breast early, allowing them to have more children, resulting in a population explosion and eventually Coachella. Unfortunately, there's no record of Bronze Age battles over whether the clay pot or the breast was best for baby. There's only evidence that this kind of feeding is, in all senses, "natural" for modern humans, a group keenly aware that making sure a baby is fed has always been more important than how that feeding takes place.

It's hard to imagine the simplicity of clay pot bottle feeding circa 2000 BCE when surveilling the paraphernalia associated with modern baby bottles. But that chemistry set–looking apparatus is less complicated than the packaging suggests. That's thanks to the fact that all mammalian babies are born with a suckling reflex. This reflex is triggered when the roof of the mouth is stimulated by an object. We use the word *object* here because the reflex does not discriminate. Babies will suck on a nipple or a finger or a silver spoon or a hex wrench. This is what their mouth was designed to do.

How to Tell if Your Baby Is Hungry

+ Licking their lips

+ Sticking out their tongue

+ Nuzzling and moving their head as if searching for a breast or nipple

+ Sucking on anything that comes close to their face like their own hands and fingers

+ Fussiness

How Much Should You Serve in the Bottle?

One of the downsides of bottles is that they get overfilled. Meaning your baby could be overserved. At the breast, where babies need to work a bit for their meal, they are better able to sense that they are full. This is why there is a persistent myth that bottle feeding leads to obese babies. It's not the bottle. It's the lack of portion control.

Serving Sizes Done Right

+ Newborns less than four weeks old: two ounces or less per bottle (two jiggers)

+ Infants over six weeks old: four to five ounces per bottle (a traditional old fashioned)

- Babies four to six months old: four to six ounces per bottle (a traditional old fashioned from a generous bartender)

- Babies over six months: rarely more than eight ounces per bottle (a half pint)

If your baby continues to grow then it is likely getting enough to eat. That said, baby growth is a somewhat subtle thing to observe. It's best left to pediatricians with the right tools and charts.

The better way for parents to keep track of feeding is via the diapers. Babies should have two to three wet diapers each day during the first week. That number increases to at least five or six wet diapers per day thereafter.

How Often Should You Feed Your Baby?

For babies who are using the bottle to supplement the breast, bottle feeding can take the place of any breastfeeding when necessary or desired. Often, fathers will take nighttime bottle-feeding duties to help a partner sleep. But when bottle feeding is supplemental to breastfeeding, it should occur less often than breastfeeding to protect from unintentional early weaning.

For parents using baby formula, or who have decided to bottle feed exclusively, the number of feedings will depend largely on age.

- Newborns: eight to twelve times every day in two- to three-hour increments

- Infants over six weeks old: every three hours

- Babies four to six months old: every three hours

- Babies over six months old: every four to five hours

A Quick Note on Nipple Confusion

Nipple confusion is when infants become so accustomed to pacifiers or bottle nipples that they have difficulty breastfeeding or refuse to breastfeed. The fear of a baby developing nipple confusion is often enough to keep parents from even attempting to bottle feed. But it's important to note that it's far from given that babies will develop a preference for artificial nipples over the real thing. By and large, research suggests that healthy, full-term infants can readily adapt to feeding methods.

That doesn't mean that nipple confusion isn't a concern. For infants with feeding problems due to preterm birth or birth defects, introducing a bottle could promote early weaning and lead mothers to stop breast-feeding sooner than the six months recommended. That could have bad repercussions not only for infant health but for a mother's health and sense of well-being.

Luckily, there are ways to protect from nipple confusion. The idea is to limit how often an infant uses a bottle, if it's supplemental to breast-feeding, and make bottle feeding as similar to breastfeeding as possible. Basically, make them work for it, as they would at the breast. That idea is central to the following skills.

How to Warm a Bottle

Never put a baby bottle in the microwave. The problem is that micro-waves can heat fluid unevenly, leaving hot pockets of liquid in an other-wise tepid bottle. This scalding liquid can damage a baby's mouth and throat.

- Prepared bottles (with formula mixed or breastmilk added) should be placed in a warm water bath until they reach body temperature.

- Test fluid temperature by placing a drop or two on your wrist. You should not feel any noticeable hot or cold sensation.

How to Hold the Baby for Feeding

- With one hand and forearm supporting the baby's back and neck, gently nestle the baby's head in the crook of the free arm. (For right-handed dads, this will be the left arm because the dominant hand needs to be free to control the body.)

- Grasp the baby's bottom and hip with the left hand and gently press the baby towards your abdomen. The baby's body should be positioned face-up along the length of the left forearm.

- Tilt the baby's body into a reclined position by lowering the left hand.

- Grasp the bottle in the dominant hand and prepare to feed.

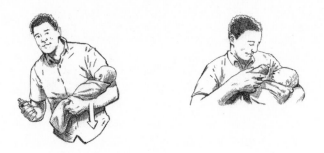

How to Hold the Bottle for Feeding

It's important to remember that you're trying to simulate breastfeeding. Those willing to go the extra mile will feed shirtless with the baby stripped to the waist. This skin-to-skin contact increases bonding and, frankly, just feels nice.

- Position the bottle so that it is relatively perpendicular to the floor, or flat.

- Angle the nipple slightly towards your baby's upper palate.

- Fill the nipple only about halfway to begin. This encourages a bit of work on the baby's part and simulates what's known as "let down" when a baby is at the breast.

- Observe a "suckle, pause, suckle, pause" rhythm. This rhythm will slow as your baby gets full. Pay attention.

- Occasionally tip the bottle back up toward the roof of the mouth, making the baby work a bit harder.

- Keep track of your flow by watching your baby's face. Frantic gulping and a surprised or worried look indicate milk is flowing too quickly.

- Feeding should only take ten to fifteen minutes.

What About Burping?

If your bottle-feeding technique is solid, there should be no need to burp. Problems with discomfort or spitting up after feeding are generally related to poor flow control and are due to a baby getting too much too quickly. That said, a burp is a satisfying sound to experience and you can coax one out with some firm, but gentle back-patting.

* Place a burp cloth over your shoulder with the majority of the cloth down your back to catch spit-up.

* Lift your baby so that its abdomen and belly are pressed against your pectoral and deltoid muscle.

* Your baby should be facing your back, head resting against the burp cloth.

* Support the baby's bottom with one hand and give the baby a few sharp, gentle pats.

* If your baby does not burp in the first few blows there's no need to keep burping.

HOW TO HOLD A NEWBORN

Courage is fear holding on a minute longer.

—General George S. Patton

At some point in human evolution, nature made a bargain with human-ity: we could have world-dominating brains, and skulls in which to carry them around, but it would mean that our offspring would be born help-less. That's unlike, say, gazelles, which have tiny brains but can run a 4.4 forty still wet with afterbirth. So human babies emerge undercooked, immobile, and, fortunately, highly portable.

Still, the prospect of holding such a small, delicate graduate-level fetus can be daunting, particularly for those unused to doing so.

(Kind of) Unbreakable

During birth contractions, the uterus exerts nearly 2.8 pounds of pres-sure per square inch on infants' skulls. That's the equivalent of being eight hundred feet underwater (about four times what your average scuba diver can handle before passing out). The point? Kids are break-able, sure, but shatterproof.

They are, however, floppy. One caveat to the resilience argument is that newborns have famously floppy necks due to their big heads and underdeveloped neck muscles. The danger with this situation is not a broken neck but a closed airway. That means the priority for anyone holding a newborn should be keeping the child's head supported in order to assure the larynx doesn't kink.

Support Your Breastfeeding Partner

Breast milk is the gold standard for infant nutrition, provided the parent is physically able to breastfeed and has the resources to succeed at the practice. This is so well-evidenced that "breast is best" is one of those rare unassailable facts, shepherded out by the federal government and for-mula companies alike.

But fathers need to remember that just because a person has breasts doesn't mean they know how to breastfeed or that it will somehow come "naturally." There is a raft of issues that can make breastfeeding difficult, including biological barriers like inverted nipples, painful conditions like sore or cracked nipple or mastitis, and even issues related to time—like a short or nonexistent maternity leave.

It can be hard to watch someone you love struggle with breastfeeding, which is often portrayed as mystically maternal in popular culture. And if you're a solution-oriented person, it can be frustrating to feel that there's little you can do to solve breastfeeding troubles. But while you may not be able to fix things, you can do plenty to help.

Talk to Your Partner

Before your kid even arrives, the first step is to find out what your partner wants to accomplish with breastfeeding:

- Would they like to breastfeed exclusively?

- Are they aiming for the recommended minimum of three months of breastfeeding?

- Do they plan on extended breastfeeding, past toddlerhood?

- Would they prefer breastfeeding with supplemental bottle feeding and pumping?

Knowing your partner's intentions will help you understand where you might be able to get in and help. And talking about it lets them know you're willing to take some pressure off. Take Your Damn Paternity Leave What does this have to do with breastfeeding? Everything. You see, breastfeeding is an all-encompassing activity, and your partner will be doing it a lot—all the freaking time, it will seem. So especially in those initial weeks of breastfeeding, you need to step up to the plate. That means doing all the housework, changing diapers, scheduling family visits, setting up doctor's appointments, paying the bills, finding great binge-worthy shows for your partner to watch while she breastfeeds. You're needed at home. Take all of your leave.

Be Empathetic and a Defender

Your breastfeeding partner could use some empathy. It's important for nonbreastfeeding parents to understand that their partners may not find feeding the kid to be a blissful, enjoyable experience. In fact, at times it can be physically uncomfortable, frustrating, and messy. It's your role to pay attention to that and offer understanding.

It's also your role to defend your partner's time and decisions from outsiders. If extended family wants to visit the baby and your breastfeeding partner doesn't want that, stick up for them. If you so much as smell a criticism about your partner's decision to breastfeed or the way they're doing it, stop it before they catch wind. Shut. It. Down.

Learn Everything Together

If your kid is delivered at a hospital, one of the first people you will talk to is the lactation consultant. You should be there for these appointments. It's possible that you'll remember tips your partner might forget. If your kid isn't being delivered in a hospital, there's a good chance it's being delivered by a midwife or doula who can double as a lactation consultant. Make sure you ask questions too.

If your partner has books about breastfeeding, crack them open and read them. Take notes and bring up interesting points in the books. Better yet, be proactive and bring some books home. Start with *Breastfeeding Made Simple* and *Dr. Jack Newman's Guide to Breastfeeding*. Put them by the nightstand. Read together in bed at night. Talk about them. Swap. Now everyone will know what to do.

Get into Coaching

There's a super-easy way to become the Jim Harbaugh of breastfeeding (if she's into it), and it's all a matter of perspective. Literally.

There are tons of breastfeeding videos out in the world, but precious few of them are shot from the breastfeeding person's perspective. This means that if you watch the videos together, you can help her adjust positions that may lead to easier feeding. It's like how she may have helped you tie a necktie.

Prepare for Problems

Breastfeeding isn't always simple. In fact, a 2012 Centers for Disease Control study found that two-thirds of mothers who plan to nurse experience problems and give up earlier than they wanted to. Those who reached their goal generally had gone through breastfeeding once and had a supportive partner.

Whether the breastfeeding person is having a problem getting the kid to latch or experiencing an infection, there are ways for you to help:

- Giving unconditional support and encouragement

- Setting up lactation consultant appointments

- Providing tea and snacks

- Keeping the nursing area clean and stocked with reading materials and supplies

- Planning a lactation-supportive menu

- Going on a cabbage run (the leaves help ease the discomfort from mastitis)

Just because the majority of fathers aren't capable of breastfeeding, doesn't mean you can't be involved in the process. Remember, that what your partner is doing is for the health and well-being of your baby. You need to be on that team and make sure they are successful.

Taking a Handoff

Babies aren't always lifted from a supine position on a flat surface. They are often being passed around from adult to adult. Receiving a baby from someone else can be a bit awkward and fraught. Here's how to get it done without fumbling.

- Position yourself so that you are facing the baby holder with the newborn between you.

- If the baby's head is on the holder's left side, place your left hand, palm up, on the infant's upper back, toward the neck. If the head is on the right, use your right hand.

- Slide your hand up the back and neck, so that it replaces the head-supporting hand of the baby holder and cradles the back of the newborn's head.

- With the newborn head supported, reach across the baby using your free hand and cradle the baby's hips and lower back in your palm.

- Acknowledge to the baby holder that you've "got it" (or whatever) to indicate that you have solid hand placement and a confident baby-holding attitude.

- ◆ Accept the full weight of the newborn and bring it close to your
  body before transitioning into the appropriate hold position.

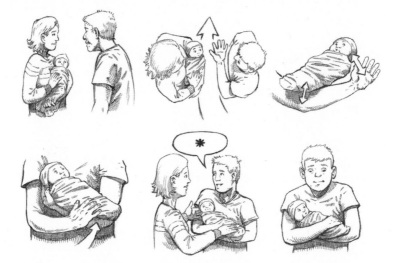

The Goal of Holding a Newborn

If a dad's not going to hurt a newborn no matter how sloppily the kid is
handled, why does it make any difference how the baby's held? Comfort,
mostly. There are three reasons to hold a child that have nothing to do
with protecting it from carnivores or changelings: calming the infant,
comforting the infant, and feeding the infant. The correct way to hold a
newborn is determined by the holder's intentions beyond not dropping
the kid. So, yes, there's a way to do it right.

Position 1: The Cradle Hold

The cradle hold situates your newborn on its
back so that you can look down into the baby's face and the baby can look up into yours.
Nervous dads can use both arms for this hold
to increase confidence. And confident dads
can use one arm, freeing the other for necessary tasks like feeding or checking scores.

1. Start with the baby positioned face up, close to your body, with one hand supporting the head and neck, and the other supporting the lower half and bottom. This is generally the default position after a baby has been passed to you.

2. Slide the hand holding the bottom of the newborn up the baby's back and under the opposite hand supporting the head and neck. The newborn's body should now be positioned so that the body extends from the hand now supporting the head, down the forearm, with feet pointed toward the elbow.

3. Now, position the infant so that the head rests, face up, in the crook of the elbow of the now free arm. The weight of the baby should transfer from one forearm to the other as the baby is positioned with head and bottom supported, respectively, in the elbow and hand of the same arm.

4. The free arm can now be used as additional support along the side of the baby.

5. The final position should have the baby's head comfortably positioned in the crook of the elbow, while your arms and abdomen form a cradle.

Position 2: The Shoulder Hold

The shoulder hold keeps a newborn more upright, which can be helpful when burping. It also presses the baby's chest and belly against your pectoral, deltoid, and trapezius muscles, which can be comforting if the baby is experiencing gas or indigestion. This hold generally feels most stable when both arms are used.

1. Begin with the newborn's body face up, with one hand supporting the head and neck and the other supporting the lower half and bottom.

2. Also, like the cradle hold, slide the hand holding the bottom of the newborn up the baby's back and under the opposite hand supporting the head and neck.

3. With both hands guiding the supported head, lift the newborn towards the shoulder closest to the baby's head. This will cause the arm supporting the baby's body to cross your chest.

4. Position the newborn so that the head rests on the top of your shoulder, with the chest and belly extending down your pectoral muscle, feet pointed towards your ribs. Both hands should be on the baby's back pressing it into your body firmly.

5. Adjust the newborn's body so that the face and nose is not pressed against your shoulder. The baby should be in a position to watch your back.

Position 3: The Panther Hold

So named because it positions your baby like a panther sleeping prone on the branch of a jungle tree, the panther hold is great for soothing fussy babies to sleep. It could also be considered a kind of inverted cradle hold because the position is largely the same save for the fact that the baby is face down. Being a one-arm hold it requires a bit more confidence. For extra soothing action, incorporate gentle rocking and swinging and pat the back in a gentle heartbeat rhythm.

1. Beginning in the cradle hold, slide your free hand and arm under the newborn cradling the head in your hand, with the baby's weight supported along the forearm of the same hand.

2. Secure and stabilize the baby's head by positioning it between the thumb, ring finger, and pinky, with remaining fingers positioned on the back of their head.

3. Carefully roll the baby toward you and position the opposite arm so that the baby's chest and belly are now resting on the forearm with head pointed to the crook of the elbow.

4. The baby's arms and legs should extend on either side of the forearm. The head should be positioned facing away from the body

with cheek pressed against the lower forearm. The hand should be positioned between the baby's thighs, cradling the crotch.

5. The free hand can now be placed on the baby's back for stabilization, or patting.

The One Way You Should Never Hold a Baby

Sam Hanke fell asleep on the couch with his four-week-old son Charlie and woke up, hours later, to find his child dead. It was April 2010, and the pediatric cardiologist had just been hoping to give his wife, who was breastfeeding, a rest.

"I just sat down on the couch to watch some TV, and he was kind of sitting on my chest. We were just hanging out and I nodded off," Hanke remembers. "A couple hours later I woke up and Charlie was gone."

Charlie fell victim to Sudden Infant Death Syndrome, a diagnosis included in Sudden Unexpected Infant Death, next to his sleeping father. The idyllic image of the dad sleeping with his kid on his chest, turned tragic. Sadly, the Hanke story—horrible and personal as it may be—is not unique. It turns out that the Instagrammable image of the tired dad with the placid baby propped on his chest depicts very real danger. Of the four thousand babies that die of SIDS annually, a significant number die on couches or in armchairs. Many perish near dad or under him because of suffocation. Emergency room doctors and pediatricians see those tragedies regularly.

As a new dad you may feel that your chest is purpose built to rest a baby. And, honestly, there are few feelings better than a newborn snoozing to the sound of your heartbeat. But fathers who hold babies on their chests need to stay awake. If you're feeling drowsy with your baby on your chest, hand them off and have a snooze or make sure there is someone alert and conscious nearby at all times.

HOW TO CREATE A BEDTIME ROUTINE

I know you're not thirsty. That's bullshit. Stop lying. Lie the fuck down, my
darling, and sleep.

—Adam Mansbach, *Go the Fuck to Sleep*

The rhythms of night and day in the womb are defined by a mother's
body movement, muffled sounds from the outside world, and light filtered through abdominal skin, membranes, subcutaneous fat, and muscle. Regardless of these clues, fetuses tend to operate on their own
schedules. Pregnant moms are often chagrined to find their unborn child
is a night owl—flipping and flopping through in-womb dance parties in
the small hours of the morning.

Once babies are born, they'll be happy to continue operating on
their own schedule. They don't know the difference between night and
day or that expectations for behavior change depending upon the position of the sun in the sky. Parents, therefore, need to teach babies
when it's time to be awake and when it's time to be asleep. It's a task
best accomplished by establishing a strong routine the moment the kid
comes home.

Routines work because they create a string of cues that help move a
baby towards sleep. When those cues are repeated nightly, babies begin
to recognize the routine as a transition from awake time to sleepy time.
It's a matter of classical conditioning, which is the same psychological
phenomenon that allowed Pavlov to make dogs drool. But in the case of
a bedtime routine, instead of drooly dogs, you get a drowsy baby (who
just happens to also be drooly).

Because the process is the key, bedtime routines can be highly specific
to a family's needs. The cues can be just about any activity, in any order,
as long as they are calm and quiet and promote a general sense of relaxa-
tion. The most important part is that the routine is implemented as soon
as the baby is brought home from the hospital and that it is completed
consistently, every night, at about the same time, forevermore. . . . Or
until they're old enough to date.

Activities for Bedtime Routines that Promote Sleepiness

Parents can get creative about the activities that they add to their routine, but there is one very specific rule to follow: activities need to be

calm. Bedtime is not a time for interesting play and bright light. It's a time for everything to be turned down to a slow soft hush.

Dimming the Lights

It's helpful to make the environment a bit dimmer about an hour before a baby's bedtime. Turn off televisions, tablets, phones, and bright lights in the home. Families with smart bulbs can even automate the process, which not only dims the lights at a certain time but acts as a nice reminder to parents that it's time for the bedtime routine to kick off.

Prebedtime Feeding

Spending some time at a warm breast or bottle is a fine way to get drowsy. You know this to be true. Think of how drowsy you get after a good meal.

Warm Bath

A warm bath is relaxing for all humans, even the new ones. Add some lavender-scented baby soap for a next-level prebed bath.

Reading

As babies relax they are in the perfect place for ten or fifteen minutes of reading. It doesn't really matter what you read, at least not for the first year. They just need to be exposed to a book and hear your voice forming new and interesting words.

Dental Hygiene

Your baby is about six months from cutting its first tooth. But that doesn't mean you should hold off on dental hygiene. You can massage their gums with your own clean fingers, soft cloth, or a super-soft silicone brush that fits on the tip of your finger. The sooner they get used to it the more likely the chore is to become a habit.

Prayer or Meditation

Some families like to establish a moment of prayer before bed. Your baby obviously can't meaningfully participate, but holding them while you say a few words of gratitude and grace, or take a mindful moment, will help them incorporate the practice into their bedtime routine when they are older.

Singing

Establishing a lullaby is a wonderful way to help babies relax. The tones and rhythm can help babies regulate their heartbeat and breathing, helping them become calm and quiet. Importantly, it doesn't matter what the song is or your singing skills. You can hit them with a slow and quiet version of Guns N' Roses "Sweet Child o' Mine" if you're so inclined.

A Final Phrase

A nice way to put a cap on the routine is to offer a parting phrase. "Don't let the bedbugs bite" is fine if you don't live in New York City, where they could definitely bite. But you could also go with something in the John Irving vein: "Goodnight you Princes of Maine, you Kings of New England." It's totally up to you.

The End of Your Bedtime Routine

Some parents believe that a bedtime routine should result in a baby that is fully asleep before they leave the room. The problem is that a baby who has gone to sleep with a parent holding them or close by will come to rely on the parent for sleep. If they wake up and the parent isn't available, they will cry or fuss because they require the parent to soothe them back to slumber.

Instead, the goal for the end of the bedtime routine should be babies who are drowsy but not fully asleep. Parents should place them in their crib and leave before sleep occurs so that their baby can get used to soothing themselves to sleep. This will pay dividends in the future.

HOW TO CHANGE A DIAPER

> God, grant me the serenity to accept the things I cannot change, the courage to change the things I can, and the wisdom to know the difference.
>
> —Serenity Prayer

Most of the skills you need for caring for your infant are some iteration of a skill you already have. Unfortunately, diaper duty combines two activities with which most people are profoundly uncomfortable: change and handling human waste. Though changing a diaper is unlikely to become your favorite thing, it is manageable, and many fathers find that getting their baby's shit together empowers them to do the same for themselves. Think of it as a mechanical task. Think of it like changing the oil. More specifically, think of it like changing the oil on a 1977 Chevrolet Chevette.

Through your diapering career, you'll go through seven thousand diaper changes, roughly the number of batters faced in a successful major league pitching career. So chances are you're going to figure out how to handle the high stuff. But first, it's critical to understand the diapering pitches, so to speak. There are two: cloth and disposable.

Remember, the first law of thermodynamics dictates that nothing is ever truly disposable. The twenty-seven billion diapers thrown out by Americans every year land somewhere. And there they stay. Cloth diapers, on the other hand, represent a vintage, ecofriendly solution.

Or do they? (This line of inquiry has been brought to you by our friends at Pampers.)

Environmentalists are fighting a pitched battle over that claim, which must therefore be treated as contentious. Some experts argue that the water and energy consumption used to launder cloth diapers neutralizes their environmental benefit. Other experts make less money and argue the opposite.

Here are the facts: a study by the UK's Environment Agency found the average global warming impact of a reusable diaper was 570 kilograms of carbon dioxide annually against the 550 kilograms generated by disposable diapers. That same report also found that consumer behavior—washing in full loads, line drying, reusing diapers on a second child—can cut carbon output by 40 percent, whereas the cost of disposables is set and profound. Disposable diapers account for nearly three hundred pounds of wood, fifty pounds of petroleum, and twenty pounds of chlorine per baby per year. In other words, environmentally conscious parents should use reusable diapers but should also have a good plan for keeping them clean.

Also, they should know that cloth diapers are a pain. They are bulkier, and some parents find that they inhibit children's movement. And, of course, the reasons disposable diapers were developed in the first place are even more salient today. Not enough time. Too much to do. Not feeling like plunging and scraping a shit-stained cloth in a toilet while your child lies on the bathroom floor staring in wonder. As far as cost goes, reusable diapers are also much cheaper. The most basic set-up—about fifty cloth diapers, a couple of fasteners, and a few covers, all of which you wash yourself—will likely run you around nine hundred dollars for the entire year. Relying on a diaper service, which drops off clean diapers and removes soiled ones, on the other hand, bumps that cost up to around a thousand dollars for the first year. Yet the real savings come in year two, when the upfront costs of your diaper setup have been amortized. Yay, diaper economics! According to some economists, over the course of a child's diaper career, reusable diapers can save you up to 60 percent. But if your kid potty trains early, it's a wash.

The biggest knock on reusable diapers is that they're a pain to put on and take off. And it is true that using a cloth diaper is like baking from scratch whereas a disposable is like using a cake mix. (Interestingly, Victor Mills, that guy who invented the disposable diaper, also developed Duncan Hines cake mix.) Yet many parents find that, after the standard learning curve, a cloth diaper and cover aren't significantly more difficult to put on. It's just a matter of practice. There's also a range of cloth diapers to choose from—from "flats," basically just cotton squares of fabric; to basic pre-folds, cotton squares with absorbent pads folded in; to more expensive all-in-ones, which function essentially the same as disposables except that they're reusable.

The point here is not to scold or even to convince but simply to lay out the two options. Ease, cultural momentum, and Big Diaper's dope marketing campaigns—all those animated bears!—versus a slightly more involved diapering process, more money, and the chance to be self-righteous at social functions. It's your call.

How to Change a Disposable Diaper

Feel free to skip this part. You'll learn soon enough what works or doesn't. There's gonna be some trials and a lot of errors. But following these steps will help skirt a few commonly avoided mishaps, such as blowouts and being peed on.

What You'll Need:

- One baby, approximately eight pounds

- One disposable diaper, size NB or 1

- One wet wipe, out of container

- One tube rash cream, if needed, cap open

- One changing table, or other level service

Directions:

1. Lay child on a flat dry surface, in a supine position, clothed.

2. Undo onesie, or other garment, to expose the old diaper, making sure to pull fabric well clear from potential poop contamination.

3. Open new diaper and position beneath the child's old diaper.

4. Carefully unstick the adhesive fasteners on the old diaper, keeping the diaper mostly in place. Hold both the infant's legs at the ankle with one hand, gently lift its legs aloft, just enough to facilitate the removal of the old diaper.

5. Using the interior of the old diaper as a preliminary catch-all, wipe as much poop from the child's butt as possible. Move diaper out of range but keep it open.

6. Moving with urgency, for this is the danger zone, use your ready wipe to completely clean the child's body. Pay attention to the lower back, where poop often resides.

7. Slide the new diaper into position. If your baby is a boy, you might want to prophylactically cover his penis with the interior of the new diaper, lest he pees and you are doused.

8. If the kid is suffering from diaper rash, rinse the affected area gently with a wet cloth, then pat dry. Apply diaper rash cream if necessary.

9. Enclose the child's loins in the new diaper, fastening the enclosures firmly but not too tightly. (You should be able to insert two fingers into the waistband.) The diaper waist should rest just under the belly button.

10. Lower the baby's legs. Now, holding the baby in place with one hand, form the old diaper into a small poop-filled ball, with used wipe(s) inside. Discard.

11. Run your finger along the cuffs of the new diaper, ensuring the cuffs aren't tucked under, a common cause for blowouts.

12. Pick up child with one arm. Pat yourself on the back with the other.

1

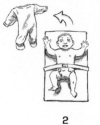

2

3

4

5

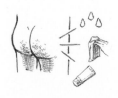

6

7

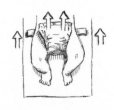

8

9

10

11

12

How To Change a Reusable Diaper

There are as many ways to fold a cloth diaper as there are types of cloth diaper. The following uses a basic prefold, the most common of the diapering choices. But you can also use this technique, called the angel fold, with basic flats too. In terms of overall setup, most cloth diapers require some sort of fastener. These used to be diaper pins, but today the only thing going, really, is rubber fastener called the Snappi, which looks like an elongated T with sticky bits on the ends. The other hardware needed is a wastebasket. These generally come in two forms: a wet bag, which you'll remember from your days white-water rafting (basically a reusable watertight bag), or a diaper pail, a specialized trash can that seals in odors.

What You'll Need:

- One baby, approximately eight pounds

- One diaper cover

- One prefold cotton diaper

- One Snappi, or other diaper fastener

- One wet wipe, out of container

- One diaper pail or wet bag, for soiled diaper

- One tube rash cream, if needed, cap open

- One changing table, or other level service

Directions:

1. Lay child on a flat dry surface, in a supine position, clothed.

2. Prepare prefold diaper by laying it on the changing table. Fold the long edges to meet in the middle, leaving the top third of the diaper open. It should look like the chest of a blazer.

1

2

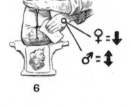

3

4

5

♀ = ↓
♂ = ↕

6

7

8

9

10

11

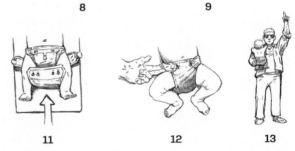

12

13

3. Undo onesie, or other garment, to expose the old diaper, making sure to pull fabric well clear from potential poop contamination.

4. Remove diaper cover and set aside.

5. Unstick the adhesive fasteners on the old diaper, keeping the diaper in place to the degree possible. Hold both the infant's legs at the ankle. With the baby's legs aloft, unstick the fasteners on the old diaper.

6. Using the interior of the old diaper as a preliminary catch-all, wipe as much poop from the child's butt as possible.

7. Moving with urgency, for this is the danger zone, use your ready wipe to completely clean the child's body. Pay attention too to the lower back, where poop often resides.

8. If the kid is suffering from diaper rash, rinse the affected area gently with a wet cloth, then pat dry. Apply diaper rash cream if necessary.

9. Place child atop the new cloth diaper. Fold the prefolded portion up between their legs to just below the child's belly button. Using the Snappi, fasten "wings" together, thus securing the diaper in place.

10. Set used diaper aside. You'll have to rinse or flush the solids, then place in diaper pail or wet bag for later pickup. If they are well soiled, you will have to swish them, most likely in the toilet. You might need a spatula or other such scraping device. This part sucks.

11. Depending on the style of cover, either slide or fold over cloth diaper.

12. Make sure the interior prefold diaper is entirely hidden by cover by tucking in where necessary.

13. Pick up child with one arm. Pat yourself on the back with the other.

The Fine Art of Diaper Reading

There was a guy in the 1960s named A. J. Weberman who was so obsessed with Bob Dylan he used to sift through the trash outside Dylan's McDougal Street apartment searching for clues to the mercurial musician's work. He called himself the first Dylanologist. We're not suggesting you become your child's poopologist. But the lesson is a lot can be picked up from waste. Honestly, this shit is fascinating. Fecal matter can, for instance, provide insight into the mercurial workings of the GI tract—

yes, in this case, your baby's intestines are the "voice of a generation"—and provide virtually instantaneous feedback on your kid's diet.

Babies poop around ten times a day for the first two months of their lives and about four times a day for the two months after that. (Adults, by the way, poop on average two and a half times a day.) As your baby—and your baby's diet—develops, so too will its stool. Once you have an eye and a nose for your baby's bowel movements, the answer to many of your questions about their health will be . . . blowing in the wind. And it all starts at the hospital.

Meconium

Though unrecorded in many baby books and unheralded with reveal parties, your baby's first poop is momentous. Nearly black, tar-like in texture, and incredibly sticky, meconium is like preelectric Dylan, edgy and enigmatic. Meconium is made up of amniotic fluid, tiny hairs called lanugo, remnant skin cells, and all sorts of other effluvia your kid swallowed in utero. Amazingly, meconium also doesn't smell, thus giving rise to the belief commonly held by many parents that their kids are so perfect, their shit don't stink.

Breastmilk and Formula-Fed Poops

The meconium phase lasts from one to a few days. After that, you're entering the taupe world of formula and breastfed poops. In terms of color palette, look for dead-moss greens and gentle taupes. *Blonde on Blonde*. The poops from a formula-fed baby tend to be slightly darker in hue. Texturally, these are still quite liquid. Neither poop type should smell terrible, and breastmilk poops sometimes smell like popcorn.

Soiled After Solids

Your baby's digestive tract is like most tracks on Dylan's *Nashville Skyline*: short, sweet, and catchy. (A baby's small intestines are only two feet long, as compared to twenty-two feet in an adult.) After introducing your child to solids, expect to see those solids manifest in their stool. Welcome to the panoply of color: the poppy orange of a resilient carrot chunk, hints of pea green, a pop of plum. Naturally, as your child's food becomes more solid, so do their poops, although harder turds don't occur until well into toddlerhood.

Bad Poop

Depending on their diet, children can poop a virtual rainbow and be healthy. Nonetheless, there are a few colors to be on the lookout for. It calls to mind the old joke: "What's black and white and red all over?" The answer is the poop of an unhealthy baby. White chalky stool, for instance, can be an indicator of a blockage in the liver's bile ducts. (Bile turns poop dark.) The cause of this blockage can be a disease called biliary atresia, which affects one in eighteen thousand births worldwide. It's pretty serious. Red stool, meanwhile, is a telltale sign of bleeding. Black stool is indicative of digested blood, which indicates bleeding in the stomach. (Although if you're really concerned about black stool, smear some on a white paper and hold to a bright light. Chances are it's dark green.) But if you see white, black, or red poop, consult a pediatrician immediately.

HOW TO PUT BABY IN A CAR SEAT

What springs from earth dissolves to earth again, and heaven-born things fly to their native seat.

—Marcus Aurelius

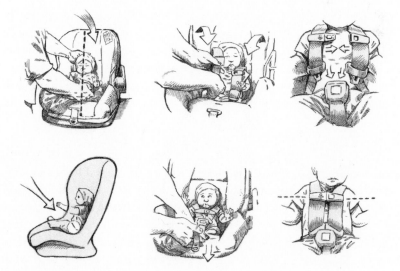

In 1990 the American Academy of Pediatrics found that only 24 percent of hospital obstetrics departments had a policy requiring infant car seats at discharge. In other words, the majority of the '90s kids could travel home in a mother's arms. As quaint as that sounds, the paucity of infant car seat consideration was a serious problem, particularly considering that infants were disproportionately the victims of vehicle fatalities that had claimed children and that a majority of the infants who died in car wrecks were unsecured.

Nearly a decade after their initial findings, the AAP created a policy that all hospitals should require an infant car seat at discharge. Now, it's nearly impossible to take your baby home without someone evaluating your ability to strap them into a car seat. The good news is that the policy appears to be working: from 2001 to 2017, child occupant fatalities in car accidents dropped over 50 percent for children age zero to four.

The upshot is that the youngest kids are way safer in cars than they ever were. Also, you're not busting your kid out of the hospital without a car seat. That makes arriving at the hospital with an infant car seat, that you know how to use, an important part of your prebirth prep work.

The Fire Station Myth

At one time, firemen were considered the go-to for car seat installation. But this is one time where the hunky fireman ain't got nothing on you. The fact is that car seat installation is not part of average firemen training.

Some (but not all) firemen are certified car seat technicians. So are some cops, and so are some average Joes. The point is that if you want a car seat tech to help you, search online before heading to your local firehouse, where they may be just as clueless and creative with their installation as you would be.

Base Camp

Most infant car seats come with two parts. The seat and the base. The base is installed in the car, where it remains. The seat can then be clicked in and out of the base with minor effort, which makes taking the car seat out of the car a much more convenient process.

But for the system to work the way it should for your baby's safety, the base needs to be installed properly. The steps are fairly simple, though care should be taken to read your model's directions prior to installing.

+ Car seat bases are directional. They have a front and a back. Make sure the base is facing the right way when installing.

- The angle of the base is crucial to keep your baby safe. Many seats will have a bubble level built into the base. Adjust the base so that the bubble is between the indicators.

- Some car seats will have a red line indicating the proper angle. This kind of seat will require you to adjust the base while eyeballing the line until it is parallel to the ground, not the car.

- If your vehicle is newer than 2007 it will have designated car seat anchors in the second row of seating (car seats should never be installed in the front passenger's side). They will be located somewhere in the crack where your vehicle's seat and seatback meet.

- Find the straps on the car seat that connect to the anchors. They may look like seatbelt clips or simple hooks. Attach these to the seat anchors.

- Tighten the straps connected to the anchors until the base has less than an inch of wiggle room in any particular direction. Make sure it's still level.

Protect Ya (Baby's) Neck

There are plenty of fine infant car seats to choose from, and they are each designed specifically to keep your baby in the optimal position for safety—rear facing and slightly reclined. When a car seat is installed correctly, and the baby strapped in right, the head should never fall forward, which could cause airway blockage. Still, infants are pretty noodly, particularly in regards to their neck. So it's not uncommon for an infant's big head to loll from side to side in the car seat, even if the baby is positioned correctly.

From the perspective of an adult whose parts are far less flexible, the way a newborn's head rests while they're in the car seat looks excruciating. If your average parents bent their necks in such extreme ways, they would probably be dead. Given that parents are hormonally primed for empathy, seeing a baby's head flopped over can lead to the visceral feeling of discomfort. This often prompts parents to make the misguided decision of adding aftermarket neck supports to an infant car seat to keep their newborn's head stable.

The problem with this seemingly logical predilection is that car seat accessories do not need to meet the rigid testing standards and qualifications required for car seats. Without those standards, you cannot know if a neck support will come dislodged and become a suffocation hazard or cause injury to your infant in an accident. And what's true for neck supports is true for any accessory you might be tempted to attach to a car seat, including mirrors or toys.

For the most part, unless advised by a certified professional car seat installer, don't add anything extra to your infant car seat.

Installing the Baby

The word *installing* is the most accurate when talking about how to put your baby in an infant car seat. It's a process with distinct steps. And those steps should be followed to the letter until the process becomes second nature.

1. Loosen all straps as much as possible and position them to the side of the seat so your baby can be placed in the seat unobstructed. Note that metal portions of buckles can get hot in the summer and cause burns.

2. Place your baby bottom snug in the seat, spine centered, and back in contact with the seat from bottom to shoulders.

3. Place the straps over the shoulders.

4. Buckle harness straps at the crotch and then buckle the chest clip.

5. Pull the strap at the center buckle so that the baby's hips are pressed firmly back into the seat.

6. Pull the chest and shoulder straps tight. You should be unable to pinch any slack in the belt at the shoulders or stick a finger between the strap and the baby.

7. Adjust the chest clip so that it is positioned at the baby's armpits.

HOW TO PACK A DIAPER BAG

Just get a bag and drop a dream in it, and you'll be surprised what happens.

—Charles Nelson Reilly

A diaper bag is no place for sentimentality. Primacy should be placed on packing items that address scenarios that ruin outings, namely blowouts, extreme spit-up situations, clothing failure, and hunger. The last thing you want is to grab a mom-packed diaper bag only to realize she didn't add a bottle because she has boobs.

Essential Items

The essential diaper bag checklist is aggressively bare. There are zero frills because frills just get in the way.

- Diapers: one per every hour you will be traveling

  - Pack these last so they are at the top of single-compartment bags. Or pack them in larger external pockets for ease of access.

- Two changes of clothes: because there's always a second "accident."

  - Pack clothing second to last. If it's under diapers it will be easy to access once diapers are removed during changing. Roll clothing items into tight bundles.

- Wipes: no need for a whole pack. Remove a few to a Ziploc and call it good.

- Plastic bags: bundles up the nastiness in a neat package to be tossed or kept separate from other diaper bag contents

  - One or two, folded neatly together

- Bottle: About four ounces of milk or formula for every feeding that will happen in the wild. No need for separate bottles as long as ounces are marked.

◆ Pack against the sides of bags or in external pockets.

◆ High-visibility luggage tag: things happen when you have a baby, so making sure your bag can get back to you if left behind is an essential consideration. The brighter the tag is, the less likely it is that you'll leave it behind.

Optional Items

Sometimes you want some extra stuff, just in case. These are the bits of gear for a variety of rare contingencies.

◆ Pacifiers: if your child uses them, pack an extra for soothing purposes.

◆ Bottled water: hydration for you or helpful for cleaning up messes in a pinch.

◆ Foldable changing pad: acts as a barrier between dirty surfaces and dirty baby.

◆ Burp cloths: nice to have, but bulky. Wipes will do for clean-up.

◆ Diaper cream: if a child is already struggling with a diaper rash or is prone to it, some good diaper cream will act as a moisture barrier and keep discomfort at bay.

Unnecessary Items

The downfall of the diaper bag packer is filling it up with crap that takes up space better used for essentials. Unnecessary items also hamper the retrieval of important gear in emergency situations.

◆ Children's books: your baby doesn't know words. Read whatever you want as long as it's not Ayn Rand.

◆ Toys: got keys? Great. Toys are redundant.

The Case for His and Her Diaper Bags

This might be a struggle for some couples. Many moms like to treat the diaper bag as a purse, which means that it can get cluttered with lip-care products, lotions, and other, often necessary feminine supplies. If sharing a bag, there's little you can do about this, and defaulting to your partner's comfort is certainly the best way to go. But there's no rule against "his and her" diaper bags. And having two can save trouble, time, and even act as a backup if one is lost.

SECTION III

GROWING
YOUR OWN

Making a baby and bringing it into the world is relatively easy.

But now comes the hard part—making sure they don't grow up

to become an asshole.

CHAPTER 11

Spoil the Child

On a hot June night in 2013, twenty-four-year-old Breanna Mitchell stepped out of her SUV onto a stranger's well-manicured lawn in the sprawling, pool-pocked suburb of Burleson, just south of Fort Worth, Texas. Shaken after a blowout, she'd swerved off the road, taking out a mailbox and haphazardly parking herself on the property of Hollie and Shelby Boyles, who came out to help and were soon joined by youth pastor Brian Jennings, who pulled over when he saw the commotion. It was nearly midnight, but temperatures were still in the mid-nineties. Heat radiated from the blacktop as these strangers, motivated by concern for the young woman, considered how to get Mitchell's SUV back on the road.

As they studied the predicament, an extended-cab Ford F-350 with blood red paint barreled toward them at more than seventy miles an hour. Mitchell, the Boyles, and Jennings had no time to react before the truck clipped Mitchell's SUV, which swung around and struck all four people. They were pronounced dead at the scene.

The truck's driver, sixteen-year-old Ethan Couch, survived. Couch was high on valium and marijuana and blind drunk from two cases of beer he'd stolen from Walmart earlier in the night. The seven people in his truck somehow survived.

For six months, the accident was treated as a local tragedy. Couch was indicted on four counts of intoxication manslaughter and was expected to plead guilty. *Texas Monthly* described him as "every cocky, rich 16-year-old in every suburb in America."[1] Then the case went unexpectedly global. Couch's attorneys, Scott Brown and Reagan Wynn, offered a stunning and headline-making defense. They argued that their client, whose father was a local sheet-metal magnate, was a victim of "affluenza," a portmanteau of the words *affluence* and *influenza*, meant to describe the supposedly sickening and contagious quality of excess and privilege.

Couch, his attorneys suggested with straight faces, was a victim of being pathologically spoiled.

Psychologist G. Dick Miller, expert for the defense, argued that Couch was incapable of knowing right from wrong because "he never learned that sometimes you don't get your way." Not content to leave it there, Miller, who spent the next several weeks on a victory tour of news networks, went on. "He had the cars and he had the money. He had freedoms that no young man would be able to handle."

What was interesting about affluenza's cultural moment was that Miller managed to refocus the attention of the public and the jury on Ethan Couch's parents, Tonya and Fred, and the corrosive nature of money and status in a capitalist society as a whole. Looking back on what went down in that Texas courtroom, it's impossible to not be disgusted by the cynicism of the moment, but it's also hard to conclude that Miller was totally wrong. Opportunistic? Sure. Wrong? That's just not clear.

Spoiling, even euphemistically described as affluenza, is not as simple as ruining a child with too many cuddles, too many toys, and too few rules. In fact, Couch could have been showered with trucks and money and still been raised to be a compassionate adult. And the flip side also is true: even without wealth and freedom, he could still have become the most spoiled brat in Texas. That's because spoiling is less about what children are given—hugs, stuffed animals, video games, money, freedom—and more about what parents withhold.

Despite pleading guilty to four counts of intoxication manslaughter and two counts of intoxication assault causing serious bodily injury, Couch received only ten years' probation and a mandatory stay at a drug treatment facility. Naturally, the sentence outraged the families of the dead as well as appalling onlookers, prompting a media frenzy over affluenza and a national conversation about what it means to be spoiled.

Miller didn't use that specific word—*spoiled*. He didn't need to. The term has been around since the 1640s, some fifty years before it was applied to food. Since then, spoilage has been used to explain away everything from poor manners to outright violence. In fact, back in 1989 psychologist Bruce J. McIntosh proposed "spoiled child syndrome" as a unique childhood condition in the pages of the medical journal *Pediatrics.*

"Spoiled child syndrome is characterized by excessive self-centered and immature behavior, resulting from the failure of parents to enforce consistent, age-appropriate limits," he wrote. McIntosh, who focused on young children, put forth characteristics of spoiling, which included re-quiring night feeding after four months, crying at night after four months, recurrent temper tantrums, and "out of control toddlers."[2]

McIntosh suggested that a spoiled child was a child who had been taught by an undisciplined parent to see no difference between their "wants" and "needs." He was basically suggesting that children were in-satiable monsters who learned to be reasonable only when their parents introduced them to discomfort.

McIntosh's spoiled child syndrome never caught on with the pediatric community, but the general premise has been taken as granted for much of Western civilization. The idea that kids need to have their nature tamed and bent towards goodness is less based on science than it is on Judeo-Christian ideas of God, sin, and redemption. The fallen state of humanity is a moral, not medical, concern brought to North America by those work-obsessed Puritans in the seventeenth century. At Plymouth Colony, parents exchanged their children so as not to be tempted to be overly kind or relent to kids' unreasonable demands, like not wanting to be beaten or burned as a witch.

What we know now is that parents' historical focus on what kids are given or allowed (or not) isn't particularly productive. There are, in fact, plenty of perfectly lovely rich kids. Indulgence isn't inherently destruc-tive. A parent can't love a child too much or provide too much attention and care. Still plenty of parents worry they could raise an awful human.

BAD NUTS

According to a 2015 Pew Research poll, 71 percent of parents surveyed said it was "extremely important" for their child to grow to be honest and ethical adults. The second greatest concern, for 65 percent of parents, was that children grow to be compassionate and caring. In contrast, only 54 percent of parents said it was important for kids to grow to be finan-cially independent, and only 45 percent wanted an adult child who was ambitious. Nobody, it seems, wants to raise a wealthy asshole. And that concern becomes particularly salient when you consider that 46 percent of parents polled by Pew say that their children's outcome reflects on their child-rearing skills.

Plenty of morality tales are aimed squarely at the parental anxiety over raising a spoiled brat, and these are often crazy violent. Consider Roald Dahl's Veruca Salt, a small girl "who lived with her rich parents in a great city far away" and meets an awful end in Mr. Wonka's chocolate factory. Veruca is given everything she wants, including her golden ticket, only found after her father's nut factory staff devotes their entire production time to finding one. She demands to be first in all things, and her parents consistently meet these demands. That is, until Veruca demands an animal from Wonka's factory, a squirrel trained to sort the good nuts from the bad. In the book these squirrels mark Veruca and her parents as Bad Nuts and attack them, sending the family down a garbage chute that may or may not end in incineration, revealing them to be literal trash. In the film version of the book, the Oompa Loompas lay out the moral of the Salts in song, leaving nothing to interpretation:

> Who do you blame when your kid is a brat
> Pampered and spoiled like a Siamese cat?
> Blaming the kids is a lion of shame
> You know exactly who's to blame:
> The mother and the father!

NEED TO KNOW

The All-Time Most Spoiled Kids

Bratty, whiny, self-centered, aggressive, and otherwise "spoiled" children have made for excellent antagonists in popular culture. That's likely because a spoiled character's bad behavior is so universally distasteful. After all, humans have been able to advance because we're willing to share. A child who demands more resources than they provide is particularly discordant.

When it comes to books, television, and film, Veruca Salt has plenty of spoiled kid competition. Some of her fellow brats are straight-up villains. Some are unlikely antiheroes. But all have shaped society's understanding of what a spoiled child is, even if they fail to shed light on how they became that way in the first place.

Angelica Pickles (*Rugrats*)

This spoiled three-and-a-half-year-old bullied and excluded the other babies, essentially becoming the villain of the *Rugrats* universe. That's a pretty significant accomplishment for someone barely potty trained.

Holden Caulfield (*Catcher in the Rye*)

Holden is pretty much the epitome of an elitist brat. He's a victim of affluenza before the term was even invented. He goes to a boarding school, he can afford to rent hotels as a teenager, and is still an insufferable jerk.

Anakin Skywalker (The *Star Wars* Prequels)

Despite humble origins, Anakin develops a pretty self-centered streak that eventually leads him to war crimes and the dark side. Maybe it's because he was told he was the "chosen one" when he was but a wee lad, but his reaction to not being able to join the Jedi council is a bit much. He killed the younglings for goodness sakes!

Draco Malfoy (*Harry Potter*)

The young Slytherin wizard will only ride the Nimbus 2000 quidditch broom and has only the best robes. And yet somehow this kid has the worst inferiority complex in the wizarding world. I guess being told you're better than everyone else tends to rot the insides.

Joffrey Baratheon (*Game of Thrones*)

Sociopathy aside, this little twerp who was born of incest was raised from birth to be a spoiled, self-entitled brat who believed he deserved everything he wanted. And when he did not get what he wanted, his cruelty knew no bounds.

Lucy van Pelt (*Peanuts*)

Assertive girls often get a bad rap, which is completely unfair. Girls should be encouraged to be leaders. But Charles Schulz created more than a mean girl when he created Lucy. She is selfish, sure. But she is also petty, insulting, and violent–particularly when she doesn't get her way.

The Boy (*The Giving Tree*)

Shel Silverstein's *The Giving Tree* can be read as an allegory for the selflessness of parenting. The tree gives and gives of itself until there is nothing left but a stump. As selfless as the tree is, the boy only takes. Not only does he take, but he wants in the most selfish consumerist way there is. First he needs money, then a house, and finally a boat to run from the troubles the money and house never solved. More than things, the boy needed values.

Mary Lennox (*The Secret Garden*)

As the main character in *The Secret Garden*, Mary has all the riches and zero adult guidance, save for the servants that give in to her every whim. It's not the giving that makes Mary so awful as much as it is her parent's absence. The good news is that of all the brats on this list, Mary shows kids can always be redeemed as she turns her attention to selflessly gardening and helping her cousin recover his health.

Narcissus (Ovid's *Metamorphoses*)

This guy is the OG brat and the literal root of the term narcissism, which defines so many "spoiled" kids. As Ovid writes of Narcissus, his beauty is unsurpassed and he knows it, causing him to believe that nobody is good enough for him. After spurning the affection of a wood nymph, the goddess Aphrodite takes revenge by causing him to fall in love with his own reflection and waste away until he becomes a yellow and white flower.

Eric Cartman (*South Park*)

Woe be to the parent of a little Eric Cartman. He demands all things be his and melts down if they are not given. He demands his authori-tay be respected without being respectful of others. He is a racist, rude, mean little jerk, but at least he's entertaining.

Around the same time that Dahl was exploring the subject in candy-colored fables, legendary developmental psychologist Diana Baumrind was looking at how parents influence children's behavior. Baumarind, who died in 2008, was a UC Berkeley researcher, and her insight into the relationships of parents and their offspring was based on observation rather than fiction.

Making careful study of several hundred Bay Area families, Baumarind defined four main parenting styles. There were authoritarian parents, who were high on demands, often employing harsh discipline, but who showed little responsiveness to their children. Then there were authoritative parents. Differing from authoritarian parents, they had high demands but were also highly responsive to their children's needs. Their discipline was thoughtful, caring, and value based, and these parents showed a great deal of love and compassion for children. Third were permissive parents, who were also highly responsive to children but never set limits. Finally there were uninvolved parents, neither demanding nor responsive to children.

As Baumarind followed her subjects over time, she found that the children of authoritative, not authoritarian, parents had the best outcomes. They were better students, emotionally stable, and most likely to avoid antisocial behaviors like drug use or dishonesty (common of children of authoritarian parents) and self-centered brattiness (common of children of permissive parents).[3]

"What you're really talking about is respect," explains developmental psychologist Nancy Darling, editor of the *Journal of Adolescence*. "You respect your child and their needs to the extent that it's reasonable. But they have a responsibility to meet the needs of others."

Darling, who has spent her career testing the premise of Baumrind's research, explains that the key to not raising the typically spoiled child appears to be finding a balance between boundaries and responsiveness.

"You don't spoil fruit by treating it carefully," Darling explains. "You spoil it by being rough with it."

Before she started conducting research into the way parental behaviors affect the outcomes of children, Darling raised children of her own. She remembers spoiling being a concern, at least for her children's grandparents, who worried that Darling was too quick to react to cries and too quick to nurse. She was, in short, McIntosh's monster parent. But her kids are just fine, and she was never worried. Why? Because she knows that indulgence doesn't spoil children. She, like a lot of parenting experts, knows about the !Kung.

The !Kung are an indigenous hunter-gatherer tribe in southern Africa who are wildly indulgent of their children. From birth, !Kung babies rarely touch the ground. They are worn by and sleep with mothers. They are fed on demand, and their desires are indulged by all members of the tribe. They rarely act up, and when they do, they are not often punished.

Placed in the context of Western culture, you'd expect this to be a tribe of assholes, but the !Kung are honest, ethical, compassionate, and caring—at least a lot of them are (some of them are still assholes). The goodness of the !Kung isn't a result of toughness or boundaries. It's a result of culture. They are supported by culture and indoctrinated into it in turn. And this works very well for them for all the reasons it can't work in America, a fiercely individualistic country in which market competition is often mistaken for morality.

!Kung kids understand that they have a responsibility to their community, which shapes their behavior. But they are not the only kids to be raised with the fundamental value is that you care for the people around you.

In 2012 author Pamela Duckerman made a great deal of money describing how the French manage this trick, in her big-time best-selling *Bringing Up BéBé*. In explaining why French children ate what was given to them, played independently, and slept through the night, Duckerman painted a portrait of parents willing to provide quality care while drawing boundaries. French parents, for instance, were famous for ignoring children when necessary, according to Duckerman, who writes "the French have managed to be involved with their families without becoming obsessive. They assume that even good parents aren't at the constant service of their children, and that there is no need to feel guilty about this."[4] It wasn't that the parents didn't show a great deal of love and concern when it was needed; it was that they drew hard boundaries that their children had to respect. But, in turn, they respected their children's abilities to be self-directed. Giving respect and requiring respect made the French system work. (As did a good Beaujolais.)

That balance of boundaries and responsiveness is exactly what Ethan Couch lacked. *D Magazine* may have been onto something when they dubbed Fred and Tony Couch the "Worst Parents Ever" in a 2015 profile. (Just a sample excerpt: "Tonya said Fred 'doesn't properly supervise Ethan.' Fred's response: 'I am not a mom.'") It does deserve mention that, based on the flurry of depositions and statements connected to civil suits after the wreck, it's clear that more is at play here than just corrosive affluence.

The relationship between Couch's parents was deeply broken. His father was often violent. Their dysfunction led to the family being visited by police cars and social services officers many times before Couch took four innocent lives and crippled bystanders. Couch's mother told lawyers in one deposition that she rarely disciplined her son. In a bid to show her affection, she replaced actual care with material goods. His father, who did sometimes discipline his son, also gave him far too much freedom. What he did not give was respect, especially in regards to Ethan's needs and limits. He argued his son was brilliant enough to drive to school at twelve without thinking that maybe that was a super shitty idea.

Can children be spoiled by parents? They can. They can be "spoiled" by lack of care and love and consideration. But we know that by another term. It's not affluenza. It's not spoiled child syndrome. It's neglectful parenting.

The fact is that Ethan Couch had been done a disservice by his parents—and that disservice wasn't being born into wealth or being given too much love. The disservice was in being given an inconsistent and contradictory set of values. His parents' behavior certainly did not appear to match their desires, and any lessons of moral righteousness were muted by decisions to leave immoral behavior unpunished.

Ethan Couch's parents socialized him to be like them and, thanks to parenting styles that took uninvolved and permissive to their logical extremes, weaponized their own carelessness. Was he responsible for his own actions? It remains ridiculous to say otherwise. But perhaps it's just as ridiculous to suppose that Ethan Couch was wholly responsible for who he became. The fact that Tonya and Fred Couch have been police blotter mainstays for over a decade is not merely a coincidence. Damaged people tend to damage the people they are raising.

But there's still hope in the final analysis. Children are wildly resilient. There are many brave and extraordinary adults who have survived neglect and abuse and have refused to allow their past to define their future. People have the capacity for change throughout their lives. But more than that, parents who were damaged by their own parents don't have to repeat mistakes. Becoming a parent offers a tremendous opportunity to find the best in yourself, and when the task of change is accepted, the biggest step toward success has already been taken. By building a strong foundation of love, moral values, and intention at the center of the family, there is little room for rot and very little that could possibly spoil.

CHAPTER 12

Welcome to the Infant–Industrial Complex

R aising children and spending go hand in hand. The average cost of raising an American child to the age of eighteen is just short of a quarter million dollars, according to the Department of Agriculture (tasked with tracking these things, for some reason).[1] But that number is actually incredibly low. It just covers necessities like food, medicine, and childcare. What's not factored in are the toys, books, strollers, car seats, play mats, baby monitors, and assorted gadgets that parents are told they need to raise a smart, safe, and healthy child. All those goods require extra cash, which parents quickly fork over, propping up a baby goods market worth tens of billions of dollars annually.

Pregnancy is a unique moment of consumption. Emotions are high. There is fear and worry and stress, and not just because of the looming arrival of a helpless creature parents will need to protect. Perhaps the only viable shortcut to feeling prepared is accumulating stuff—thus the cultural emphasis on baby showers. Before parenthood, most couples don't have the gear that marks people as parents. It's like the old directive to "dress for success," except instead of corporate power suits, parents-to-be outfit themselves with burp cloths, baby wraps, and nursing bras. In the absence of real calming know-how, having the stuff that parents have operates as a reassuring shorthand for being truly prepared.

In the turmoil of the transition, brands step in to provide products marketed as a kind of reassurance. They help new parents feel like good new parents while also offering solutions to common fears and pain points. In many circumstances, where markets meet parents, the outcomes are beneficial. Parents do need a bunch of new shit and so some spending is necessary. Unless you're planning on carrying your child in a papoose until they can walk, you'll need a stroller, a car seat, and probably some board books to keep the kid occupied. There's nothing wrong with any of that. But problems can arise when the spending stops being so much about the needs of the kid and becomes about the anxieties of the adult.

A market worth billions doesn't grow when parents stick to rational purchases. And the baby market has been growing despite the birth rate in the US having been in decline for half a decade and currently sitting at the lowest rate seen since 1985.[2] How are industry leaders pulling this off? It's all about the upsell.

Consider baby monitors. The connected devices range in price from as low as forty dollars for basic audio-only models to four-hundred-dollar top-of-the-line artificial intelligence–enabled technological wonders. The purpose-driven reason for buying a baby monitor is safety. But a baby does not get any safer the more money is spent on a baby monitor.

Yes, parents who buy high-tech baby monitors get more information, including respiration rates, nursery temperature and humidity, heart rate, sleep cycle data, and an alert when the baby poops (as if the crying and smell didn't do that already). But none of those features are required to be standardized or regulated. And none can save a baby from Sudden Infant Death Syndrome. In fact, the American Academy of Pediatrics does not recommend the use of smart baby monitors to keep babies safe during sleep.[3]

That guidance came after a 2018 Children's Hospital of Philadelphia study that tested smart baby monitors and found the accuracy of the pulse and breathing data to be problematic. When compared to FDA-approved medical monitors used in hospital settings, one high-end baby monitor was inconsistent in recognizing low oxygen levels, and one model displayed a false and consistently slow baby heart rate.[4] There's a reason FDA guidelines prohibit smart baby monitor manufacturers from making medical claims.

Instead, baby monitors are marketed as providing peace of mind. Ad copy for the Owlet Smart Sock, which retails for a cool $399, focuses on helping parents worry less. The Owlet purports to help parents by giving them a "complete picture of your baby's safety."[5]

This proposition is for the comfort of the parent and not necessarily the baby. That's key, according to Richard Gottlieb, CEO of the consultancy firm Global Toy Group. "At the basic level you're buying a baby monitor because you think your kid will die," he says.

Gottlieb takes a rose-tinted view of baby product marketing, explaining that manufacturers aren't building businesses by taking advantage of the high emotions of parents. He notes that the baby product industry is earnest in trying to create good products that offer value to parents' lives.

"To be heard out of this huge confluence of messaging that people get every day, you have to figure out what triggers parents," Gottleib says. "The triggers are not all fear related. They are not all anxiety related. Some are aspirational. Companies do look for triggers specifically, but they didn't create them. The industry did not create anxiety."

NEED TO KNOW

The Weird History of Diapers and . . . Pringles

Until the highly lucrative development of disposable diapers in 1958 by Johnson & Johnson, all diapers were, at least in theory, reusable. They were simply pieces of cotton wrapped around a kid's junk that, when soiled, were washed and reused. (The word *diaper* originally referred to the cloth, not the use.)

But that laborious process of washing and drying–and the desire by mothers to enter (or stay) in the workforce after World War II–combined with technological advances gave rise to the disposable diaper. The first prototype was developed in 1946 by a New York housewife (and all-round genius) named Marion Donovan using an old shower curtain and a surplus army parachute to contain military-grade dookie.

But it wasn't until 1961 that Johnson & Johnson launched Pampers. The product was developed by a guy named Victor Mills, who also invented Pringles ("Once you poop, the fun don't stoop"). Cut to 2020. The global diaper market is worth more than $59 billion. Big Diaper is spending millions of dollars on R&D, developing everything from ruffle technology (remember Jerry Seinfeld's puffy shirt?) to superabsorbent polymer crystals of sodium polyacrylate (according to Pampers, they can absorb up to thirty times their own weight)–and it's worked. Disposable diapers carry 66 percent of the market share. The reasons why are easy to see. Disposable diapers are exceedingly easy to use. They are convenient. They're cheap-ish and, most importantly, you throw them out! No one wants to wash diapers. That's a human truth.

This is surely true, but the baby product industry isn't exactly trying to calm anyone down.

Robin Raskin, founder of Living in Digital Times, which produces events at the annual bacchanal that is the Consumer Electronics Show in Las Vegas, points out that brands need parents to err on the side of safety (if not neurosis) to survive, much less grow.

"A kid tracker is a perfect example," Raskin says of the electronic devices that can be slipped into a kid's pocket so parents can follow them via GPS. "On the one hand it's horrible to think about leashing your kid to an electronic tether. On the other hand, stuff happens. So it becomes very personal how much you buy into the fear and how much you let things go."

But Raskin notes that when parents engage with companies, buying to assuage anxiety, the consumption creates a weird feedback loop. In the case of kid trackers, a parent might be terrified of their child being abducted. Yet a look at the statistics would show the parent that abductions by a stranger are vanishingly rare. But all the proof many need that a kid tracker is needed is the existence of kid trackers. Yes, the anxiety existed before the product, and the product is designed to alleviate the anxiety, but the existence and marketing of the product actually reinforces the initial concern, however groundless.

BLOWING OFF STEM

Capitalizing on anxiety is nothing new, but it is worth pointing out that the infant-industrial complex has managed to create some new anxieties along the way. Witness the growth of the STEM (science, technology, engineering, math) toy market. In 2019, the Toy Association released a survey of two thousand parents who felt, on average, a child should be on a career path by around five years old. Some 75 percent of parents wanted their child to end up in a career related to STEM, and another 85 percent of parents planned on encouraging their child to learn to code.[6] This report was intended to underline the importance of STEM toys, but a logical leap was required for parents to conclude that buying a $500 coding rig for a six-year-old made sense. For the STEM trend to justify itself, STEM toys would have to provide children with a meaningful economic advantage.

But there's really no reason to believe this is true.

The Fisher-Price Code-a-Pillar is a futuristic, grinning caterpillar made for three-year-olds. Launched in 2016, the toy has large anime eyes and two rakish blue antennae. Its body is made of shining white plastic, with a design that looks like it might have sprung from a toddler Steve Jobs's sketch book. It lights up and chirps happily and practically begs to be touched by little hands. But most importantly, its body is made of segments that operate as commands: go left, go right, stop. When placed in sequence the segments become a code that causes the Code-a-Pillar to move as prescribed. It's adorable and about ninety dollars retail.

The question is this: will the Code-a-Pillar help a three-year-old get an early step on the career path to coding? No. And not because it's a bad toy. That's just not how play works. Kids use play to learn about the world, understanding causality and motivations. What does a coding toy teach kids about binary that Simon Says does not? Essentially nothing. Patterns are patterns. If there is a correlation between the purchase of STEM toys and academic success, it likely has far more to do with parents' disposable income and academic values than it has to do with what's going on in a child's head.

SCENES FROM THE STROLLER WARS

But anxiety about a child's current or future well-being isn't the only trigger that can get parents to buy irrationally. Where safety anxiety doesn't work, status anxiety does the trick. Enter the stroller industry. "You're seeing a lot of competitive parenting, a lot of 'My rig is better than yours,'" Raskin notes.

Objectively, there's very little a $2,000 battle stroller can do that a forty dollar folding umbrella-style one can't. They have wheels and seats and roll. That's basically the deal. But between those price points exists a wild array of options and abilities. The American baby commerce site Buy Buy Baby lists six categories of strollers and twenty-four brands representing hundreds of strollers each. It's basically the automotive industry writ small, but luxury vehicles account for more of the spending. Ferrari, in partnership with Cybex, makes a stroller. Mima charges $1,999 for the Xari Black Chassis Stroller in black and yellow, a contraption that looks like something out of a 1970s sci-fi film and features a psychedelic umbrella.

Richard Gottlieb extends this car metaphor even further. "There's a sense of status for a stroller in an urban area," he says. "Do you want a

Ferrari, Fiat, Volkswagen, or Ford? They all do the same thing. They get you from A to B. But in what style do you want to get to A and B?"

Just like a car, a stroller says a lot about how parents want to be seen. But the signaling is a bit more complex. It's not just about having money; it's about choosing to spend it on their child. Parents want the best for their baby and wish to be seen wanting the best for their baby. But when the best is out of reach, things get complicated—specifically because the market isn't defined by need, but by aspiration.

"In America we fool ourselves into thinking there is an average American," Gottlieb explains. "Today, we have a bifurcated population of parents, some with a lot of money to spend and some who don't. But we market and produce as if there were an average American."

FOOD FOR THOUGHT

In 2019, the organic baby and toddler food purveyors Tiny Organics attempted to introduce frozen food options to compete with the sugary, pureed fruit and grain pouches ubiquitous among on-the-go-parents. Co-CEO and cofounder Sofia Laurell created veggie-laden and textured options with far less sugar, sent frozen by mail, but at a premium price around $4 per meal, compared to a $1.50 for pouches. They kicked marketing into high gear. Then, disaster.

"We had an ad campaign around the baby food category being reinvented and how many of the options had high sugar content," Laurell says. "The response was, by and large, not positive. If that's the only thing you can afford or that you know, you will feel ashamed. For sure."

Tiny Organics had pissed off a lot of parents who couldn't afford their product by implying that they were doing something wrong instead of selling them on something more. They changed the campaign, leaning into the idea that parents know what's best for their child. This was done out of sensitivity—"We would love to get the price point down to be an option for all children and not just people on the coasts," Laurell says—but also ignored a hard truth. Sugary pouches aren't good for kids. Laurell's product actually was and is healthier.

And therein lies the paradox of marketing to parents. It's critical to play off their anxiety that they're doing something wrong, but making a direct case that they are doing something wrong will create serious headwinds in a hurry. This is perhaps the best proof conceivable that most baby products are ultimately being sold as signifiers of parental identity.

The baby product market will likely become even more bifurcated and bizarre in the coming decades as one type of parent makes decisions based on personal notions of parenthood and self and another type of parent makes decisions based on a limited budget. In all likelihood, this will lead to an arms race in two directions, with companies driving prices toward extremes to cater to audiences anxious about entirely different things.

This is not to say that the irrational purchases parents make are bad or that the companies that make products for this audience are doing anything evil. Itches beg to get scratched. No, a coding toy won't turn a three-year-old into a genius programmer, but if it helps a parent feel more relaxed about the child's future, is it that bad? If the Owlet's stream of data allows a parent to rest easy, is it delivering against its promise of relief despite offering little of statistical or medical value? Perhaps so.

Parents should have clarity on their reasons for buying what they buy because buying a lot of stuff won't help. In fact, it will increase anxiety by dinging the bank account. It's also a pretty inefficient method for coming to terms with change and fear of transitions, which will be something that happens throughout the process of parenting. Still, basic baby stuff can help parents ease their way into a new role and make life practically easier.

"It's fine to buy things for yourself that are also for your kid," says Gottlieb. "Buy selfishly."

Or, just don't.

CHAPTER 13

Your Job Is to Roughhouse

Under the hot lights, in an arena built inside a Miami, Florida, hotel, Ulysses "The Monster" Diaz squared off against Donelei Benedetto. It was November, and despite a virus raging, the two men had only one thing on their mind: inflicting damage to the other.

Diaz and Benedetto stared at each other—their fists up and cocked to strike, wrapped in the least possible protection allowed by the Bare Knuckle Fighting league rules. It was the championship bout, and the atmosphere was charged with malice.

Then, the ring ref dropped his hand, a ring bell rang, and several actions occurred very quickly: Diaz surged forward. Benedetto stepped back and tried to raise his right fist. Diaz slapped the hand down with his left while simultaneously firing a right hook to Benedetto's cheek. And with the last resonant tones of the bell still ringing, Diaz's opponent fell back like a toppled monolith at the edge of canvas.

Officially, the knockout took just three seconds. In actuality the whole thing happened in maybe two and a half. Either way, it was the fastest knockout in Bare Knuckle Fighting history.

The moment is so fast and so violent, and Diaz (who goes by Uly) is so focused and intense, that it's hard to imagine the man using his shredded muscular physique and brutal speed for anything as silly and joyfully unbridled as a playful backyard wrestling match with a grade schooler.

"I have a twenty-three-year-old son, I have a nineteen-year-old daughter, I have a seven-year-old son and an eight-year-old nephew who I have custody of, who I also raise," Diaz says, standing on the lanai of the Miami home he sometimes shares with girlfriend and World Wrestling Entertainment superstar Dana Brooke. "I roughhouse with all of them."

He gestures broadly at his backyard, complete with a small boxing ring, an assortment of mats, and punching bags. "This is the Rough House," he says, chuckling.

One would imagine that rough housing with the thirty-nine-year-old Diaz is probably on another level than tossing kids around the family room rug while growling like a cartoon bear. After all, the tattooed five-foot-ten, 190-pound fighter, with his solid square jaw and a nest of dreads piled on top of his head, has trained to make men submit—or render them unconscious.

But Diaz says that physical play with children changes him. "I rough-house with them from the time they wake up to the time they go to sleep. It's all in good fun; it's all in all in love; it's never bullying." He smiles broadly. "I make a memory every day with these guys."

But he's making more than memories. Like every dad who gets on the floor with his kids for some grappling, throwing, and rolling around, Diaz is making healthy human beings, both physically and mentally. That's his job as a dad.

Typically mothers emerge as the physical nexus of the family. Motherhood, like bare-knuckle boxing or mixed martial arts, tends to be a full-contact sport. There's breastfeeding, baby wearing, and direct infant care like changing, picking up, rocking, and cradling. It's enough to make some moms want to tap out.

Yes, modern dads do get in on some of the action too. It's not uncommon to see a dad sporting a baby wrap or sling, absentmindedly bouncing in place. But the majority of dads provide less direct care to babies, particularly in the early months, and so they have less physical contact with their baby than moms do.

The good news is that a dad's engagement with his kid does appear to grow as the child gets older. And while the time with his kids continues to lag compared to Mom's, it does increase. But more than that, the way Dad engages with his child becomes distinct from the way Mom engages.

Decades of observational studies from around the world, starting as early as the 1970s, have shown that when dads engage with kids, interactions are physical and intense. Child development researchers tend to use words like *rough-and-tumble*, *exhilarating*, and *rambunctious* when describing the way dads play. Comparatively, mother's play is described as "conventional," relying on words instead of yelps and grunts.

Diaz would agree. "It makes me feel like a kid," he says. " One time I went to the beach with my oldest son. At that time I outweighed him by a hundred pounds. I was 225 and strong as heck. We were wrestling on the beach and he got the best of me. I could not get this skinny kid off me. It made me a super proud dad. It was amazing."

Dads roll around with kids on the ground, chase, tackle, jump, tickle, and poke, whereas mothers role-play and discuss. This sounds sexist—"Dad, Tarzan. Mom, Jane."—and is likely derivative of historical gendered expectations, so there's a bit of a chicken and the egg dynamic at play. But the behavior is the behavior and data shows profound consistency on this point. A 2011 study from the Pittsburgh State University observed differences in play between fathers and mothers and found that mothers objectively provided more guidance, structure, and empathy in play, "whereas fathers tend to engage in physical play, behave like agemates, follow the child's lead, and challenge children."[1]

Fathers are more likely to throw their kids around. And there's value in that.

NEED TO KNOW

The Counterintuitive Link Between Roughhousing and Violence

On a mild morning in August 1966, twenty-five-year-old marine and architectural engineering major Charles Whitman dragged a dolly up the stairs of the famed University of Texas clock tower on his way to the observation deck. From his perch about three hundred feet up, Whitman could see the students closing out the summer term and others preparing for the new academic year greeting one another on the genteel South Mall of the sprawling campus, the sculpted mermen splashing in the Littlefield Fountain on the far side. He sorted through the seven firearms and seven hundred rounds of ammunition he'd carried up the stairs, picking a Remington 700 6-mm bolt-action hunting rifle that felt comfortable in his hands.

Between 11:30 a.m. and 1:24 p.m., Whitman, who had already murdered his wife and his mother and shot and killed a guard in the tower, rained bullets from the twenty-eighth-floor balcony. The rampage ended only after officers Houston McCoy and Ramiro "Ray" Martinez reached Whitman's perch and gunned him down.

At the time, the University of Texas shooting was the deadliest mass shooting by a lone gunman in US history. In the wake of the horror came the inevitable inquest. Why had an ordinary if somewhat tempestuous marine killed two women he loved, much less sixteen people he didn't know? An autopsy found a tumor close to Whitman's amygdala, but a commission convened by Governor John Connally declined to conclude the tumor was the cause of his behavior.

The inquiry was aided by the University of Texas Psychology Department, where assistant professor of psychiatry Stuart Brown, an expert on violence, was tasked with going through Whitman's extensive journals and diaries. Brown interviewed Whitman's family and friends and developed a picture of a life—a childhood in Florida, a young adulthood in Texas. Brown was struck by one curious fact: Whitman's father had purposefully kept young Charlie from playing, demanding instead that he focus on excellence in education and skills like playing the piano.

Brown did not know what, if anything, to make of this. Millions of Americans with awful or abusive fathers don't commit acts of stunning barbarity. But the fact seemed significant, so Brown decided to see if there was a connection between restricted childhood play and acts of adult violence. He started visiting America's prisons and studying the childhoods of the criminal class. Brown found something odd: whereas the average thief had a fairly normal—though disproportionately economically disadvantage—childhood, the average killer had not been allowed to play. Some 90 percent of murderers Brown spoke with had been denied access to rough-and-tumble play.

"If you sequentially sort of watch a life emerge, and you look at what play offers from early infancy into adulthood, when crucial experiences are missed, the ability to regulate emotions and to establish empathy and to live with trust with one's companions is definitely attenuated, or definitely constricted," Brown said in a 2014 public radio interview on his work.

After his inquiry into Charles Whitman, Brown spent decades advocating for free play and championing the importance of roughhousing. He became a crusader for stupid, seemingly pointless fun, which he was convinced actually had a critical purpose: teaching kids how to be people. Without play, Brown had concluded, humans can lose their humanity.

Roughhousing isn't only a behavior of humans. Turn on just about any nature documentary, and you'll see it in action as baby elephants, lions, or wild dogs spar and tumble and charge one another between feedings—all while ringmaster David Attenborough calls the shots.[2] Naturalists call this "play fighting," but it's no different than roughhousing. It teaches cubs and pups and kittens and children too.

Brown notes that roughhousing, particularly between children, is very important for socialization. In his 2009 book, *Play: How It Shapes the Brain, Opens the Imagination, and Invigorates the Soul*, Brown writes:

"Play sets the stage for cooperative socialization. It nourishes the roots of trust, empathy, caring, and sharing. When we see another human in distress, that distress becomes ours. Games, sports, and free play between kids sets the foundations for our understanding of fairness and justice."[3]

In humans there appears to be a strong social and emotional benefit in rough-and-tumble play. And that benefit is particularly salient in relationships with children and fathers.

ROUGHHOUSING:
A Different Kind of Play

Roughhousing helps children build social and emotional skills in ways distinct from other types of play. For instance, it's helpful to compare rough-and-tumble types of play to pretend and imaginative play, which largely sit in a mother's domain. When children pretend by dressing up and adopting different characters, they're engaging in lessons of perspective taking. They are free to take risks by trying on new personas in simulated scenarios. If there is danger or adversity in pretend play, it's imagined, and therefore more easily managed—kind of like an "emotional rehearsal," according to Erin O'Connor, developmental psychologist and director of New York University's Early Childhood Education.

"Humans have this higher-level executive control function. We're able to make sense out of role shifts. We can see what it looks like to pretend to be a mother and explore what a mother does. Animals don't have that ability," she says.

Roughhousing is different because by its physical and rambunctious nature, the risks and danger are far more real, O'Connor notes. "Rough-and-tumble play is the way we learn about boundaries and self-control in a positive way," she says. "It's how we learn the limits between having fun and being uncomfortable. And learning that lesson in a space with your parent is ideal. You can only learn these things by experiencing them."

Being the powerhouse he is, "The Monster" Diaz has had his fair share of accidental bonks while roughhousing. "Without meaning to, we go too far; we get too much into the game. But they know at the end of the day I'm their dad, and it's never ill will or bad intention," he explains. "If something happens I catch myself, check in, say I'm sorry, let them know it was a mistake and then we keep going. Life is rough; what you get from me as a dad is just a small piece of what really happens in life."

In that moment, Diaz is modeling some serious skills, including empathy, concern, remorse, and reparation. Pausing the play helps a child understand restraint and the need to rest when things are uncomfortable or hard. Restarting play even after an accident promotes resilience.

"In this acceptance of risk, there's an implicit message that fathers are there for their children even if things get a bit chaotic," O'Connor says. "You don't have to be perfect. Things happen. You get knocked around and hurt sometimes. But the message is, 'I'm here for you even if things go off the rails.'"

NEED TO KNOW

The Heart of Roughness

Roughhousing fires up the senses. And as a child's senses are stimulated, neural pathways are activated in the brain. The more the pathways are activated, the more they are reinforced. The vestibular system, for instance, is crucial for balance. When rough-and-tumble play challenges balance by a kid being pushed, pulled, spun, or turned upside down, the vestibular system activates. When this happens enough, the time between sensory input (going off balance) and vestibular system activation (correcting the center of gravity to regain balance) becomes faster. In other words, a child's balance improves.

Proprioception is the brain's ability to know where the body and limbs are in space and where they are in relation to each other. Proprioception is activated by movement like changing heights—crouching, jumping—pushing, pulling, throwing a ball, or swinging an object. Rough-and-tumble play that involves these characteristics helps children know where their bodies are in the world, a skill that is crucial to survival.

"Roughhousing involves multiple sensory systems at the same time," says occupational therapist Cheryl Albright. "Touch sensation is a given but also vestibular and proprioception as well as smell if the parent wears cologne or any other scent from soap or deodorant. These senses are all important in development for motor skills and learning how to do everyday activities. You cannot put your pants on if you don't have the sensation of where you are in space."

Understanding the parts of the brain that fire during roughhousing helps clarify what type of activities are included in the term. The basic parameters are simple: rough-and-tumble play should include movements that challenge balance and coordination. It should also include movements that change where a body is in space, like climbing, crouching, and jumping. Roughhousing should also include other less obvious sensory inputs like touch, texture, pressure, and smell.

That scaffolding can support a wide variety of activities. Albright is particularly fond of using pillows in play, either for pillow fighting or wrestling. But she also notes that an activity as simple as freeze tag could also be considered roughhousing. Many dads who find themselves ready to roughhouse might default to a John Cena–like wrestling style. But Albright encourages the fathers she works with to expand their rough-and-tumble repertoire. Tag is a good option. Chase is fine too. But whatever you play, she says, kids also need to learn how to calm down.

"If you think of an adult working out, you do a cooldown to bring down your heart rate. Bring the child's heart rate back down and demonstrate how this is done," she says. "So when they feel their heart race from something that happens at school or if they have a meltdown, they now have a calming strategy to slow their heart rate."

Fatherhood and rough-and-tumble play are inextricably linked. It seems almost that Dad is biologically programmed for roughhousing, as evidenced by the first time he feels irresistibly compelled to toss his baby in the air and scare the shit out of his partner.

Roughhousing is undeniably a form of care and should be considered an important part of child-rearing—not only for the developmental benefits it gives to children but for the benefits to fathers too. Physical play gives fathers who would otherwise lack a sense of self-efficacy to grab on to a parenting purpose. Fathers who engage in physical play feel comfortable with and connect to their children in the arena of breathless fun and joy, so play can help establish a trusting relationship that can last.

Roughhousing is like a conversation. It requires a certain amount of give and take. But when children are preverbal, a father has even more of a responsibility than normal to make sure he understands his child's side of the conversation. In the best circumstances, roughhousing allows children to develop trust in their own abilities and in their fathers.

Diaz understands the kind of trust that's built on rowdy, physical clashes with dad. He's delighted about the relationship and trust that's built from the breathless clashes.

"When your kids come running at you at full speed, they know that dad has their back. He's not going to go anywhere, and they're not going to get hurt when they hit him at full speed," Diaz says. "Even at seven and nine years old, they know that. They know that roughhousing is love. They might get hurt here or there, but you know what? They'll cry for two seconds, get a hug from dad, and everything's all right again."

Diaz notes that he was never able to grow that kind of trust as a kid. "I never had a father figure growing up. I never had a male role model in my life. I never knew right from wrong from somebody teaching me. I had to learn that on my own," he says. That's part of what fires the joyful physical play he gets into with his kids.

"When I roughhouse and play with them and I see them using these little techniques that they learned, it makes me so proud," Diaz beams. "I stop them in their tracks and tell them, that's amazing what you just did. I give them credit. Kids need that."

IT'S NOT JUST FOR BOYS

For boys, this is critical because it teaches constructive engagement. Watching Dad, boys learn how to take a breath when things get a bit too wild. For girls, rough-and-tumble play can encourage confidence and resilience. O'Connor notes that when fathers engage in rough-and-tumble play with girls, they teach some lasting lessons about how to be in the world.

"Girls have been taught for so long that they are not the ones setting the boundaries," O'Connor says. So when a physical father acknowledges his daughter's boundaries in play, the idea that she has agency is reinforced. "Rough-and-tumble play is a good example of where you can work through reinforcing your boundaries. It's really important for girls to learn that skill, and it is a skill."

Unfortunately, discussions of roughhousing tend to be highly gendered. When boys wrestle and roll around it's considered just the thing that boys do. When a girl does the same, she is labeled a tomboy—a weird species of quasi boy with dirt on her cheeks who frightens gender conformers. Stuart Brown found a lack of rough-and-tumble play in male killers, but he makes no mention of female killers—likely because female mass killers are so rare. But that doesn't mean that a lack of rough-and-tumble play doesn't affect girls.

In the 1980s, famed Stanford psychologist Carol Dweck was studying learned helplessness in middle-grade girls. She found that when otherwise highly intelligent girls were given tasks slightly beyond their abilities, they rarely rose to the challenge to solve them. Instead, they opted to give up, believing that their abilities were innate and unchangeable. Smart boys, however, would tackle the problems, attempting to solve them, believing that with enough effort they could overcome the limits of their knowledge to find an answer.[4]

Dweck hypothesized that the reason girls tended to give up was because they were often praised for innate abilities, unlike boys, who were praised for their ability to overcome and achieve. Rough-and-tumble play is part of this. When fathers roughhouse with boys, their abilities are challenged and their effort praised. The goal of physical play is often for the kid to best the big man who, after rebuffing some frontal charges, might feign being conquered. The message is that success comes with practice, and failures are simply ways to learn how to be better. Dweck calls this a "growth mindset."[5]

"If parents want to give their children a gift, the best thing they can do is to teach their children to love challenges, be intrigued by mistakes, enjoy effort, and keep on learning," Dweck told *Psychology* magazine in a 2016 interview. "That way, their children don't have to be slaves of praise. They will have a lifelong way to build and repair their own confidence."[6]

NEED TO KNOW

The Rules of Roughhousing

As is the case in all interpersonal touch, consent is key. A kid who doesn't want to be tickled or wrestled shouldn't be. Parents need to know that in the context of play, "no" and "stop" don't lose their meaning. And adults following those directives given by children can actually help children understand and strengthen their personal boundaries and the agency they feel over their own bodily autonomy.

Of course, in the heat of the moment—say, at the pinnacle of a bed-bouncing body slam—it can get complicated. Kids' cues can be confusing. How is a dad to make sense of a kid who is shouting "Stop! Stop!" but also saying it playfully, while laughing maniacally?

First, take the stop at face value. Then look for nonverbal cues that can reveal how a kid is really feeling. "Connection is key," says occupational therapist Cheryl Albright. "Just because a child is laughing doesn't mean they're having a good time. It could be a nervous giggle. Look for signs of fight or flight. Signs of distress."

Those signs might include dilated pupils, a change in breathing pattern, a red nose or ears. Even if children are saying they're fine, these signs could indicate that their nervous systems have gone into overdrive.

Of course it all depends on the child, Albright notes. "Everybody's nervous system is wired differently. I'm not a big fan of light touch. I don't like being tickled, but some kids crave it. It's about knowing your own child."

So go ahead and let the wild rumpus start. Just make sure you keep watch for signs it's time for the game to end.

The paradox of roughhousing is that it's incredibly important but can't be made to feel like work. For children, roughhousing should feel like unbridled, pointless physical and exhilarating fun.

For dads, there's really just one practical measure to keep in mind: kids need to wind down after a round of roughhousing. It's a health thing and also a critical skill. Getting wound up is a natural process. Learning to cope with it isn't.

That cardiovascular insight gets to the heart of the matter. To be alive is to be tossed, rolled, and flung by the oversized hand of fate, happenstance, or—if you go in for that sort of thing—God. Who we become is in essence a product of how we react to being overpowered, sideswiped, or seized. Roughhousing, an act of love perpetrated as an act of aggression, contains almost all the elements of the socialized human experience. There's pain, pleasure, bafflement, and the opportunity to punch Dad in the dick. What better way is there to train a child to confront the vicissitudes of life? None, really. Roughhousing is practice for life, and no matter what noted child development expert Allen Iverson has said in the past, practice matters.

Practice matters not only because the great game of life has personal stakes but because society is built on the fundamental assumption that adults know how to give and take. Those who don't do damage.

Diaz puts it succinctly: "People who don't have roughhousing grow up to be bullies," he says. "The guys I grew up with who had blackbelts were always the kindest guys. The guys that I knew in gangs, who didn't know what they were doing? Who didn't roughhouse? They were assholes in my opinion."

He stops for a moment and ponders. "In combat sports, we kick each other's ass and then we shake hands and hug it out," he says. "That's a gentleman's sport."

And it would seem, in its own way, roughhousing is too.

CHAPTER 14

The Only Discipline You Need Is Self-Discipline

With the coronavirus pandemic lockdown in full effect, Celeste Kidd, thirty-eight years old and perhaps the most respected child development specialist in the country, was holed up with her three-year-old son at home in the Berkeley hills. She'd called off a speaking tour and had taken her eponymous Kidd lab virtual. She was spending a lot if not most of her time on the phone and Zoom, which had become her lecture hall. She wasn't happy, but no one else was either. She knew she had to keep moving forward—if not for her own sake, for the sake of her son.

In the spring of 2020, Kidd was watching her son stress. Every time another child passed outside their window he would yell out a greeting. If the other kid didn't return the greeting, he melted into a puddle of sadness and despair. When Kidd got on the phone, he ran into the room to yell loud nonsense or find another way to distract her. She watched this behavior. Then she started to manage it by giving the three-year-old chocolate and treats—a kind of chocolate-to-stop-bad-behavior system—which worked pretty well right up until the moment it didn't. That moment came when Kidd was on another phone call. Her son removed the cushions from the couch, stacked them in a pile, stood on them with his arms outstretched, and fell as if he were stage-diving at Woodstock '99.

Being a developmental psychologist, Kidd is professionally observant. She built her career on the back of a freakish ability to ferret out causalities and understand behaviors as the externalization of internal states.

Still, Kidd didn't know why things had escalated to the point of free fall. Then she remembered: chocolate. After seventeen years researching child behavior, Kidd had made an incredibly basic error. She'd reinforced her son's disruptive behavior by rewarding it. Like Nielsen during the heyday of *Jackass*, she'd provided an incentive for her little Johnny Knoxville to engage in increasingly risky behaviors.

"He understood something about the situation that I had failed to realize," Kidd says. "He saw it as an opportunity. He's a very good statistical learner."

Lines from *Anchorman* comes to mind: "I'm not even mad. I'm just impressed."

Kidd had enough context for the situation to know that her son's behavior made perfect sense and was ultimately a result of her own. So she changed tactics and deployed a different tool. She took a reasonable breath, sat with him, and then changed the way she responded. She used discipline. Self-discipline, to be exact.

Discipline means different things to different people. For some, specifically those who grew up in rigid households and maybe got super into the Misfits when they were seventeen, discipline is synonymous with punishment. For others, specifically those who could sight-read Misfits bass lines by age seven, it's synonymous with training. But discipline—that thing that all kids purportedly need—is neither of those things. Discipline is a set of self-regulatory behaviors. It is something that a kid is taught, not something that is inflicted upon them. Parents cannot create the kids they want through sheer force of will. Tiger dadding the kid won't make him a perfect Cub Scout. This is not to say that kids can't be forced into obedience and compliance. Of course they can. They are very small and generally pretty easy to bully. But passivity and fear aren't discipline. They just look that way until the kid steals the keys to the Camaro.

THE DISCIPLINE OF TEACHING DISCIPLINE

As it turns out, kids do need discipline, but they don't often get it from enforcement. Discipline is passed down from parents to children when children have the opportunity to observe their parents keeping their impulses and emotions in check. Kids learn from how they are treated. Think of it as a perversion of the Golden Rule: do unto others as you have seen others do unto you.

This will sound counterintuitive to new parents because, well, babies can be unbelievable jerks. So can toddlers. Never once has a coworker looked you straight in the face while dropping a banana slice on the floor . . . then done it again. Adults don't behave like that. Why? Because adults aren't experimenting. Adults don't play scientist with their everyday reality. Kids do.

Generally, the action is intended to cause an instructive reaction. Thus the couch dive. The answer for Kidd wasn't to stop the sweets but rather use them to reinforce the best behaviors. The child is quiet? You get candy! The child is well-behaved? Congratulations, you get candy! The child butts in on a conference call with incredibly smart people whose time is literally money? No candy for you!

"Babies and toddlers are noticing that somebody else may want me to do something different than I want to do. They are noticing that other people may do something different than they would do in that situation," Kidd explains. "All of those observations are important in collecting data to help a baby reach the understanding that different people have different temperaments, desires, and goals. It helps them make sense of the personal world."

Put differently, treating other people well is extraordinarily difficult if you don't understand that there's such a thing as other people. That needs to be learned, and from there, further work must be done to understand how those people are likely to react. What more efficient way is there to do that than to defy specific instructions and rain banana slices on the carpeting?

This is why toddlers are often infuriating. At around eighteen months old, they develop "Theory of Mind," which means they understand that every person has thoughts and experiences unique to themselves. But this isn't a particularly stable idea for them, and they don't necessarily understand which experiences are likely to be annoying. They genuinely don't. "The goal of a child is very rarely to cause harm to a parent," Kidd says. "What you're thinking the action means is very different than what the action probably means."

Behaviors are questions, not statements. And how parents react to those behaviors is the core of discipline. Hugs won't get the job done, but neither will yelling. Parents who react calmly and confidently are the parents who teach their children how to be a successful human.

Parents can sometimes mistake natural developments for parenting wins, focusing on the first words, steps, and potty poops instead of the initial conflicts. But parenting consists largely of what happens when the kid throws an iPhone in the tub or a fit in the middle of a supermarket. Handing out time outs is easy. Tagging in and handling the situation is hard. It takes . . . what's the word? Discipline.

OBSERVATION AND CONSEQUENCES

The idea that parents can teach behavior to children through modeling is based on social learning theory developed by psychologist Albert Bandura in the 1960s. His breakthrough was the proof that learning occurred in a social context and, most notably for parents, that it could occur through observation of behavior or the consequences of behavior.

Bandura tested his theory with his now infamous Bobo doll experiment, which can be found in just about any Psych 101 book. In his experiment, children were exposed to an adult model who would either ignore or beat the crap out of and verbally assault an inflatable clown-faced Bobo doll. Bandura found that children who were exposed to the adults' violent interaction with the Bobo Doll were more likely to mimic the behavior when left alone with the doll to play. Moreover, they were more likely to display novel aggressive behavior to other toys.

NEED TO KNOW

The Greatest Hits of Albert Bandura, Canada's Freud

At ninety-four years old, the Stanford professor and National Medal of Science winner was still working on social cognitive theory—the premise that humans learn primarily through observation. His work has influenced hundreds upon hundreds of developmental psychologists who have been working to understand how kids develop social skills and behaviors. It turns out that much like a late '70s antimarijuana commercial, they learn it by watching you, all right!? They learn it by watching you. That's to say that Bandura helped birth the idea that parents were important models. Here are some of his very best insights:

Why You Should Believe in Yourself

"People must have a robust sense of personal efficacy to sustain the perseverant effort needed to succeed. Self-doubts can set in quickly after some failures or reverses. The important matter is not that difficulties arouse self-doubt, which is a natural immediate reaction, but the speed of recovery of perceived self-efficacy from difficulties. Some people quickly recover their self-assurance; others lose faith in their capabilities. Because the acquisition of knowledge and competencies usually requires sustained effort in the face of difficulties and setbacks, it is resiliency of self-belief that counts."[1]

Why You Should Tell Yourself You're a Good Parent

"A strong sense of parental efficacy yields dividends not only in emotional well-being and quality of caretaking but also in shaping children's developmental trajectories. Parents who believe they can influence the course of their children's development act on that belief in ways that cultivate their potential. They build their children's sense of intellectual efficacy and aspirations, which, in turn, contribute to their social relations, emotional well-being, academic development, and career choice and development. Moreover, parents of high efficacy are strong advocates for their children in interactions with social institutions that affect their children's development during the formative period of their lives."[2]

When (and When Not) to Spy on Kids

"Parental monitoring is likely to be viewed as enabling and supportive when based on children's disclosure in an atmosphere of open communication, but as intrusively controlling when parents try to keep track of their children's activities by surveillance means."[3]

Where Cruelty Comes From

"Given appropriate social conditions, decent, ordinary people can be led to do extraordinarily cruel things."[4]

Why You Should Believe in Your Family's Abilities

"The more efficacious groups judge themselves to be, the higher their collective aspirations, the greater their motivational investment in their undertakings, the stronger their staying power in the face of impediments, the more robust their resilience to adversity, and the higher their performance accomplishments."[5]

Why the Internet Is So Powerful

"New ideas, values, behavior patterns, and social practices are now being rapidly diffused worldwide by symbolic modeling in ways that foster a globally distributed consciousness. Because the symbolic environment occupies a major part of people's everyday lives, much of the social construction of reality and shaping of public consciousness occurs through electronic acculturation."[6]

Why You Should Think Out Loud in Front of You Kid

"Much human learning is aimed at developing cognitive skills on how to gain and use knowledge for future use. Observational learning of thinking skills is greatly facilitated by having models verbalize their thoughts aloud as they engage in problem-solving activities. The thoughts guiding their decisions and action strategies are thus made observable for adoption."[7]

Critics have argued that because children were exposed to adult violence on the toy, Bandura's experiment was unethical. That does not mean it wasn't incredibly well designed. Despite the small sample size of seventy-two children selected from parents who were enrolled in Stanford, a fairly homogeneous group, the study offered strong support for Bandura's hypothesis that aggression and conditions like anxiety and stress can also be passed through modeling. In 2016, Bandura was awarded the National Medal of Science by President Barack Obama.

In his seminal paper on the subject, Bandura noted that the lessons of aggression children learn can change as they extrapolate the general effects of aggression on the world. So while watching an adult kick a Bobo doll might teach a kid to do the same thing, the aggressive behavior might become more generalized. "Models teach more general lessons as well," Bandura writes. "From observing the behavior of others, people can extract general tactics and strategies of behavior that enable them to go beyond what they have seen or heard."[8]

Here's how deep this goes: A 2011 study from the Max Planck Institute of Psychiatry in Munich, Germany, examined how environmental factors in early childhood can influence a child's future mental health. Researchers found that early childhood stress causes changes in a child's gene expression, affecting the way their body releases hormones in response to stress. These changes persist over a lifetime, making it difficult for the body and brain to react efficiently and positively to adversity.

When a parent yells or engages in harsh discipline, children's bodies respond to the stress and, in a sense, store it. The possibility that unhealthy interactions over a prolonged period of time could change a child's gene expression is very real. Bandura was right about the psychology, but it's biology as well.

TRAIN YOURSELF, NOT YOUR KIDS

That is particularly obvious in situations when parents mistake physical punishment for discipline, according to Andrew Grogan-Kaylor from the University of Michigan School of Social Work. Grogan-Kaylor was co-author on a massive 2016 literature review looking into the long-term outcomes of children who were spanked. He and his colleague, Elizabeth Gershoff of the University of Texas at Austin, looked at seventy-five studies with longitudinal data representing 160,927 children who had been spanked to see if their outcomes were different than those of children who had been more obviously abused. What they found was that spanking was not associated with any positive outcomes. In fact, spanking was linked with mental health problems, addiction, and violence. What's more, the outcomes of children who were spanked were consistent with children who had been physically abused.[9]

This makes sense. If young children's behavior is best understood as an inquiry, the kids who got spanked and the kids who got slapped received roughly the same answer.

Yes, children can be punished in productive ways. But punishment rarely begets discipline as a set of behaviors. Time-outs may provide an opportunity for kids to practice self-talk and self-regulation, but they need to have those skills first. Which is why when it comes to discipline, parental self-discipline is pretty much the whole ball game. When a parent calmly expresses frustration and provides a corrective, children are shown a path forward that is both practical and prosocial. Think of explaining it as unspanking and you get it.

"Ultimately the idea about discipline is teaching kids to be self-disciplined in their own right so that they can engage in good decision-making, good choices, and doing the right thing depending on the situation," explains psychologist Jim Taylor, who consults with the United States Tennis Association and the US Ski Team on issues related to super high-performing children. Taylor teaches young athletes' parents how to treat the Bobo dolls unique to their situation and, in so doing, give their children the opportunity to be their best selves. As anyone who's ever been to a junior soccer game might guess, it's hard work.

"The first thing parents need to do is look in the mirror and see the emotional baggage they bring to parenting," Taylor says. "Baggage is a part of the human condition because we're flawed, sensitive creatures."

NEED TO KNOW

Do Time-Outs Work?

The disciplinary time-out was created in the 1950s by psychologist and behaviorist Arthur W. Staats, who used them on his own children. He describes their use as a gentle punitive measure basically meant to remove a misbehaving kid from a supportive environment to one where they can get it out of their system on their lonesome.

"I would put her in her crib and indicate that she had to stay there until she stopped crying," Staats said of the technique he used on his two-year-old daughter. "If we were in a public place, I would pick her up and go outside."

But since Staats, time-outs have become an altogether different kind of animal. Time-outs hit their popular stride in the early 2000s largely thanks to reality TV parenting expert Jo Frost of *Supernanny* fame. Frost stressed time-outs and the "naughty chair" on which they would occur as her preferred discipline option, and week after week, the families she worked with on her show would be transformed by the technique. It was the time-outs' greatest hour.

But what does science say? The effectiveness of time-outs depends entirely on how parents use them. If a time-out is mainly punitive and administered with yelling, blame, and name-calling, it will be destabilizing for a kid. If the goal is correction and isolation, children may learn to obey blindly but not how to control their emotions and change behaviors. Time-outs are particularly useless during tantrums. By the time a child is melting down, they've lost the ability to process why they're being put into time-out in the first place.

Time-out is not effective as "a stand-alone parenting strategy; rather, it was part of a stepped process, in which effective implementation was dependent on mastery of positive reinforcement of the child as a first step," University of Sydney researchers Mark Dadds and Lucy Tully wrote in a 2019 study reanalyzing data around the effectiveness of time-outs. "In other words, enhancing the positive relationship between parent and child ('time-in') was necessary for time-out to be effective."

To make time-outs work, they have to be codified and consistent and end in positive relationship building. The process of a time-out should include age-appropriate explanation of why the time-out is happening and an exploration of what the better behavioral choices might have been. But even after that talk, parents should consider whether there will be additional natural consequences so a kid can make reparations. Those reparations can include everything from an apology to cleaning up a mess.

A time-out without talk, reparation, and a mending of the relationship is just punishment. It's a brain spanking and can be just as damaging as a smack on the butt.

Often, Taylor notes, a parents' baggage will cause them to react to children in anger or frustration, when those emotions are largely unhelpful to resolving conflict. Fortunately, there are plenty of tools available to help a parent get an understanding of what they carry into parenthood. Taylor recommends self-help books, therapy, and practicing mindfulness. In a sense, it's all the same. Introspection is the key, and it doesn't much matter how parents manage to get there. Once parents understand what sets them off, they can explain it and handle the rodeo bull that is the hyperemotional amygdala, the source of humans' fight-or-flight impulses. When parents train themselves to use their more rational prefrontal cortex, they demonstrate to their kids that fight and flight are just two not-particularly-good options among many.

Fetishizing rationality can get ugly, but there's a lot to be said for demonstrating a bit of stoicism. Importantly, that doesn't necessarily mean hiding your emotions, just controlling them. The ability to control one's emotions makes it far easier to control one's kids.

Taking a step back allows parents to engage in pattern recognition and behave like Kidd—disrupting feedback loops that aren't working. One might say that Kidd's ability to understand her son's behavior saved her from disciplining her child, but that's not precisely the point. Kidd's ability to understand her son's behavior allowed her to teach her son how to discipline himself. The chocolate was an indulgence, sure, but even an indulgence can teach discipline if deployed smartly.

If parental love is unconditional, parental discipline is purely tactical. And that's fine. Sometimes the best way to provide care is through calculation.

Should I Get My Kids Vaccinated?

Yes.

Screen Time Is a Parent Problem

On December 9, 1993, Senators Joe Lieberman and Herb Kohl called executives from Sega and Nintendo before the Senate Governmental Affairs Committee in Washington to answer questions about violence in video games. The grandfatherly Kohl, with reading glasses perched on his nose and wearing a somber gray suit, opened the hearings by acknowledging their yuletide timing. Parents, he noted, were already holiday shopping for kids. And on many lists were sure to be gaming consoles like the Super Nintendo and Sega Genesis.

Along with the consoles, kids would be asking for a surfeit of games—not all of them as innocent as the ode to Italian plumbers *Super Mario Brothers.* The ultraviolent fighting game *Mortal Kombat,* for instance, allowed players to perform gory "finishing moves" like pulling an opponent's spine out of its body. And the scandalous live-action horror video game *Night Trap* featured a scene in which a nightgown clad woman had her blood drained from her neck via an augur. Somebody, Kohl warned, had to think of the children.

Lieberman, in his opening statement, amped up the rhetoric to full moral panic. "Violence and violent images permeate more and more aspects of our lives, and I think it's time to draw the line. I know that one place parents want us to draw the line is with violence in video games," the senator intoned soberly to the chamber. "Like the *Grinch Who Stole Christmas* these violent video games threaten to rob this particular holiday season of a spirit of goodwill. Instead of enriching a child's mind, these games teach a child to enjoy inflicting torture."

At the time of the video game hearings, "screen time" writ large as we understand it today had yet to become the enemy of the family—mostly because screens hadn't mobilized past the den or computer desk. But that hadn't stopped parents from feeling threatened by the boob tubes and "idiot boxes" that haunted their living rooms.

Those parental concerns were first addressed in a 1961 book called *Television in the Lives of Our Children: The Facts About the Effects of Television Based on Studies of Over 6,000 Children* by Wilbur Schramm, director of the Institute for Communication Research at Stanford University. The book attempted to answer burning questions about what happened when kids propped themselves up in front of the fuzzy warmth of the cathode ray tube. Researchers found that contrary to popular belief, television wasn't bad on the eyes. Also, counterintuitively, it did not necessarily appear to disrupt sleep. And in terms of social status quo, TV and its programs was not likely a cause of delinquency, although they could potentially "feed the malignant impulses that already exist."

Despite the lack of evidence for widespread harm, Schramm offered a dire warning. Children exposed to too much television, he said, could become inured to wonders of life because "there is little they have not seen or done or lived through, and yet this is second-hand experience. When the experience itself comes, it is watered down, for it has already been half-lived but never truly felt."

The moral concerns related to screens simmered just below full blown panic until technology enabled children to progress from watching GI Joe cartoons to actively shooting up the bad, bad guys with 1988's *Contra* for the Nintendo gaming system. By the time the 1993 video game hearings happened, screen panic for American parents hit a rolling boil. This was a new threat. The age of kids just passively "vegging out" in front of the television had passed. Through video games, kid became active participants in the media. And through that participation, screens had developed a new ability to turn America's precious angels into little torture junkies (proof apparently be damned).

The pressure from the hearings was enough that just a year later, in 1994, the video game industry voluntarily created the Entertainment Software Rating Board (ESRB). The board is responsible for rating video games in much the same way the motion picture industry rates movies. The end result is a video game industry held accountable for their product and parents with a better understanding of what they're buying for their children. An unsteady détente among parents, screens, and kids persisted until technology changed the game yet again.

In 2007 Apple released the iPhone, and within years screens were boundless. Easily clutched in even the stickiest toddler hand, screens could follow children from room to room and out of the house. Now between tablets, phones, televisions, and laptops there appears to be no safe haven from screens. Worse, each one can act as a portal to content, including games, videos, and apps that are far more difficult for parents to control and understand.

The panic has coalesced, focusing now directly on the screens, in all forms, as the arbiter of generational decline. But even in the literal bright, screen-filled future, old arguments have emerged echoing midcentury accusations that were leveled at televisions. Parents agonize that screens are disrupting sleep, contributing to obesity, causing eyestrain and promoting depression, anxiety, and antisocial behavior.

Even scarier is the prospect that screens connect children to a vast network of pedophiles or introduce them to practically supernatural villains that will coax them to suicide and self-harm. Consider the specter of the weird, bird-faced Momo, who emerged as a menace in 2018 when it was reported the shadowy internet character coaxed a twelve-year-old girl to her death via the so-called Momo Challenge. Even Kim Kardashian was not immune to the spooky story, begging YouTube to scrub Momo from its platform.

Importantly, no such challenge existed, and the delirium around the story was largely propped up by media outlets, boosting specious stories from overcautious law enforcement. Yes, it was a hoax, but it was a viral hoax, which was good for driving internet traffic. That's the thing about panic: it's easy to exploit.

The problem for parents when it comes to children and screens is in sorting out the reliable information from the fear mongering. Science can help, but it's limited by its need to constantly progress. For instance, research has largely abandoned the idea laid out by Schramm in 1961, that the experiences lived through the screen would deaden children to the experiences of real life. On the other hand, where Schramm noted watching television was unlikely to disrupt sleep, science has discovered that the blue light from modern screens can trick the pineal gland into disrupting melatonin release and, therefore, sleep. So how do you sort it all out? A measured and skeptical approach is necessary.

SCREEN TIME AND THE BRAIN-CHANGE PANIC

In November 2019, the journal *JAMA Pediatrics* published a headline-grabbing study on screen time and child development—"Associations Between Screen-Based Media Use and Brain White Matter Integrity in Preschool-Aged Children." The new research sounded alarming. Researchers from Cincinnati Children's Hospital Medical Center suggested more screen time meant lower expressive language, less ability to rapidly name objects, and decreased literacy skills. They'd also found physical changes to the brain—specifically lower brain white matter integrity in a portion of the brain directly impacting language and literacy skills.

The researchers came to this conclusion after giving MRIs to forty-seven preschool-aged children. In addition to the brain imaging, participants also completed a battery of literacy and language assessment tests. The brain scans and test scores were compared to a measure of screen access, frequency of use, and content gleaned from a fifteen-item screen time questionnaire linked to the American Academy of Pediatrics (AAP) screen time guidelines.

Those guidelines, updated in 2016, are no screens outside of video chatting for children under eighteen months. Toddlers up to twenty-four months should not use screens without adult coinvolvement. And children over the age of two should have no more than one hour per day of "high-quality programming."

What researchers found was that children who participated in screen time beyond the AAP guidelines had "lower microstructural integrity of brain white matter tracts supporting language and emergent literacy skills." Moreover, those brain changes were consistent with the lower scores in literacy and language assessment tests among children who received more than the recommended screen time.

That all sounds very scary and damning for screen time, but there are some important caveats to the research. For one, the sample size of forty-seven children is hardly representative of a larger population. Additionally, researchers readily admitted that their study had no way to tease out related reasons for their results.

"A critical question is whether neurobiological differences are directly associated with properties of screen-based media itself," researchers posited. "Or indirectly associated with differences in human interactive (e.g., shared reading) time, which tends to decrease with greater use."

It's also important to acknowledge that while researchers found brain changes, there was no way of knowing what those changes might mean for preschoolers' developmental outcomes. In short, without a longitudinal study, there is nothing in the study that might suggest children with more screen time are doomed to lives of illiteracy.

NEED TO KNOW

The Longshot Hope of Learning via Screens

Futurists have been traditionally bullish about tech-enabled learning. And looking at your favorite mobile app store, it would seem that tech developers are going all in using mobile technology to meet children's learning needs.

But the promise of learning through a screen may be dimming as research catches up with the glut of applications. A couple of recent studies suggest that screen-enabled learning does not work as well as face-to-face interactions.

In 2017 researchers from Vanderbilt University set out to test if children's physical interaction with a touch screen via tapping or swiping was actually beneficial to children's learning. In one study, they placed iPads with a lab-designed, flashcard-based, word-learning app in the hands of kids between the ages of two and five years old. The app featured a portion in which children were instructed to not tap the screen, followed by an activity where tapping the screen made butterflies flutter. Researchers then tested children to determine if the words had been learned.

A second study also included a university-made word-learning app, though this time on a Galaxy tablet. The game included a passive learning portion and an experimental portion. The experimental portion required the kids, this time between the ages of two and four, to help an object cross a river by tapping or dragging or simply watch the object cross the river. They were also tested on word-learning ability.

In both studies, researchers found that boys learned fewer words when asked to interact with the app through dragging or tapping. On the other hand, girls learned more when asked to interact with the app than when instructed to passively watch. They were also less likely than boys to tap at a screen willy-nilly when instructed not to.

Researchers concluded that the incessant tapping from boys "is consistent with a reliable sex difference in self-regulation reported in the research literature—specifically, that young males have lower self-regulation than females do." And as far as having trouble learning through dragging objects on a screen, researchers suggested, "a partial explanation for this sex difference may be more advanced fine motor development in girls during the preschool years."

In a nutshell: little boys may lack sufficient self-regulation or require too much concentration on tasks that involve fine motor skills for screen interactivity to be effective.

This is just one of many studies suggesting that learning via screen is not a panacea. There is a chance it could help some kids, but there are far too many variables that can confound the ability of kids to learn from a screen. A child's gender is one of those factors, but so is a child's home environment, the parents' investment in caregiving, and the child's age.

The fact is that social and societal norms have always had the opportunity to change the course of normal childhood development. When children in nineteenth-century America wore long gowns for the first eighteen months or so of their childhood, they rarely learned to crawl. Instead, they log-rolled when they wanted to get somewhere. And when it became the norm to place children on their backs to sleep, babies' ability to roll over was delayed by about a month on average, leading to the creation of tummy time. If they had MRI machines in 1842, scientists likely would have found that learning to crawl changed the brains of children.

That's all to say that, yes, big social changes like the increased availability and access of screens for children may, in fact, be changing their bodies and their development. But that doesn't mean that those developmental changes lead to worse outcomes for children and society at large.

More than that, it's intriguing that most of the adverse effects listed in anti–screen time studies are incredibly similar to the adverse effects of parents who've decreased reading and interacting with their children. Is that because of screens? Possibly. Could parents compensate for more screen time by increasing their reading and interaction? Probably.

But cognitive issues aren't the only fears related to screen time. There's also the issue of the "blue light" emitted by screens.

THE BIG BAD BLUE LIGHT SPECIAL

Light emitted by artificial electronic sources is packed with bright, blue-hued short waves. This kind of light is emitted from LED bulbs and pretty much any screen in the home, from televisions to phones.

This blue spectrum of light is also what shines through our morning windows as the sun rises. Before windows existed, as humans evolved in the out-of-doors, our brains developed a way to help us become alert after sleep, using the blue morning light as a cue.

The key to the interaction is the pineal gland, a structure in the brain tied to regulation of the hormone melatonin, which causes humans to feel drowsy and promotes sleep. When the short wavelength blue light enters the eye, even when filtered by the eyelids, the optic nerve sends signals to the pineal gland to suppress the release of melatonin, promoting a sense of alert wakefulness.

As the day progresses, the light from the sun's rays are filtered towards warmer long wavelength hues. This light signals the pineal gland to ramp up melatonin release and cause a sense of drowsiness that will eventually lead to some good shut-eye.

The thing is that the nerves can't recognize the source of the light. Sun? Screen? For our autonomic nervous system, the one that performs crucial tasks without requiring conscious thought, it's all the same. Yes, the sun shouldn't be shining into your eyes as you lay in bed at midnight. But as you scroll through social media feeds with a phone close to your face, the pineal gland is still working as if it were high noon.

The problem is slightly exacerbated for kids, according to a 2018 study from the Sleep and Development Laboratory at the University of Colorado Boulder. It suggested that exposing kids to bright lights, including smartphone or tablet screens, too close to bedtime can alter their sleeping habits.

To conduct the experiment, researchers measured levels of melatonin in a group of ten children ranging from ages three to five. Initially, the children were put on a regular sleep schedule for five nights, with researchers monitoring their saliva several times a day to check their melatonin levels. Then, on the sixth day, the kids' homes were transformed into "low-light" areas, which meant covering up all the windows with black plastic and using low-wattage light bulbs instead of regular ones.

In addition to spending the night in low-light conditions, the children spent the next day there as well. Except that for an hour before bedtime, the preschoolers were exposed to bright light, playing on a light table meant to replicate the effects of using a smartphone or tablet. The researchers then measured the children's melatonin levels one last time and discovered that their levels had dropped dramatically after being exposed to bright lights.

"We found that the bright light exposure suppressed melatonin by almost 90 percent, and the effects persisted even after the kids returned to dim light," said Lameese Akacem, an instructor at the University of Colorado Boulder and the lead author of the study. According to the study, even fifty minutes after the light was gone, the majority of the children were still not back to 50 percent of the melatonin levels they were experiencing the day before.

Here again, it's difficult to extrapolate larger possible trends from the surprising results because of the small sample size of ten children. Still, based on what we know about how blue light affects humans, it all makes sense. Luckily, there are ways to manage the effects of blue light before bed. It's as simple as extinguishing screen light an hour or so before bed.

Which is to say that it would appear that panic is unnecessary in the blue light of reason—or in the reasonable use of blue light. Which is not to say that screens should not warrant any kind of concern. But it might be better to focus on the content on the screens rather than the delivery system.

THE PREDATOR ON THE SCREEN

"At any given moment of time, when a child goes online, there are fifty thousand offenders attempting to have contact with children," explains Camille Cooper, the vice president of Public Policy for the Rape, Abuse and Incest National Network (RAINN). "The scale of the problem is far greater online than it is in your backyard."

Nevertheless, as children have increasingly moved indoors, parents have barely put up a fight against these new dangers. "Parents are hovering in the real world but they're not even paying attention to what their kids are doing online," Cooper says. "When you allow your kid to go online, you're giving the entire world access to your child. It's a parent's job to be vigilant."

It's critical to note that the fifty thousand online predators are not simply hanging out in forbidden corners of the internet waiting for children to stumble into the wrong place at the wrong time. Rather, they are logging in to the apps, games, and online spaces where kids congregate.

They exploit the social functionality of these spaces in order to make contact. And they do make contact.

Forty percent of kids in grades four through eight connected or chatted with a stranger online. More than half gave them their phone number and 15 percent attempted to meet the stranger in person.

This is why the danger is not in the access of the internet, but the way the internet enables communication. Chat features are built into almost every app, game, and social media platform to make the experience more communal, real, and immediate. These functions also allow kids to be contacted by virtually anyone.

The problem is not the screen. It's parental oversight. And if parents don't provide oversight in the earliest years, they will have little say as a child gets older.

According to a Pew Research poll related to online monitoring, 40 percent of parents did not check the website their teenagers were visiting. Another 40 percent did not check on their teens' social media usage. Less than half of parents ever looked at their teen's texts or phone records. Even more damning, only 39 percent of parents reported using parental controls to block, filter, or monitor their child's online activity.

There's a good likelihood that the lack of oversight might come from the backlash against helicopter parents (a backlash we've been a part of). Few parents want to be seen as overbearing and overprotective. After all, parents are told again and again that helicopter parents and their machine-parenting counterparts—the snowplow and lawnmower parents of the world—have practically ruined the upcoming generation of children. The children of helicopter parents are said to be depressed, stressed out, and virtually incapable of doing anything themselves. But letting them go online themselves is just not worth the risk.

As the director of K–12 safety for the educational and home internet monitoring platform Securly, Mike Jolly compares the lack of oversight to just tossing an inexperienced kid the keys to the car. "It's like saying 'good luck!' without ever driving with them or putting them through drivers' education," he says. "When parents let their kids have open access, they're putting them at risk for cyberbullying and seeing things that can be harmful to them."

The more you look at the panic over screen time it seems to be misplaced. The panic is framed as a kid issue. But perhaps the concern would be better focused not on a child's behavior but in the adult's behavior.

THE KIND OF SCREEN TIME THAT MATTERS MOST:
Yours

The still-face experiment is disturbing. At first, a parent and baby play together, dad smiling and cooing, baby clapping her hands and laughing. Then, prompted by the researcher, the dad turns his face away from the stroller and when he turns back his face is completely expressionless. Baby tries to get dad to smile again, but he keeps up the flat affect, remaining neutral and unresponsive. Within a few minutes, the child dissolves, crying, squirming, and desperately trying to make a connection. On a second prompt, dad turns away again, and when he looks at baby again he's his normal self, soothing the baby who quickly recovers. Baby forgets all and gets back to playtime as if nothing happened. Only the viewer is left shaken.

Edward Tronick, the creator of the still-face experiment, didn't conclude that parents needed to bathe their kids in unending attention. When he began the test, "we just didn't have any idea how powerful the connection with other people was for infants, and how, when you disconnected, how powerfully negative the effect was on the infant," Tronick told the *Washington Post* in 2013. The experiment shed light on the impacts of childhood neglect in real time: "When it goes on long enough, you see infants lose postural control and actually collapse in the car seat. Or they'll start self-soothing behaviors, sucking the back of their hand or their thumbs. Then they really disengage from the parent and don't look back." Further research finds that such neglect could last through adulthood, becoming a generational cycle that is exceedingly difficult to break.

"Someone playing with a modern smartphone is exactly like a still-face paradigm," says Caspar Addyman, developmental psychologist and director of the Goldsmiths InfantLab at Goldsmiths University of London in the United Kingdom. He notes that on YouTube, people have shared videos of their own still-face paradigm experiments with a smartphone instead of a blank stare.

A large part of the reason smartphone use mimics the still-faced experiment is eye contact, which is a crucial part of normal parent–child interactions, says Addyman. Researchers have found that when mothers and babies look at each other their brain waves actually sync up, he says. If you aren't looking at your baby's face because you're scrolling on a cell phone, you and the baby can't possibly be in sync, interrupting that parent–child interaction.

While Addyman isn't aware of research specifically on the disruptive power of smartphones and parent–baby interactions, he suspects studies of babies and television can offer a clue as to how parental smartphone usage could influence young children. Television itself is not bad for babies, but it tends to replace live interaction between the parent and child. The hours spent in front of a television is time that could have been spent with someone talking and interacting with the baby, which is how babies develop language and other skills. Babies are active learners, and any time parents are on the screen is time they're not interacting and baby isn't learning.

"You're a partner for the baby to let them learn how to interact with people," says Addyman. In any face-to-face interaction, babies are learning skills like how to take turns and have a conversation, even from their earliest days, he says.

Though playing peek-a-boo or talking to your baby while feeding mushed carrots may not feel like work, children learn a lot through these interactions. Some of what they're learning is emotional. Children pick up on lack of engagement and enthusiasm, even on a subconscious level, when they are really young. Positive attention, on the other hand, helps children feel loved, cared for, safe, and nurtured, she says. Babies are also learning important life skills, like turn taking and social interactions, how to control their behavior and manage their emotions.

The still-face experiment works because it breaks the way parents and children naturally interact. Fortunately, most parents do actively engage with their children most of the time.

What screen time panic fails to take into account is that screens are often needed structural support for parents who are already overburdened. If anything, the 2020 COVID-19 pandemic brought that need into stark relief. Many parents could not have coped without the television holding children's attention just long enough to get through a Zoom meeting. And most children would have lost valuable education without screen time.

Screens will be a tool for many parents. When articles and studies demonize screen time, parents can feel attacked and guilty and even more stressed out. Raising kids without screens in a world that demands so much from parents and insists on screen use for cultural relevance is a wildly unreasonable expectation. Parents should not feel guilty using a tool that has been given to them. Particularly when that tool is more affordable than childcare and there's very little enthusiasm to give parents any meaningful social support that would make screen time unnecessary.

That said, it makes sense that some parents might be wary. That's okay too. If parents are motivated to reduce their children's screen time, then there's absolutely no reason to not follow AAP guidelines. But for parents who find themselves with few alternatives, the screen time panic is terribly unhelpful. Besides, the most important thing parents can do for a kid is to show them love. That has never changed.

CHAPTER 17

The Life-Changing Art of Teaching Your Child Happiness

There's no table read for life and no guarantee of resolution, much less a happy ending. To varying degrees, all parents struggle with this, but rich parents seem to struggle most of all, pressing their advantage in service of what they perceive to be their child's best interests. All those tutors, extracurriculars, overpriced STEM toys, and private schools are supposed to de-risk life in a capitalist society. And to a degree they do. But they don't guarantee happiness. Kids have to pursue that.

Still, it's hard to separate the happiness of American children and the deviousness of American money.

On September 13, 2019, Felicity Huffman, famous for her star turn on *Desperate Housewives*, stood before a judge in Boston's John Joseph Moakley US courthouse, smoothing a wrinkle from her tasteful black dress and reciting lines punched up by her lawyer.

"I am deeply ashamed," she stated.[1] One year previously, Huffman had enlisted the help of William Rick Singer, a con man specializing in fraudulent test scores and sports credentials, to ensure her daughter had a top-tier SAT score. At that time, most University of California campuses had an admission rate in the upper 30 percent—presumably a bit higher for the wealthy children of Hollywood stars. Huffman, not liking those odds, arranged for her unknowing daughter to take the SAT at a rigged testing center.

She knew better.

"I thought to myself, 'Turn around. Just turn around,'" Huffman told Judge Indira Talwani, letting out a small sob. "To my eternal shame, I didn't." Then she recalled her daughter's reaction when she found out: "I don't know who you are anymore, Mom. Why didn't you think I could do it on my own?"

So why didn't Huffman turn around? In Hollywoodspeak, what was her character's motivation? It seems as though she was pursuing happiness with all the subtlety of her horny, profligate character on *Desperate Housewives*. Her intent was to bring it home like a trophy kill and lay it bloodied at the feet of her child.

Hers was the classic American blunder. Like Barry Bonds, Richard Nixon, Lance Armstrong, and Charles Foster Kane, she conflated happiness with achievement and abandoned the beauty of process for the inhumane relief of guaranteed results. The only difference was that she did it for her kid—or for the *idea* of her kid anyway. And, in a sense, that's normal. How many upper- and upper-middle-class parents have called in a favor to get their children an internship or subsidized a fledgling career or bought a library at Harvard? More than a few. Harvard has 70 libraries.

IT'S ALL ABOUT RESILIENCE

It's easy to vilify Huffman and other parents like her. They acted like villains. But it's also easy to understand why. As soon as "pursuit" and "happiness" become separate concepts, adversity starts to look optional, and cheating starts to look like a smart move. After all, income inequality has been steadily increasing in the United States since the 1970s. Over the last fifty years the nation's top earners are outpacing the bottom earners by 20 percent. The top 5 percent of earners make over two hundred times that of median income earners.[2]

When life on the wrong side of the widening economic divide looks like struggle, stress, and sickness, money well spent looks like the ultimate vaccine.

And like most vaccines, money works—to a point. A 2010 study from Princeton by economist Angus Deaton and Nobel Prize–winning psychologist Daniel Kahneman looked at poll data from Gallup for over five hundred thousand Americans and found that income was correlated with happiness, as measured by daily moods and stressors. But this was only true up to $75,000 a year. Above that income, daily well-being became decoupled from money—which is to say, it became more strongly correlated with resilience and personal relationships.[3]

In other words, Huffman risked way too much in an attempt to ensure her daughter could clear the $75,000 mark (especially considering the kid probably could have gotten there on syndication residuals alone). Had Huffman been poor, her behavior would have actually made sense. Where moneyed parents have the luxury of teaching their kids to be happy, cash-strapped parents must focus on providing *access* to happiness. These are dissimilar situations, and the public ridicule Huffman faced seems to have been, at least to some degree, a reaction to her further undermining a system already thoroughly rigged in favor of wealthy children.

That said, parents aren't playing a zero-sum game. There are not a discrete number of spots in Well-Being University's freshman class.

Unless you're John Wick, happiness is not a warm gun. It is, according to psychologists and social scientists, best understood as a pervasive sense of well-being. And people who feel a strong sense of well-being generally share the same set of qualities: resilience, a sense of purpose, spirituality, gratitude, and healthy, meaningful relationships with family, friends, and community.

Resilience appears to be key. What good is happiness if you are derailed by and dwell on adverse setbacks? To have a sense of well-being is to know that you can make it through the hard stuff, says Joan Durrant, associate professor of Family Social Sciences in the faculty of Human Ecology at the University of Manitoba. To get there, some hard stuff is required. And Durrant knows from hard stuff. She studies violence in families and ways that parents can orient towards positivity and well-being to build better relationships.

"Inner happiness is really a sense that you're going to be okay," she explains. "You're going to survive it, and you're going to integrate it into your life."

When parents say they just want their kids to be happy, they are often considering happiness as the state of being possible only in the absence of pain, stress, or adversity. The goal becomes erasing the trials and tribulations from a child's life and attempting to manage away negative emotions. When those emotions emerge—there is no scenario where they don't—parental frustration leads to anger and, much of the time, stupidity. We think of the parent telling his child to "get over it" as fundamentally dissimilar to the parent haggling with teachers over a child's grades. But those are flip sides of the same coin. Parents who attempt to sidestep adversity rather than teaching kids to handle it create chaos both inside and outside their homes. And it seems as though these parents are becoming more common every year.

Durrant cites an example from her own childhood. When she was a little girl, she was devastated by the loss of a balloon that she'd let fly away. Her parents sat with her and let her feel her feelings because that sadness and loss wasn't something to be feared or chased away. There was no urgency to move on, she says. By simply being with her in her moment of pain, her parents helped Durrant realize that loss is hard and life goes on.

"Eventually, they died," Durrant says. "Those are big balloons to lose. But because they never invalidated my feelings, I was okay. Being happy does not mean having no sadness in your life but having an inner contentment."

FIRST, TEACH YOURSELF HAPPINESS

Durrant notes that there's no real trick to happiness, that it's basically a product of classical conditioning—a kind of Pavlovian reinforcement built on brain connections. But kids don't learn to drool at the sound of a bell (they're probably drooling already); they learn to adjust in the face of adversity. Punishment doesn't teach this. Neither does success. Life teaches this, and so it becomes incumbent upon parents to be honest about what life is: "what happens to us while we are making other plans," in the memorable and shockingly biologically accurate formulation of cartoonist Allen Saunders.

There's a phrase often trotted out by neuroscientists that backs up Durrant's claim: neurons that fire together wire together. That's why classical conditioning works the way it does. Every time neural pathways in our brain fire, connections between neurons are made. Sometimes these connections are fleeting. But if those pathways fire consistently, they are reinforced and become stronger. While this works for getting dogs to drool on cue, it also works in changing the way we perceive the world. The trick is in catching our brains experiencing contentment and happiness and dwelling on those moments when they occur—in common practice: mindfulness and gratitude. That recognition helps the neural pathways get stronger.

Of course, it's hard for parents to help a kid understand mindfulness when they have a hard time practicing it themselves. This is why, according to positive psychologist Robert Zeitlin, parents should start working on changing their own minds before a baby even arrives. In his private practice, Zeitlin leverages the emerging science of happiness to help the families he works with increase their joy and well-being. He notes that pleasure is often the unconscious drive that drove his clients before they became parents in the first place.

"I don't think many parents are prepared for the onslaught of unconscious motives that kick in, driving their behavior all the way through parenting," Zeitlin says. "The sooner partners can have a conversation and find ways to make those unconscious motivations more conscious, the better things will be. If you're not aware of these things, they will rule the day."

This style of parenting requires its fair share of intention and focus. And it can be difficult to find that intention and focus when a parent's happiness is tied to discrete moments of pleasure or material gain.

There's science behind why this is the case. Pleasure is tied to the neurotransmitter dopamine, which causes feelings of euphoria, alertness, focus, and motivation when it floods the brain. But dopamine fluctuates. It comes and goes. And when it goes, humans seek to trigger another release. It's partly why humans enjoy sex so much. It's why others bungee jump or buy big, expensive toys. But because dopamine is fleeting, the pleasure doesn't last. Advertisers know this. It's why they can compel us to upgrade our devices regardless of the functionality of the ones we have.

There's nothing wrong with pleasure or dopamine for that matter. Pleasure is wonderful when it's recognized as a perk of living. But when pleasure is considered the point of living, people tend to misallocate energy and resources, and their sense of well-being wanes.

Zeitlin offers an example of a family he worked with who noticed that their child displayed an early aptitude for math. "They went all in," Zeitlin says. Sensing an opportunity to exploit an edge, the family invested a tremendous amount of money and time. Their child played along until his sophomore year of college, until he realized he didn't actually like math. An identity crisis ensued. His parents had seen a fulfilled future for him because they thought he liked math. Maybe he did, but he was a kid and kids change overnight.

"The world is more volatile and ambiguous than we're giving it credit for," Zeitlin says. "We're really bad at predicting what our children will like when they grow up. Making gambles potentially undermines our children's well-being."

Predicting who a child will become is impossible. But predicting what character strengths will ensure long-term well-being is not. Over the last two decades, positive psychologists have used observation and experimentation to identify and classify twenty-four unique character strengths. These strengths are valued and recognized in almost every culture around the world and are largely independent of political orientation or even religious dogma.

The character strengths are organized under six essential human virtues: wisdom, courage, humanity, justice, temperance (or moderation), and transcendence. The character strengths organized under the virtue of wisdom include creativity, curiosity, open-mindedness, love of learning, and perspective. But those are just a quarter of the diverse traits catalogued, which include bravery (under the virtue of courage), kindness (under the virtue of humanity), leadership (under justice), mercy (under moderation), and humor (under transcendence).[4]

Character strengths do not develop by setting discreet goals. Instead, they operate as unique values that parents naturally try to build in their children by encouraging kids to be fair or practice self-control, kindness, and honesty. Research has found that while most people find value in all twenty-four character strengths, every individual builds a personal hierarchy of which strengths are most important to them. One person might prize love of learning more than any other strength. Another might value bravery.

Positive psychologists posit that the path to long-term personal fulfillment and well-being is found by engaging in pursuits and activities that build on the strengths a person values most.

"One of the beautiful things about the character-strengths model is that it's so open ended," Zeitlin says. "It's not in the spirit of a career-advancement model, which sorts people into one category. For instance, you can take the strength of appreciation of beauty in multiple ways and even combine it with other strengths that leads to natural growth." And that growth is what creates a lasting sense of fulfillment.

Given that there are twenty-four strengths, parents might feel daunted to figure out the strengths that connect to their kid. It sounds complicated. But the point isn't to run children's behavior through some kind of diagnostic tool to pinpoint the strength that drives them. The idea is to do what good parents already do: be cautious and observant about what lights up their child's face. One child who loves sports, for instance, might love sports because it fulfills their sense of bravery. Another child might like sports because it fulfills their desire for leadership. If parents use the twenty-four character strengths as a guide, Zeitlin says that it's possible to distinguish the motivating strength far earlier than parents might expect.

NEED TO KNOW

The Twenty-Four Character Strengths of Positive Psychology

Positive psychologists suggest that every human being is driven by twenty-four character traits related to six universal virtues. These traits occur in every culture and nationality around the world, but every individual will value certain traits over others.

A central tenet of positive psychology is the idea that when we live our lives in such a way that we amplify and support those traits we most value, we will feel more fulfilled and content with the world. The following is a list of all twenty-four traits with a brief explanation of each.

THE VIRTUE OF WISDOM AND KNOWLEDGE

Creativity

This one's pretty self-explanatory. It's about having a love of making by leveraging imagination.

Curiosity

When the whos, whats, whys, whens, and hows turn you on.

Open-Mindedness

You're willing and ready to hear new ideas and reserve your judgement.

Love of Learning

When answering the whos, whats, whys, whens, and hows turns you on.

Perspective

It's about seeing the big picture from different angles and making connections.

THE VIRTUE OF COURAGE

Bravery

You like to overcome the daunting challenges.

Perseverance

The going gets rough, but you relish the chance to carry on.

Honesty

The truth matters even when it's difficult to tell or accept.

Zest

You have a balls-out love of life that is undiminished by bullshit.

THE VIRTUE OF HUMANITY

Capacity to Love and Be Loved

You're a lover, not a fighter, although you may fight for love.

Kindness

You're animated by a wealth of compassion and the doing of good deeds.

Social Intelligence

Empathy and sympathy rule. You enjoy feeling what others feel and reacting appropriately.

THE VIRTUE OF JUSTICE

Teamwork

It makes the dream work and helps you get motivated.

Fairness

You're excited by the idea that there's enough for everyone and everyone should have enough.

Leadership

It feels good when people look to you for guidance, and you're fired up by taking pole position.

THE VIRTUE OF TEMPERANCE

Forgiveness and Mercy

You're animated by clemency, reparations, and the belief that people can change.

Modesty and Humility

It's not all about you. In fact, the more it's not about you, the better.

Prudence

Caution and careful consideration is the most fulfilling way for you to approach life.

Self-Regulation

You feel best when you enjoy moderation in all things.

THE VIRTUE OF TRANSCENDENCE

Appreciation of Beauty and Excellence

It's not that you're beautiful or excellent, it's that when you see it, up close and personal, you're filled with joy.

Gratitude

You're #blessed every day and you know why.

Hope

You're motivated by the assumption that things can and will get better.

Humor

Not only do you appreciate a laugh, you appreciate the ability to make others laugh with you.

Religiousness and Spirituality

Whether it's Big G God or a connection to a higher power, you are comforted and boosted by the knowledge there's a force beyond humanity that influences the universe.

But this is different than looking for aptitude. A parent who believes happiness comes from the discreet goal of a good job might see a child who enjoys blocks and point them towards engineering. They might invest in more building toys and enroll in extracurricular STEM classes or engineering subscription boxes. But a child could enjoy building for other reasons. If they prefer building with others, they might be keyed into the character strength of leadership or teamwork. A child may simply enjoy the aesthetic quality of their work, appreciating the artistry rather than the skill required to build their structures.

Instead of going all in on things, parents who make observations based on character strengths can then offer their child more opportunities to engage in teamwork, leadership, or the appreciation of beauty. Indulging in activities that boost these character strengths reinforces them and helps children understand that fulfillment isn't necessarily in having things but in doing things that connect to their character, their unique perspective, and identity.

DEFINE YOUR FAMILY'S VALUES

Character strength can be used more broadly too, to focus a family's values. It's notable that strengths like creativity, bravery, kindness, fairness, and justice would be at home on a coat of arms, as a family motto. That's because the strengths are connected to essential core human values.

"A family can pick values from the menu of character strength while also honoring an individual family member's strengths," says Zeitlin.

That's essentially what forty-five-year-old stay-at-home dad and one-time University of Miami football coach Joseph Fowler and his partner, Kristine, did, before even having their first child. The pair began focusing on their values shortly after she became pregnant. What they learned is that they were driven by curiosity, particularly when it came to travel.

"We knew money was going to be tight as a single-income family. So we wanted to prioritize experiences and not indulge in consumerism," Joseph says.

Their clarifying motto became a family hashtag that they adopted in their social posts, almost in lieu of a motto: #ExperiencesNotThings. Looking at it from a character-strength perspective, the Fowlers had prioritized the virtues of wisdom and transcendence with their focus on love of learning, curiosity, and appreciation of beauty. From the outset, the Fowlers were set on exploration. Their children are eleven and nine years old now, and they've been around the country and even traveled to Cuba in 2019. The focus on adventure has clarified how the family lives and how the children have grown. And it has changed the family's relationship with money.

"If we go out to eat it will be eighty bucks at least because there are four of us," Joseph says he's told his children. "If we spend that money on dinner, that's less money that we have for an adventure. So do we want to go out for hamburgers or save that money for a fun adventure?"

The choice is adventure, nine times out of ten.

Researchers have repeatedly found that consumers overestimated the sense of the value of material goods. It makes sense then that the Fowler family, who prioritize shared experiences, seem so happy. They have respect for the journey and, having put on some miles, understand that nothing goes smoothly all the time, least of all life. This informs not only the family's ability to handle adversity day to day but how Joseph thinks about the future. He's not complacent, but he's also not Huffman-esque.

"If it's not college, then I'll be happy if they are productive members of society and find a career that they find joy in and supports them," Joseph says. "Most of us are just regular folks who want to be content with life and what we've earned and been given."

Notably, Joseph Fowler may have an easier time helping his kids achieve that goal of contentment than many parents. That's because he's content himself, and modeling that quality to his children does much of the work for him. But his condition isn't necessarily common. Parents, on average, aren't the happiest people in the world.

A 2014 study published in the journal *Marriage and Family* titled "Parenthood and Life Satisfaction: Why Don't Children Make People Happy?" looked at longitudinal data from over sixteen thousand parents between the years 1994 and 2010. Researchers found that while children did, in fact, improve life satisfaction, that satisfaction was blunted by the cost and time associated with raising a child. It's hard to be happy when you are overworked and undercompensated.[5]

This brings us back to money. Parents stressed by financial concerns are less likely to be resilient in the face of their child's own behavior or perceived failings. Bad SAT scores aren't so easy to shrug off after you work extra hours to pay for the tutor and you lack the funds to cheat. Those scores can matter, and college admission can matter, and happiness and access to opportunity aren't unrelated. But they also aren't the same thing. Money can't buy you love. Love, however, can substantially change your relationship with money.

There's a quote from *Desperate Housewives* that comes to mind: "It isn't easy giving up power admitting that we might need help from friends and neighbors, deciding that a loved one might know what's best for us, giving up our better judgment for a slightly darker agenda, but for some, the hardest kind of power to give up is the power to control their own desires."[6]

Felicity Huffman should have read the script more closely.

Skills

Milestones that Matter

THE ONLY MILESTONES THAT MATTER

Milestones, as they relate to navigation, are markers along a path offering an indication of precisely how far a traveler's advanced toward a destination. On a highway, you usually will miss them, since they're mostly indistinguishable green signs that fly by while you're focused on the yellow lines—and on your full-throated car karaoke rendition of "I Would Do Anything for Love." If your car breaks down, however, you'll be glad the milestones are there. You can call for help, offering a precise marker for a mechanic to come in and make all of it better for a price that's totally fair and not at all taking advantage of your dire straits.

In reality, although not usually in practice, child development milestones are much the same. Used to describe an ability—like crawling or babbling—that a child should acquire at a certain point in life, milestones can be useful under the discerning eye of an expert. But as far as parents are concerned, developmental milestones are mostly a distraction—a stressful, overwhelming distraction.

Milestones were initially developed to give physicians a broad understanding of how an average child grows. So in the aggregate, "most" kids will begin walking by twelve months. But depending on where they grow up in the world, how much space they have to explore, and how much freedom they are given by parents, babies can start walking as early as six months and as late as sixteen months. The truth is whether they start at six months or sixteen, the vast majority of kids will be walking by age two.

So why does everyone care so much about milestones? When it comes to parents, they just can't help themselves.

In the best circumstances parents will take their child's development in stride and use the milestones as a general guide for how baby should grow. But sometimes, like that dad during the Little League game, parents become competitive and overly fixated about when their baby achieves the milestones. This fixation can become stress, or even panic, should a child inevitably not reach a milestone when a parent expects, reach a milestones out of order, or skips them altogether.

Some parents might be inclined to buy special tools or toys that will help a kid reach a milestone like talking or walking. This is the equivalent of buying a batting cage and pitching machine for a disinterested Little Leaguer. If they're not that into it, they're not that into it. Adding special toys or tools can't really speed up that process. Besides, everything those tools do can be accomplished with parental attention, touch, and play. That parental engagement is the real secret to helping kids develop motor and cognitive skills over time.

It helps to remember that children outside of the average a milestone represents aren't somehow advanced or deficient. In fact, by the time children are in grade school, most are operating on the same developmental level regardless of whether they've developed some abilities more quickly or more slowly than their peers.

And a child who is slow to reach milestones isn't necessarily showing signs of disability. Many other factors can slow development. Children who are born prematurely will develop at a speed commensurate with that early arrival. Expect a child who arrived a month early, for instance, to reach their milestones a month late.

Temperament also has a great deal to do with milestone achievement. An outgoing, adventurous, risk-taking child may be quicker to crawl in order to explore and discover. On the other hand, a cautious child might rather stay in one place or stay by their parents rather than strike out into the world.

More than anything, for kids to develop at their unique optimal pace, they just need a supportive parent who gives them plenty of opportunity to practice their babbling, wiggling, face making, grabbing, scooching skills.

This is not to say that developmental milestones are meaningless for parents. There are certain milestones that act as important developmental markers; they just might not be the milestones that most parents will be familiar with. Knowing which milestones to pay attention to can relieve some of the parental stress during a baby's first year.

The One-Month Developmental Milestones that Matter

Milestones in the first month of a baby's life are all about getting control of their limbs, which at birth seem to have a mind of their own. They also begin to develop their senses, allowing them to become more aware of the sights, sounds, and smells of the world that surrounds them. Their nervous system is getting organized, so weird things may happen. That's a sign that the brain is learning and everything is moving at a pretty good clip—just like it should. The only things that should cause any real concern is a lack of reaction to outside stimuli.

Moving Hands to Face and Mouth, Making Fists

Your baby's brain is figuring out how to coordinate arms and legs, but they can't do the brain's bidding just yet. Because of that, movements may seem jerky and random and will include bringing the hands up to the face and mouth.

Red Flags: If your baby appears to be moving slowly, or if its limbs seem to be too floppy or too rigid, you may want to bring it to the attention of your pediatrician. Jerky and trembling movements are normal, but a constantly trembling chin or jaw when they aren't crying or excited could be a sign of neurological issues.

What You Shouldn't Stress About: Don't stress if your baby has a floppy neck, twitchy movements, or self-inflicted scratches. It's all normal as babies develop control over their bodies.

Reacting to Loud Noises and Turning Head Toward Sounds

By the end of the first month, the baby's hearing should be fully developed. Baby will be listening and might turn to you at the sound of your voice. Dads who talked to their babies in the womb might be surprised that their kid recognizes their dulcet tones.

Red Flags: If your baby does not seem to react or startle to loud or sudden noises, it may be a sign that there is a hearing problem. A baby who doesn't react to loud noises could be affected by hearing loss or other neurological disorders.

What You Shouldn't Stress About: There's no need to worry about babies not making eye contact when you talk to them. That's a bit advanced. There's also no need to worry about babies who don't turn their heads toward the sound as long as they react to it.

The Rooting Reflex

Babies likely have what's known as the rooting re-
flex, which means they will turn their head toward
a touch on the cheek or lip and make sucking
movements. This helps them feed when presented
with a nipple. The rooting reflex helps your baby
feed either from the breast or the bottle.

Red Flags: More important than the reflex itself
is how your baby is feeding. If sucking is weak or
feeding is too slow, you should contact your pediatrician.

What You Shouldn't Stress About: Don't worry about a baby that sucks
on its own fist or seems to be rooting toward dad's chest. All good stuff
there. And while feeding, don't worry if sucking seems to happen in
bursts with pauses in between. That's normal. So is spit up, so take that
in stride too.

Other Things to Think about during the First Month

Considering how little babies are, one-month milestones are limited.
You're likely to run into the Moro reflex, which you'll recognize when
the baby splays out arms and legs as if in the sensation of falling. It can
disrupt their sleep and it's completely normal (if strange). Swaddling can
help. Other than that, enjoy the slow month. Things will be getting much
more interesting pretty soon.

The Two-Month Developmental Milestones that Matter

Around the second month, an infant's movements will start to be better
coordinated by the nervous system—that's why most two-month developmental milestones focus on how a baby moves in response to environmental stimuli. Because parents are such a huge part of that
environmental stimuli, many of those milestones are measured in how
two-month-olds react to their parents. But that puts some pressure on
how those parent–child interactions should feel, which can make the
two-month milestones particularly fraught. Luckily, there are really only
a couple of crucial two-month milestones for babies at this stage of development.

Lifting Head During Tummy Time

Tummy time wasn't always a thing, but now that we know children
should always be placed on their backs to sleep, babies have less

opportunity to practice their "prone skills." Those skills, like pushing up with their arms and turning their head and neck, can only be done when babies are backside up, which helps them develop important neck and arm muscles—thus, the need for tummy time.

At two months old, babies should be able to lift their heads during tummy time and look around. Will they always enjoy them-selves during this time? Nope. But they should have some neck strength as they fuss. This ability is emblematic of a healthy nervous system that's communicating with a baby's muscles.

Red Flags: When two-month-olds are not able to lift their heads or hold them steady, it could be a sign of a serious issue. But it's important not to consider that in isolation. Babies get tired just like everyone else. Sometimes it simply takes longer for muscles to strengthen and develop, particularly if a baby was born premature. If your two-month-old also seems lethargic, however, with loose "floppy" limbs or overly stiff and shaky limbs, you will want to notify your pediatrician.

What You Shouldn't Stress About: Babies at this age aren't supposed to be rolling over or playing with toys in a specific and focused manner. Also, babies might naturally be fussy during tummy time. It's not the most fun a baby can have. So don't panic if your baby "hates" tummy time.

Developing a Personality

So you won't find "develops personality" on most infant milestone lists. It's too subjective for those compiling the scientific data. Most milestone lists break this down into more ob-jective minutiae: smiling, cooing, responding to a parent's voice, fussing when they want needs met. But for a parent who has been pay-ing attention to their kid, it all boils down to the feeling that their child is developing a per-sonality—it seems the baby is becoming more of a person.

With that personality comes a focus on the parent. You will likely see a lot of cute responses when you interact with your baby. On the other hand, when things get too monotonous, your kid may fuss out of bore-dom. (And you thought that wouldn't come until they were a tween.)

Red Flags: There is a lot to be said here about who parents understand their babies to be. Some babies have a very watchful and mellow temperament. Babies may sometimes be incredibly fussy because of issues like colic. Other times babies are curious and excited. So recognizing the red flags at this stage is more about keeping track of babies' physical response to their environment in the context of what a parent knows to be normal for their child. Babies who don't follow a novel object or a parent's face with their eyes may need to be seen by a pediatrician, for instance. The same goes for a baby that does not respond to a parent's voice or loud noises. These could be signs of neurological issues.

Other Things to Think about during the Second Month

Around month two, much is said about a baby being able to smile. But parents should be relaxed and patient on this front. Some babies are not as easy to make smile. This doesn't necessarily indicate a child having an autism spectrum disorder, for instance. Babies who are premature might smile later. Babies suffering from colic may not smile that often. And babies with parents who aren't very smiley may not respond to them with smiles.

That's why it's important to stay calm if a baby hasn't flashed a gummy grin by two months. It'll show up eventually. And because babies are sensitive to their parent's emotions, a stressed-out parent may not have a supersmiley kid. That said, parents who feel there has been a change in their child's demeanor, or see that their child is not particularly responsive in general, will want to speak to their pediatrician. Trust your gut.

The Three-Month Developmental Milestones that Matter

In the third month of your baby's life, you should expect to see increased strength and social interaction. If you saw only glimmers of personality in month two, you should see babies starting to display joy, boredom, and frustration in the coming weeks. With blossoming personality and strength comes the ability to indulge their curiosity. So this month's main infant milestones are about reaching out to touch someone (or something).

Much More Social

Your baby might have been slow to smile in the second month, but as the third month progresses, parents should see baby flash a smile in response to play and activity. Along with that smile should come a change in facial expressions along with a bit of babble. Baby won't be saying mama or dada yet, but you may hear some breathy gahs, ohs, guhs, and oos. The babble may be subtle or pronounced. It will definitely be pretty slobbery.

If you're lucky, you may be able to coax a belly laugh from your kid while you play. On the other hand, your three-month-old baby may start crying when play is done. These are all great signs of on-point development, but they also require a little coaxing from parents. Playing with baby (at this point, this means making different sounds and facial expressions) is essential for the kid. Without this interaction, babies can't practice their mimicry and may be a bit slower to gain their social skills.

Red Flags: Parents need to leave room for babies who are hesitant to offer social responses, but there is a difference between a baby who appears reluctant or slow to react to parents and a baby who appears incapable of a social response. The red flag here is more about the absence of a set of behaviors. A baby who doesn't laugh or coo but does smile is likely just taking its time. The same goes for a baby that looks interested in a parent, coos, and babbles, but doesn't smile. You may simply want to take some time to see if anything changes in the coming weeks. But a baby that seems completely disinterested or does not babble, look at parents, or smile may need to see the pediatrician sooner rather than later. This could be a sign of any number of neurological disorders that can be addressed with early intervention.

What You Shouldn't Stress About: At this age, it's normal for babies to fuss and cry, particularly when they are bored or something they enjoy has been taken away. They may also cry when they are put down. This is normal. If you suspect there is a deeper issue, there's no harm in talking to your pediatrician.

Reaching for and Grasping Objects

At three months old, the spark of play is lit. Babies should be able to reach and grasp for things they are curious about and may start to explore cause-and-effect by bopping things that make noise when grasped or jostled. Granted, this play is primitive and might look more accidental than intentional. Still, embedded in the play is proof that on a physical level things are clicking along. Newborns who can play in these very basic ways are showing that they can see and track objects and coordinate their limbs. Babies that repeatedly bop or kick an object that makes sound show that they are developing muscle strength and that they can respond to auditory cues.

Red Flags: Babies who seem to be unable to reach and grasp or who do not take any interest in loud noises may be experiencing neurological issues. The same goes for babies who appear too tense in their limbs or too floppy. An inability to lift their head during tummy time over the next four weeks should be brought to the attention of your pediatrician.

What You Shouldn't Stress About: Babies at three months old will grab and hold just about anything that they can get their hands on. So if they are pulling hair, beards, or their own private parts, it's not an issue. It's just something that happens.

Other Things to Think about during the Third Month

Newborn sleep starts to normalize over the next few weeks. And as babies are able to bring hands to their mouths and suck their fists, they should be learning to self-soothe. Also, at three months, as babies start learning to roll over, their risk of SIDS begins to decline. All of this means that babies can move into their own nurseries and parents can begin thinking about sleep training. If you haven't thought about how you plan to do it, this would be the time for research.

The Four-Month Developmental Milestones that Matter

In the fourth month of life, infants become natural experimenters, and while their experiments can be disruptive—"what happens when I drop my pacifier this time?"—they are important. Because four-month-olds are starting to learn about their world and, just as important, trying to make sure you know about the world they're discovering.

More Communication

Baby communication is a bit subtler than you might imagine. Absent the capacity for language, kids have to rely on the tools they do have to try and get your attention. What are they? Crying, cooing, grabbing, dropping, kicking, giggling, making faces, and looking.

These methods of communication aren't always pleasant. After all, you only want to pick up the dropped toy so many times, and crying is never fun. But these behaviors are important because they signal your baby has developed some important skills. Smiling at you to get you to smile back means the baby is becoming aware of their personhood. Dropping objects for you to pick up means the baby is gaining an understanding of cause and effect. Watching your face and listening to your voice before making a response means that the baby is beginning to understand your emotions.

When a baby becomes more communicative, in its special baby way, it means that motor development and cognitive development are beginning to work in concert. And as these systems come together, they are beginning to connect your baby to a wider world outside itself. Most important, not every baby will communicate in the same way. Look for your baby's special mode of communication.

Red Flags: If your baby isn't following objects with its eyes or doesn't vocalize or react to your face by four months, it could indicate an issue with cognitive development. While there's no reason to be terribly worried if your baby's health is otherwise sound, it's definitely something you'll want to discuss with your baby's pediatrician.

What You Shouldn't Stress About: Being communicative does not mean that your baby will be signing or saying actual words. Mostly, babies just want to make sure they have your attention. Give it to them, for sure, but also let them lead. There's no sense in trying to teach them more words through DVDs or flashcards. Those things won't help. Just talk to them as you normally would.

Getting Stronger

Physically, typical babies' motor systems seem to "turn on" in a specific way—from head to toe and from the middle of their body outwards. Which is to say they develop control and dexterity over these systems in a top-down, middle-out manner. As they practice using all these muscles, from neck to core to legs, and from arms to hands to fingers, they will become stronger.

It's not as if babies will be lifting weights at four months, but they should be using their systems in concert in order to explore their world. They might push themselves up and be able to reach out during tummy time. They might keep their arms taut and pull as parents help them into a sitting position. They will look fairly stable and be able to look around freely, reaching out to play and explore. And when parents hold them in a standing position they should be strong enough to support their weight without their knees buckling.

Red Flags: A baby whose movements are erratic and who does not seem to have control over its head may not be developing typically. Babies who are struggling with physical development might tend to keep their limbs tucked up and may simply seem listless and floppy.

What You Shouldn't Stress About: At four months, there's no need for your baby to need to know how to roll over. If babies are otherwise strong and alert, the movement will eventually come, as will the ability to sit independently and eventually move around on their own.

Other Things to Think about during the Fourth Month

Four-month-olds should be taking a couple of naps during the day along with a full night of sleep. So that's a very good sign. Keep in mind that sleeping through the night doesn't mean soundless sleep. They will naturally wake between sleep cycles just like adults. So before you rush in, see if they can settle on their own.

Also, take a look at your baby's eyes. Weirdly, the color might be changing a bit, and you may not know what color the eyes will settle on for a few more weeks. This is natural, if a little sad. Goodbye, baby blues.

The Six-Month Developmental Milestones that Matter

From here the initial rush of development begins to slow down. That means you'll only need to check in on the milestones every couple of months. The most useful six-month milestones look at global behaviors and traits rather than a set of specific skills. Keep in mind that you've got six months of experience with the growth of your child. If something seems off, it probably is, but if you feel your baby is progressing at the same clip as the previous months, then everything is likely fine.

Increasing Curiosity

More than any little thing that parents are told to look for at six months, parents will want to see a general inclination toward curiosity. How do you know if your baby is curious? If you find yourself asking your baby questions like, "What was that? What is that? Did you hear that? Do you see that?" it's very likely that you are responding to your baby's curiosity cues. Babies may look around if they hear a new sound or stare intently at a new sight or new person. They might reach out and bat at a new object. They might chew on toys and turn them over in their hands. They will splash in liquids and drop objects.

This curiosity feeds off of itself, and its presence means that systems are integrating and working together. A six-month-old's curiosity means that it's beginning to recognize what's novel and what's familiar. The ability to explore objects with hands and mouth shows that muscles are developing correctly and your baby is developing dexterity. Reaching out for objects or listening intently to new sounds shows that a child's hearing and sight are coming along too.

Red Flags: You'll want to talk to your pediatrician if your baby isn't showing at least some pointed curiosity in their day-to-day life. That's particularly true if the lack of curiosity is paired with listlessness or a disinterest in parents.

What You Shouldn't Stress About: If your baby is a bit quiet or slow to explore its surroundings, that's not really a huge concern as long as it's showing some inclination toward curiosity. Place your baby's behavior in the context of the previous months. If baby has always been slow to react and explore it's more likely a product of its particular temperament rather than a developmental delay. Still, any concerns should be brought to a pediatrician.

Making Moves

At the six-month mark some babies have actually started to master movement (time to get on baby proofing your home!). A small number of babies in the six-month range can actually get on their hands and knees and crawl. But while some babies can, many others aren't ready to. Some babies will skip crawling altogether for butt scooting, rolling, scuttling, tripod walking, or dragging. If it works to get them where they want to go, it honestly doesn't matter.

At six months, many babies will have developed the core strength to hold themselves in a quasi-seated position, using their hands to prop themselves up. When on their belly, some babies have figured out how to roll over; others can kick themselves forward toward an object they find interesting.

The upshot is that a six-month-old should be a physically active creature and relatively purposeful in its activity.

Red Flags: At six months, babies should have a pretty strong core and the ability to coordinate their limbs around a task. Parents should tell their pediatrician if their baby seems particularly floppy or seems unable or unwilling to move, turn its head, or coordinate its limbs.

What You Shouldn't Stress About: Don't worry about crawling specifically—this isn't the end-all goal for your soon-to-be bipedal kid. Some babies crawl, some babies don't. Some babies go from rolling over to cruising to walking. You don't need to spend an inordinate amount of time getting your baby to crawl. Just give opportunities to explore the world.

Other Things to Think about during the Sixth Month

Around six months of age you'll hear and read a lot about your baby's ability to recognize "object permanence." That's the concept that objects and people don't just disappear when they are out of sight. But there is some controversy as to whether babies are just starting to understand object permanence at six months or if they are just developing the ability to show that they already understood the concept.

The Nine-Month Developmental Milestones that Matter

At this point, parents are looking for the marquee developmental milestones, like crawling, saying first words, eating new solid foods, and cruising. But at this point your baby may not hit important milestones at the same rate or in the same order as other children.

When considering the following nine-month milestones, it's important to place them in the context of how your baby has been developing since birth. Look more at broad collections of behaviors and abilities rather than the minutiae. If you feel that something has changed dramatically in terms of your baby's pace of development or abilities, there may be cause for concern, but most likely if babies continue to gain abilities, they are growing as they should.

Moving and Sitting with a Purpose

Between six and nine months old, babies' natural curiosity and developing strength should compel them and enable them to explore. But how far and how often they explore is very much connected to their surroundings and their temperament.

What that means is that some babies may be naturally inclined toward caution and the conservation of movement. Other babies will be adventurous and seemingly indefatigable. Neither type of temperament is better than the other.

How that temperament manifests will also be contingent on the baby's surroundings. A high-energy and super curious baby in an urban apartment with plenty of furniture and shelves to pull up on might start cruising sooner than expected because there aren't that many places to crawl and explore. A cautious baby with plenty of room to roam may keep crawling or scooting longer than other children because it is not inclined to go beyond its parents or the toys within reach.

Red Flags: At nine months, crawling is less important than whether your baby has developed the core strength to prop itself up and move its body with a sense of coordination and purpose. You will want to talk to your pediatrician if your baby seems limp or will not put weight on its legs when held in a standing position. Additionally, if a baby's movement continues to seem random or it tends to move or use one side of its body over the other, there may be developmental issues to consider.

What You Shouldn't Stress About: Most parents will have recognized their baby's temperament by nine months old. So any expectations of reaching big milestones like cruising or crawling should be placed in the context of their baby's natural activity patterns. Babies that are content to sit and play are fine as long as they are active and curious about what they have at hand. Babies that army crawl all over the house at a fantastic clip are also fine, as long as they are moving with a sense of curiosity. Taking steps, cruising, or four-on-the-floor crawling is unimportant as long as a child is active and interactive with the environment.

Plenty of Playing Around

Nine months into baby development, play is becoming an increasingly important way for babies to show you their abilities. As they become more coordinated, their natural curiosity will help them to find joy in manipulating objects, reaching, grasping, and passing toys from hand to hand. They should also become pretty adept at a pincer grasp: that is, picking up smaller objects between thumb and forefinger.

Play also helps reveal a nine-month-old baby's cognitive development. A baby who delights in peek-a-boo or reaching into boxes to remove objects is showing an understanding of object permanence and has started building memory skills. The baby knows that when objects can't be seen they do not simply disappear and that an object that has been hidden away can be retrieved.

Back-and-forth play with parents will also be super fun for babies, and they should show a connection to parents with smiles, mimicry, and good old-fashioned babble.

Red Flags: A baby who doesn't want to play is very different from a baby who can't, and parents need to make that distinction. Talk to your pediatrician if your baby seems unable to play because they are unable to focus, meet your gaze, sit up, or manipulate objects in a purposeful way.

What You Shouldn't Stress About: At nine months, baby babble is fine. Parents shouldn't expect full words that indicate a particular object or person. In fact, some babies may get what they need through other cues like pointing or crying or looking, making specific words kind of unnecessary. Parents also shouldn't put too much concern into a baby who prefers to explore or play with things rather than people or other babies. As long as babies have the ability to play, their preference in what they play with isn't too much of a concern.

Other Things to Think about during the Ninth Month

At nine months old many babies are able to start exploring new foods. Parents who are interested can start supplementing formula or breastfeeding with child-safe, soft finger foods that babies can gnaw on. Aim for whole foods rather than processed, and lean on stuff like bananas, avocado, peppers, and maybe the occasional pudding if you want to let your baby play with a spoon. This process will be wildly messy, but don't sweat it.

The Twelve-Month Developmental Milestones that Matter

By the time a child reaches their first birthday, parents should be learning exactly who their child is. The coming of the first birthday should reveal your child to have opinions and preferences. And they should be standing, responding, and interacting to make sure you understand what those opinions and preferences are.

Developing Desires, Opinions, and Preferences

It's not that babies didn't have preferences and desires before twelve months. It's just that they are finally able to convey those desires, opinions, and preferences to you via body, language, voice, and facial expressions.

Of course, the preferences and how a baby expresses them can't be generalized. Some babies will like things other babies don't. Some babies may show fear of strangers by being clingy. Some might cry when a parent leaves. Some may point to ask for a toy, and some might babble to get attention and interaction. Some babies might do all of these things. What's most important is that your twelve-month old is showing an interest in the world around it and in communicating interests and displeasure with you through vocalization or gestures.

Red Flags: A twelve-month-old should be able to use body language, facial expressions, or movements in a purposeful way. You may want to speak to a pediatrician if your twelve-month-old cannot point, wave, or shake its head to communicate needs or desires.

What You Shouldn't Stress About: Many parents are hoping to hear a real first word around twelve months. If you want, you can totally decide that a babbled mama or dada is the first intentional word, but best not to put too much stock in it. Notably, a parent who talks more to their kid will have a kid who talks more and sooner. So if you're the silent type, you may have to wait a bit longer. Also, if your child is getting along just fine with a gesture or a point, what's the use in saying anything?

Responsive and Interactive

At the end of your baby's first year, you're likely to have noticed that its communication abilities have truly bloomed. In fact, beyond simply conveying happiness or displeasure at the world, babies can now recognize and respond to your cues. And sometimes, the give and take can feel downright conversational.

At twelve months old, your baby may mimic your movements or the baby's babble may pick up your style of inflection. Babies pay attention to you (when they want to) and should be able to respond to specific simple commands (again, when they want to) like "no."

This interactivity will make playing and story time that much more fun. You can hide objects and your child will seek them out. You can point to pictures as you read and your baby should follow your finger and your gaze. Bang on an object like a cooking pot, and the baby should delight in banging on the pot with you.

Some of this interactive play might be prompted by your baby too. The problem is what is play for your baby may not feel playful to you. For instance, repeatedly dropping a beloved toy from the high chair might seem inexplicable, but for a twelve-month-old it's a fun experiment to see how you react.

Red Flags: If your child has been responsive and interactive and appears to stop or regress, it's important to speak to a pediatrician. But keep in mind that regressions may not be sudden, and they will need to be placed in the context of your child's development. An hour or even a day of a less responsive and interactive baby does not necessarily indicate a problem.

What You Shouldn't Stress About: Every baby will have a different personality. Some twelve-month-olds are more exuberant and active than others, and some are relatively sedate. It's important to not compare your baby's level of activity to others. Instead, look for significant changes that seem out of place with your baby's disposition to date.

Starting to Stand

At twelve months old, babies who have been given the opportunity generally have the ability to stand on their own two feet, either with the help of a parent or a piece of furniture. How long they stand and what they do when they get to a standing position, however, will vary wildly. Some twelve-month-olds will simply plop back down on their bottoms, while others may take a step or two.

Red Flags: Talk to your pediatrician if your baby appears to be dragging one side of its body when moving or can't stand and hold up its body with support.

What You Shouldn't Stress About: At twelve months, parents probably are pushing for those first steps. But there is no hard and fast rule about when these steps should happen. If your baby isn't taking steps now, just take a deep breath. It will happen eventually as long as your baby has the time and space to practice.

Other Things to Think about during the Twelfth Month

At twelve months old your baby will still be putting things in its mouth on a regular basis. Don't sweat it. There are a lot of sensitive sensory organs on babies' faces, so it makes sense that they would explore their world orally. Just make sure to keep choking hazards out of arm's reach. The general rule is that if it can fit through a toilet paper tube, it's not safe.

The Eighteen-Month Developmental Milestones that Matter

Again, the developmental milestones that matter at eighteen months are less about physical and cognitive skills and more about the developmental trajectory of your particular kid. It's less about what your child can do by eighteen months than it is about missed skills that may be red flags for developmental problems.

Toddling

At eighteen months, most typically developing infants have started walking. That caveat
is important. Some children have started
walking long before that and some are just
getting the hang of it. The onset of walking
is likely due to a number of factors that will
include kids' temperaments, the opportunities they have been given, and how much
encouragement they have received.

Red Flags: Eighteen-month-olds who appear to be unable to stand or support them-
selves for long despite some effort may have deeper developmental issues. Look for signs that your toddler is favoring one side overwhelm-ingly or seems unable to coordinate its limbs in a way that allows for mobility.

What You Shouldn't Worry About: If your kid isn't particularly good at walking yet, don't sweat it. There is no need for your toddler to know parkour at eighteen months. If your baby is taking steps, that's all that really matters. Some milestone guides will suggest your child should be able to go up and down stairs, but keep in mind, a kid who doesn't expe-rience stairs regularly probably will not have figured this out. What's important is that babies' muscles are strong and they are mobile with an inclination toward getting on their own two feet and taking steps. Some kids might stay cautious cruisers for a little bit longer.

Exploring the World Cautiously

Toddling and exploration go hand in hand. They have a symbiotic rela-tionship: a desire to explore fuels a push to walk, and walking allows kids to explore more. The way kids explore will tell you a lot about how they are developing. Children interested in things they encounter might point them out to parents and try to name them. Other toddlers might carry the object around and show it to people. Some kids can be directed by parents where to explore and where not to.

These behaviors not only show that a toddler is developing physical strength and dexterity but indicate cognitive development through communicating discovery and taking simple direction. Still, toddlers' abilities to move and communicate are still fairly limited compared to their desires. Because their limits are in conflict with their ambitions, don't be surprised if toddlers tend to melt down in frustration.

Red Flags: An eighteen-month-old's willingness to explore should not be confused with complete standoffishness. Most neurotypical toddlers will return to the safe home base of their parents after exploring independently. If a toddler seems unconcerned about parents leaving or doesn't show any interest in, fear of, or connection with other people, it may be a sign of developmental delay.

What You Shouldn't Worry About: Because they want to do more than they're able, you can expect toddlers to melt down. You can also expect them to be clingy as they regroup from their exploration. Basically, don't sweat it if your toddler appears to have big emotions around this time, and maybe cut your kid, and yourself, some slack. It's not easy being a toddler. Or a toddler's dad.

Pretending

Pretend play really starts kicking off around toddlerhood. You might see your toddler mimicking your behaviors, like looking at a phone. Toddlers might pretend to take care of or talk to stuffed animals and dolls, or they might pretend to be another creature. During this pretend play a toddler will also likely be displaying other developmental skills, like language, laughter, and an ability to connect with other people.

What toddlers pretend is less important than *that* they are pretending. And parents should make sure kids have plenty of opportunities to exercise their imaginations.

Red Flags: If a toddler seems to have lost any abilities, you should see your pediatrician. These kinds of regressions may be a sign of developmental issues.

What You Shouldn't Worry About: Some parents might expect their eighteen-month-old to be talking, but keep in mind that some kids can get by through nonverbal forms of communication and don't see the need to speak. If a kid is communicating through gestures, the important part is the communication.

Other Things to Think about at the Eighteenth Month

Your toddler is likely looking more like a little boy or girl than a baby. This can be an emotional time for parents. You can also look forward to your toddler's molars coming in. Finally, look for your toddler to start losing some naps around this time.

SECTION IV

REFERENCE

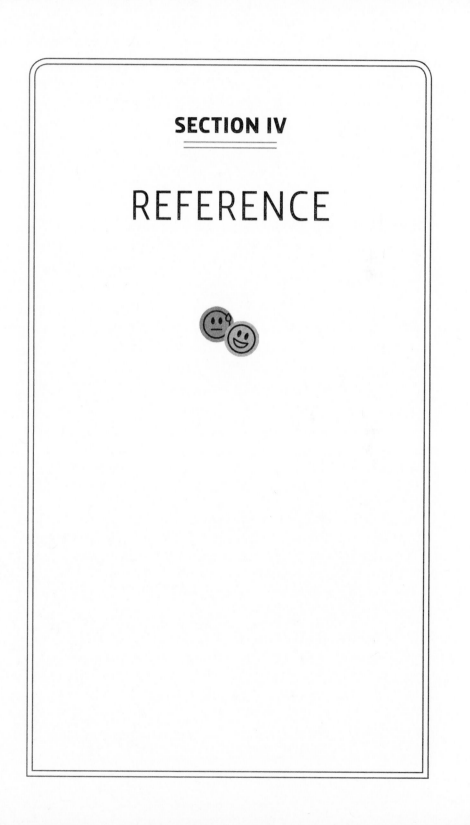

Acknowledgments

This book would not have been possible without the work and energy of Fatherly founder Michael Rothman, who recognized that fathers deserved a platform for support and information that suited their unique needs and roles. His tireless nurturing of the Fatherly brand has been and remains the foundation on which the essential father-focused news, information, and advice has been built. This book was also made possible thanks to the support of the entire Fatherly staff, who have spent years listening to, researching, and living the realities of modern parenting. Thanks to Fatherly alumnus Andrew Burmon for his leadership, his words, and giving the book life and direction. Deep gratitude extends to Tyghe Trimble, current Fatherly editor-in-chief, for taking the project over the finish line. Thanks to Fatherly Visuals Editor Anne Meadows and illustrator Conor Nolan for helping make this book look as good as it reads. Special thanks to the editors of Scary Mommy, who offered crucial guidance and a close read. Additional appreciation goes to the staff of Harper Horizon, particularly Amanda Bauch and freelancer Nat Atkins, who have guided the process with gentle hands and extraordinary insight. Finally I would like to thank my wife, Kitty Coleman, and my children, Atticus and Sebastian Coleman, for their love and support and for being the engine of inspiration that drove the contents of this book and continues to drive my work at Fatherly. I am so lucky to be your partner and poppa.

PATRICK ALAN COLEMAN
Parenting Editor
Fatherly.com

Endnotes

CHAPTER 1

1. Mark Lino et al., *Expenditures on Children by Families, 2015*, Miscellaneous Publication No. 1528-2015 (Washington, DC: US Department of Agriculture, Center for Nutrition Policy and Promotion, 2017).
2. *Survey on Workplace Flexibility 2013* (Scottsdale, AZ: WorldatWork, 2013).
3. Personal interview with Ferne Traeger.
4. Brad Harrington, Fred Van Deusen, Beth Humberd, *The New Dad: Caring, Committed and Conflicted* (Boston: Boston College Center for Work & Family, 2011).
5. Michelle J. Budig, "The Fatherhood Bonus and the Motherhood Penalty: Parenthood and the Gender Gap in Pay," *Third Way*, September 2, 2014, https://www.thirdway.org/report/the-fatherhood-bonus-and-the-motherhood-penalty-parenthood-and-the-gender-gap-in-pay.
6. Tesa E. Leonce, "The Inevitable Rise in Dual-Income Households and the Intertemporal Effects on Labor Markets," *Compensation and Benefits Review* 52, no 2 (April 2020), https://doi.org/10.1177/0886368719900032
7. Stewart D. Friedman, "Children: The Unseen Stakeholders at Work," *Business and Society Review* 104, no. 1 (1999).
8. Harrington, Van Deusen, Humberd, *The New Dad.*
9. Steward D. Friedman and Jeffrey H. Greenhaus, *Work and Family—Allies or Enemies? What Happens When Business Professionals Confront Life Choices* (Oxford: Oxford University Press, 2000).

CHAPTER 2

1. E. E. LeMasters, "Parenthood as Crisis," *Marriage and Family Living*, 19, no. 4 (1957), 352–355.
2. Marsha Pruett et al., "Enhancing Father Involvement in Low-Income Families: A Couples Group Approach to Preventive Intervention," *Child Development* 88, no. 2 (March/April 2017): 398–407, https://doi.org/10.1111/cdev.12744.
3. Marion O'Brien and Vicki Peyton, "Parenting Attitudes and Marital Intimacy: A Longitudinal Analysis," *Journal of Family Psychology* 16, no. 2 (June 2002): 118–27, PMID: 12085726.
4. John DeFrain and Sylvia M. Asay, "Family Strengths and Challenges in the USA," Marriage & Family Review 41, nos. 3–4 (2007): 281–307, https://doi.org/10.1300/J002v41n03_04.

CHAPTER 3

1. Department of the Navy, *Marine Corps Doctrinal Publication 5: Planning* (Washington, DC: United States Government, 1997).

2. Theresa Morris and Katherine McInerny, "Media Representations of Pregnancy and Childbirth: An Analysis of Reality Television Programs in the United States," *Birth* 37, no. 2 (June 2010): 134–140, https://doi.org/10.1111/j.1523-536x.2010.00393.x.
3. Richard K. Reed, *Birthing Fathers: The Transformation of Men in American Rites of Birth* (New Brunswick, NJ: Rutgers University Press, 2005).
4. Julie Ann Tharp, Susan MacCallum-Whitcomb, eds. *This Giving Birth: Pregnancy and Childbirth in American Women's Writing* (Madison, WI: Popular Press, 2000).
5. Donald Caton, "Who Said Childbirth Is Natural? The Medical Mission of Grantly Dick Read," *Anesthesiology* 84 (April 1996): 955–64, https://doi.org/10.1097/00000542-199604000-00024.
6. Caton, "Who Said Childbirth Is Natural?"
7. Laura Kaplan, "Changes in Childbirth in the United States: 1750–1950," *Hektoen International* 4, no. 4 (Fall 2012).
8. Kaplan, "Changes in Childbirth."
9. Kaplan, "Changes in Childbirth."
10. Jessica Martucci, "Beyond the Nature/Medicine Divide in Maternity Care," *AMA Journal of Ethics* 20, no. 12 (December 2018): 1168–74, https://doi.org/10.1001/amajethics.2018.1168.
11. Adrienne Rich, *Of Woman Born: Motherhood As Experience and Institution* (New York: Norton, 1976).
12. Margaret Talbot, "The Way We Live Now; Pay on Delivery," *New York Times Magazine*, October 31, 1999.
13. A. M. Durik, J. S. Hyde, and R. Clark, "Sequelae of Cesarean and Vaginal Deliveries: Psychosocial Outcomes for Mothers and Infants," *Developmental Psychology* 36, no. 2 (March 2000): 251–60, https://doi.org/10.1037//0012-1649.36.2.251.
14. Anne Lyerly, "Ethics and Pursuit of the Good Birth" (lecture, Thirty-Fifth Annual Disciplinary Series 2016–2017, University of Chicago, Chicago, IL, November 9, 2016), https://www.youtube.com/watch?v=4CGrHpxhSjQ.
15. Thomas Sartwelle, James Johnston, and Berna Arda, "Electronic Fetal Monitoring, Cerebral Palsy, and Medical Ethics: Nonsense of a High Order," *Medical Law International* 17, no. 1–2 (March 2017): 43–64, https://doi.org/10.1177/2F0968533217704883.
16. Department of the Navy, *Marine Corps Doctrinal Publication 5: Planning* (Washington, DC: United States Government, 1997).

CHAPTER 4

1. "Gordon Ramsay: I Didn't Want to See My Kids Being Born," *CelebsNow* (blog), *Now Magazine*, July 30, 2008. https://www.celebsnow.co.uk/latest-celebrity-news/gordon-ramsay-i-didn-t-want-to-see-my-kids-being-born-235071.
2. Richard K. Reed, *Birthing Fathers.*
3. Y. Parfitt and S. Ayers, "The Effect of Postnatal Symptoms of Posttraumatic Stress and Depression on the Couple's Relationship and Parent-Baby Bond," *Journal of Reproductive and Infant Psychology*, 27, no. 2 (April 2009): 127–42.
4. Parfitt and Ayers, "Effect of Postnatal Symptoms."

CHAPTER 5

1. Judith Walzer Leavitt, *Make Room for Daddy: The Journey from Waiting Room to Birthing Room* (Chapel Hill, NC: UNC University Press, 2009).
2. Shane K., "Cigar Traditions Explained: After a New Baby is Born," July 19, 2019, Holts Clubhouse, Holts.com, https://www.holts.com/clubhouse/cigar-culture/cigar-traditions-new-baby.
3. Karen K. Gerlach et al., "Trends in Cigar Consumption and Smoking Prevalence,"

Publication of the National Cancer Institute, https://cancercontrol.cancer.gov /sites/default/files/2020-08/m09_2.pdf].

4. Ipsos Mori, *Fatherhood and Social Connections* (Los Angeles: Movember, 2019). https://cdn.movember.com/uploads/images/News/UK/Movember%20 Fathers%20%26%20Social%20Connections%20Report.pdf.

5. Shefaly Shorey and Lina Ang, "Experiences, Needs, and Perceptions of Paternal Involvement During the First Year After Their Infants' Birth: A Meta-Synthesis," *Plos One*, January 7, 2019, https://doi.org/10.1371/journal.pone.0210388.

6. Eleonora Bielawska-Batorowicz and Karolina Kossakowski-Petrycka, "Depressive Mood in Men After the Birth of Their Offspring in Relation to a Partner's Depression, Social Support, Fathers' Personality and Prenatal Expectations," *Journal of Reproductive and Infant Psychology* 24, no. 1 (2006): 21–9, https://doi .org/10.1080/02646830500475179.

SKILLS:

HOW TO HAVE A BABY

1. Lydia A. Futch Thurston, Dalia Abrams, Alexa Dreher, Stephanie R. Ostrowski, and James C. Wright, "Improving Birth and Breastfeeding Outcomes Among Low Resource Women in Alabama by Including Doulas in the interprofessional Birth Care Team," *Journal of Interprofessional Education & Practice* 17 (2019); K. B. Kozhimannil, R. R. Hardeman, L. B. Attanasio, C. Blauer-Peterson, and M. O'Brien. "Doula Care, Birth Outcomes, and Costs Among Medicaid Beneficiaries," *American Journal of Public Health* 103, no. 4 (2013), e113–e121.

CHAPTER 6

1. Soranus of Ephesus, *Soranus' Gynecology*, trans. Owsei Temkin (Johns Hopkins University Press, 1991).

2. J. Locke and P. Nidditch, *An Essay Concerning Human Understanding* (Oxford: Clarendon Press, 1975).

3. *Rousseau's Emile; or, Treatise on Education*, trans. William Harold Payne (New York: D. Appleton, 1908), 33.

4. William Cadogan, "An Essay Upon Nursing and the Management of Children, from Their Birth to Three Years of Age," https://quod.lib.umich.edu/e/evans /N09700.0001.001/1:1?rgn=div1;view=fulltext.

5. William Buchan, "Advice to Mothers, on the Subject of Their Own Health, and on the Means of Promoting the Health, Strength, and Beauty, of Their Offspring," https://collections.nlm.nih.gov/catalog/nlm:nlmuid-2544038R-bk.

6. Walter W. Sackett, *Bringing Up Babies: A Family Doctor's Practical Approach to Child Care* (New York: Harper & Row, 1962).

7. Jane E. Brody, "Final Advice From Dr. Spock: Eat Only All Your Vegetables," *New York Times*, June 20, 1998.

8. Ruth Gilbert, et al., "Infant Sleeping Position and the Sudden Infant Death Syndrome: Systematic Review of Observational Studies and Historical Review of Recommendations from 1940 to 2002," *International Journal of Epidemiology* 34, no. 4 (August 2005): 874–87.

9. American Academy of Pediatrics Council on Communications and Media, "Media and Young Minds," *Pediatrics* 138, no. 5 (November 2016).

10. Y. C. Chen, W. C. Chie, P. J. Chang, C. H. Chuang, Y. H. Lin, S. J. Lin, and P. C. Chen. "Is Infant Feeding Pattern Associated With Father's Quality Of Life?" *American Journal of Men's Health* 4, no. 4 (December 2010): 315–22. doi: 10.1177 /1557988309350491. PMID: 20413386.

11. S. Madigan et al., "Association Between Screen Time and Children's Performance

on a Developmental Screening Test," *JAMA Pediatrics* 173, no. 3 (March 2019): 244–50.

12. Diana Baumrind and Allen E. Black. "Socialization Practices Associated with Dimensions of Competence in Preschool Boys and Girls," *Child Development* 38, no. 2 (1967): 291–327. *JSTOR*. www.jstor.org/stable/1127295.

13. S. O. Roberts, C. Bareket-Shavit, F. A. Dollins, P. D. Goldie, and E. Mortenson, "Racial Inequality in Psychological Research: Trends of the Past and Recommendations for the Future," Perspectives in Psychological Science 15, no. 6 (November 2020): 1295–1309. doi: 10.1177/1745691620927709.

14. Elizabeth A. LeCuyer and Dena Phillips Swanson. "A Within-Group Analysis of African American Mothers' Authoritarian Attitudes, Limit-Setting and Children's Self-Regulation." *Journal of Child and Family Studies* 26, no. 3 (2017): 833–842. doi:10.1007/s10826-016-0609-0.

15. C. M. Super, "Environmental Effects on Motor Development: The Case of 'African Infant Precocity,'" *Developmental Medicine and Child Neurology* 18, no. 5 (October 1976): 561–67.

16. L. B. Karasik, C. S. Tamis-LeMonda, O. Ossmy, and K. E. Adolph, "The Ties That Bind: Cradling in Tajikistan," *PLoS ONE* 13, no. 10 (2018): e0204428. https://doi .org/10.1371/journal.pone.0204428.

17. Oskar G Jenni et al., "Infant Motor Milestones: Poor Predictive Value for Outcome of Healthy Children," *Acta Paediatrica* 102, no. 4 (2013).

18. Matthey J. Salganik et al., "Measuring the Predictability of Life Outcomes with a Scientific Mass Collaboration," *Proceedings of the National Academy of Sciences* 117, no. 15 (April 2020).

19. S. S. Woodhouse et al., "Secure Base Provision: A New Approach to Examining Links Between Maternal Caregiving and Infant Attachment," *Child Development* 91, no. 1 (2020).

CHAPTER 7

1. J. F. Paulson and S. D. Bazemore, "Prenatal and Postpartum Depression in Fathers and Its Association With Maternal Depression: A Meta-Analysis," *JAMA* 303, no. 19 (2010).

2. "Depressed Fathers Risk Not Getting Help," *ScienceDaily*, November 6, 2017.

3. R. S. Edelstein et al, "Prenatal Hormones in First-Time Expectant Parents: Longitudinal Changes and Within-Couple Correlations," *American Journal of Human Biology* 27, no. 3 (May–June 2015): 317–25.

4. K. A. Donovan et al., "Psychological Effects of Androgen-Deprivation Therapy on Men with Prostate Cancer and Their Partners," *Cancer* 121, no. 24 (December 15, 2015): 4286–99.

5. Ana Martinez et al., "Paternal Behavior in the Mongolian Gerbil (*Meriones unguiculatus*): Estrogenic and Androgenic Regulation," Hormones and Behavior 71 (May 2015): 91–95, https://doi.org/10.1016/j.yhbeh.2015.04.009.

6. Martinez et al., "Paternal Behavior in the Mongolian Gerbil."

7. Stephen J. Blumberg, Tainya C. Clarke, and Debra L. Blackwell, "Racial and Ethnic Disparities in Men's Use of Mental Health Treatments," *NCHS Data Brief* 206 (June 2015): 1–8.

8. S. Rosenbaum et al., "Does a Man's Testosterone 'Rebound' as Dependent Children Grow Up, or When Pairbonds End? A Test in Cebu, Philippines," *American Journal of Human Biology* 30, no. 6 (November/December 2018): 23–80.

CHAPTER 8

1. E. A. Cannon et al., "Parent Characteristics as Antecedents of Maternal Gatekeeping and Fathering Behavior," *Family Process* 47, no. 4 (December 2008): 501–19.
2. Gretchen Livingston and Kim Parker, "8 Facts About American Dads," *Pew Research Center, Fact Tank,* June 12, 2019.
3. Sarah M. Allen and Alan J. Hawkins, "Maternal Gatekeeping: Mothers' Beliefs and Behaviors That Inhibit Greater Father Involvement in Family Work," *Journal of Marriage and Family* 61, no. 1 (February 1999): 199–212.
4. US Bureau of Labor Statistics, "American Time Use Survey," Table A-7A. Time spent in primary activities by married mothers and fathers by employment status of self and spouse, average for the combined years 2015-19, own household child under age 18.
5. Claire M. Kamp Dush, Jill E. Yavorsky, and Sarah J. Schoppe-Sullivan, "What Are Men Doing While Women Perform Extra Unpaid Labor? Leisure and Specialization at the Transition to Parenthood," *Sex Roles* 78, no. 11–12 (June 2018): 715–30.
6. H. F. Harlow, R. O. Dodsworth, and M. K. Harlow, "Total Social Isolation in Monkeys," *Proceedings of the National Academy of Sciences of the United States of America* 54, no. 1 (July 1965): 90–97.
7. Allen and Hawkins. "Maternal Gatekeeping."
8. Joyce A. Martin et al., "Births: Final Data for 2018," *National Vital Statistics Reports* 68, no. 13 (November 27, 2019).
9. Cannon et al., "Parent Characteristics."

CHAPTER 9

1. "The Grandparent Boom! Record 70 Million Americans Have Grandchildren," *AARP Bulletin*, May 4, 2017.
2. Patty David and Brittne Nelson-Kakulla, *2018 Grandparents Today National Survey: General Population Report* (Washington, DC: AARP Research, April 2019).
3. S. M. Moorman and J. E. Stokes, "Solidarity in the Grandparent-Adult Grandchild Relationship and Trajectories of Depressive Symptoms," *Gerontologist* 56, no. 3 (June 2016): 408–20.
4. Lois M. Collins, "BYU Study: Grandparents Help Kids Be Kinder, More Involved," *Deseret News*, November 20, 2011.
5. A. Flamion, P. Missotten, M. Marquet, and S. Adam, "Impact of Contact With Grandparents on Children's and Adolescents' Views on the Elderly," *Child Development* 90 (2019): 1155–1169.
6. Laura Hess Brown and Sara B. DeRycke, "The Kinkeeping Connection: Continuity, Crisis and Consensus," *Journal of Intergenerational Relationships* 8, no. 4 (2010): 338–53.

CHAPTER 10

1. Noam Shpancer, Jessica Bowden, Melanie Ferrell, Stacy Pavlik, Morgan Robinson, Jennifer Schwind, Erica Volpe, Laurie Williams and Jessica Young (2002) The Gap: Parental knowledge about daycare, Early Child Development and Care, 172:6, 635-642, DOI: 10.1080/03004430215108.
2. Xiaoli Huang, Liling Chen, and Li Zhang, "Effects of Paternal Skin-to-Skin Contact in Newborns and Fathers After Cesarean Delivery," *Journal of Perinatal & Neonatal Nursing* 33, no. 1 (2019): 68-73.

3. E. M. Chen, M. L. Gau, C. Y. Liu, and T. Y. Lee. "Effects of Father-Neonate Skin-to-Skin Contact on Attachment: A Randomized Controlled Trial," *Nurs Res Pract.* (2017):8612024. doi:10.1155/2017/8612024.

CHAPTER 11

1. Michael J. Mooney, "The Worst Parents Ever: Inside the Story of Ethan Couch and the "Affluenza" Phenomenon," *D Magazine*, May 2015.
2. Bruce J. McIntosh, "Spoiled Child Syndrome," *Pediatrics* 83, no. 1 (January 1989): 108–15.
3. Thomas G. Power, "Parenting Dimensions and Styles: A Brief History and Recommendations for Future Research," *Childhood Obesity* 9, no. S1 (August 2013): S14–21.
4. Pamela Druckerman, *Bringing Up Bébé: One American Mother Discovers the Wisdom of French Parenting* (New York: Penguin Press, 2012).

CHAPTER 12

1. M. Lino et al., "Expenditures on Children by Families, 2015," *Miscellaneous Publication No. 1528-2015. U.S. Department of Agriculture, Center for Nutrition Policy and Promotion.*
2. B. E. Hamilton, J. A. Martin, and M. J. K. Osterman, "Births: Provisional Data for 2019," *Vital Statistics Rapid Release* 8 (May 2020).
3. Christopher P. Bonafide et al., "Accuracy of Pulse Oximetry-Based Home Baby Monitors," *JAMA* 320, no. 7 (August 21, 2018): 717–19.
4. Bonafide, "Accuracy of Pulse Oximetry-Based Home Baby Monitors."
5. Owlet Monitor DuoSmart Sock 3 + Cam, https://owletcare.com/products/owlet-monitor-duo, accessed October 7, 2020.
6. The Toy Association, "STEM/STEAM Formula for Success," *The Toy Association Report*, 2019.

CHAPTER 13

1. Aesha John, Amy Halliburton, and Jeremy Humphrey, "Child–Mother and Child–Father Play Interaction Patterns with Preschoolers," *Early Child Development and Care* 183, no. 3–4 (2013): 483–97.
2. *David Attenborough Wildlife Specials*, episode 14, "Elephant: Spy in the Herd," aired on July 20, 2003, on BBC.
3. Stuart L. Brown, *Play: How It Shapes the Brain, Opens the Imagination, and Invigorates the Soul* (New York: Avery Penguin, 2009), 197.
4. C. S. Dweck, T. E. Goetz, and N. L. Strauss, "Sex Differences in Learned Helplessness: IV. An Experimental and Naturalistic Study of Failure Generalization and Its Mediators," *Journal of Personality and Social Psychology* 38, no. 3 (March 1980): 441–52.
5. Katty Kay and Claire Shipman, Claire, "The Confidence Gap," *The Atlantic*, May 2014.
6. Kendra Cherry, "Carol Dweck Biography," Explore Psychology, July 18, 2016. https://www.explorepsychology.com/carol-dweck-biography/.

CHAPTER 14

1. Albert Bandura, "Human Agency in Social Cognitive Theory," *American Psychologist* 44, no. 9 (1989), 1175–1184. https://doi.org/10.1037/0003-066X.44.9.1175.
2. A. Bandura, G.V. Caprara, C. Barbaranelli, C. Regalia, and E. Scabini, "Impact of Family Efficacy Beliefs on Quality of Family Functioning and Satisfaction with Family Life," *Applied Psychology* 60 (2011): 421-448. https://doi.org/10.1111/j.1464 -0597.2010.00442.x.
3. A. Bandura, G.V. Caprara, C. Barbaranelli, C. Regalia, and E. Scabini, "Impact of Family Efficacy Beliefs on Quality of Family Functioning and Satisfaction with Family Life."
4. Albert Bandura "Selective Moral Disengagement in the Exercise of Moral Agency," *Journal of Moral Education* 31, no. 2 (2002), 101–119, DOI: 10.1080 /0305724022014322.
5. Albert Bandura "Personal and Collective Efficacy in Human Adaptation and Change," *Advances in Psychological Science* (1998).
6. Albert Bandura "Social Cognitive Theory of Mass Communication," *Media Psychology* 3, no. 3 (2001), 265–299, DOI: 10.1207/S1532785XMEP0303_03.
7. Albert Bandura, "Social Cognitive Theory of Mass Communication."
8. Albert Bandura, "Social Learning Theory of Aggression," *Journal of Communication* 28, no. 3 (September 1978): 12–29.
9. Jiang Shui et al., "Epigenetic Modifications in Stress Response Genes Associated with Childhood Trauma," *Frontiers in Psychiatry* 10 (November 2018).

CHAPTER 17

1. Alexia Fernandez, "Felicity Huffman Describes Her 'Deep' Shame for College Admissions Scandal in Letter to Judge," *People.com*, September 6, 2019.
2. Juliana Menasce Horowitz, Ruth Igielnik, and Rakesh Kochhar, "Most Americans Say There Is Too Much Economic Inequality in the U.S., but Fewer Than Half Call It a Top Priority," *PewSocialTrends.org*, January 9, 2020.
3. Daniel Kahneman and Angus Deaton, "High Income Improves Evaluation of Life but Not Emotional Well-Being, *Proceedings of the National Academy of Sciences* 107, no. 38 (September 2010): 16489–93.
4. Christopher Peterson and Martin Seligman, *Character Strengths and Virtues: A Handbook and Classification* (Oxford: Oxford University Press, 2004).
5. M. PollmannⴲSchult, "Parenthood and Life Satisfaction: Why Don't Children Make People Happy?" *Journal of Marriage and Family* 76, no. 2 (April 2014): 319–36, https://doi.org/10.1111/jomf.12095.
6. *Desperate Housewives*, season 8, episode 20, "Lost My Power," directed by David Grossman, aired on April 29, 2012, on ABC.

Index

Notes Pages

CONVERSATION ONE: Should Past Be Precedent?
("Nine Months, Six Conversations," pages 16–17)

CONVERSATION TWO: Division of Labor
("Nine Months, Six Conversations," page 18)

CONVERSATION THREE: Faith
("Nine Months, Six Conversations," page 19)

CONVERSATION FOUR: Health
("Nine Months, Six Conversations," pages 19–20)

CONVERSATION FIVE: Discipline
("Nine Months, Six Conversations," pages 20-21)

CONVERSATION SIX: In-Laws
("Nine Months, Six Conversations," page 22)

OUR MISSION STATEMENT
(See "Nine Months, Six Conversations," pages 23–24)

OUR BIRTH PLAN
(See "The Trouble with Birth Plans," pages 25–38)

_____

_____
_____
_____
_____
_____
_____
_____
_____
_____
_____
_____
_____
_____
_____
_____
_____
_____
_____
_____
_____
_____
_____
_____
_____
_____
_____
_____
_____

MOMENTS TO HOLD ONTO
FROM PREGNANCY

A LETTER TO MY CHILD, NOW JUST AN INFANT

The Makers of *Fatherhood*

ABOUT FATHERLY

Founded in 2015 by Mike Rothman and Simon Issacs, Fatherly was built on the understanding that dads are an underserved community in parenting media. Their goal, made explicit in Fatherly's mission statement, is to empower men to raise great kids and lead more fulfilling adult lives. Fatherly has met this aspiration over the years by putting journalism and expert insights first, offering fathers and dads-to-be the best information, advice, and recommendations suited to their specific needs. Fatherly now reaches more than eight million readers monthly through its website, social handles, newsletter, podcast, and books.

The brand has accrued its share of accolades: a Webby Award for the Best Parenting Site; a Peabody nomination for the podcast, *Finding Fred*; and another Webby Award for Best Newsletter for the pandemic-centered *Homebodies*. But the staying power of the brand lies in the impact it has on men and dads. Fatherly readers not only share and engage with the brand's articles, videos, and events, they engage more with their children and partners, building stronger families in the process.

PATRICK ALAN COLEMAN

Patrick Coleman, a father of two, joined Fatherly in 2016 as the site's first Parenting Editor. He used his extensive experience as a journalist to build the brand's core of research-based child wellness and parenting articles. His work at Fatherly has put him in conversation with some of the world's preeminent child health, development, and parenting experts, including Yale University's Sterling Professor of Psychology and Child Psychiatry Dr. Alan Kazdin, 2017 Time Person of the Year Dr. Celeste Kidd of UC

Berkeley's Kidd Labb, and Director of the Vaccine Education Center Dr. Paul A. Offit.

With over five years of inquiry, study, and conversations about parenting issues (a great deal of which he has applied to his own family), Coleman has built an uncommon understanding of what it takes to raise good kids. With his unique reporting and research, *Fatherhood* expands on a central thesis that raising good kids is less about practical advice and tactics than it is about working to become a better man and partner with a strong sense of values.

THE EDITORS OF FATHERLY

Fatherhood is an extension of the advice, skills, and insights found on Fatherly.com, where the brand's insightful staff of editors and writers delve into all aspects of a man's life.

Under the guidance of Andrew Burmon, Fatherly's Editor-in-Chief from 2017 to 2020 and current Editor-in-Chief Tyghe Trimble, Fatherly has built a body of work that includes news and family policy reporting, insights into parenting media and popular culture, and thoughtful explorations of parental relationships, sex, and mental health.

The work continues. *Fatherhood* is just one part of the brand's rich offering of information and entertainment, which includes the critically acclaimed *Finding* podcast series, Fatherly's annual Family Car and Best New Toy awards, interviews with luminaries like Eddie Murphy, Gavin Schmidt (NASA's top climatologist), and President Barack Obama, and even congressional testimony on family leave by CEO Mike Rothman.

Fatherly's writers, editors, and staff continue to delve into the heart of what it means to be a father and strive to build relationships with listeners, viewers, and readers that will grow along with their children. Join us, won't you?